Foreign Currency Trading

From the Fundamentals to the Fine Points

RUSSELL R. WASENDORF, SR.
RUSSELL R. WASENDORF, JR.

McGraw-Hill
New York • San Francisco • Washington, D.C. • Auckland
Bogotá • Caracas • Lisbon • London • Madrid • Mexico City
Milan • Montreal • New Delhi • San Juan • Singapore
Sydney • Tokyo • Toronto

Library of Congress Cataloging-in-Publication Data

Wasendorf, Russell R.
   Foreign currency trading / Russell R. Wasendorf, Sr., Russell R.
Wasendorf, Jr.
     p. cm.
   Includes index.
   ISBN 0-7863-1167-3
   1. Foreign exchange futures. I. Wasendorf, Russell R.
II. Title.
HG3853.W37 1997   97-27935
332.63'2--dc21   ·   CIP

McGraw-Hill

A Division of The McGraw·Hill Companies

1 2 3 4 5 6 7 8 9 0 DOC/DOC 9 0 2 1 0 9 8 7

ISBN 0-7863-1167-3

The sponsoring editor for this book was Stephen Isaacs, the editing supervisor was
John M. Morriss, and the production supervisor was Suzanne W. B. Rapcavage. It was set
in Times Roman by Lisa M. King of Editorial and Production Services.

Printed and bound by R. R. Donnelley & Sons Company.

McGraw-Hill books are available at special quantity discounts to use as premiums and sales promotions, or for use in corporate training programs. For more information, please write to the Director of Special Sales, McGraw-Hill, 11 West 19th Street, New York, N.Y. 10011. Or contact your local bookstore.

 This book is printed on recycled, acid-free paper containing a minimum
of 50% recycled de-inked fiber.

*To Connie and Debbie for the love and patience
they consistently bestow on us*

CONTENTS

PREFACE

This book is intended for everyone with an interest in the flow and exchange of currencies. A financial analyst, individual investor, importer/exporter, or banker is likely to find the simplified explanations herein useful in gaining a broader knowledge of this marketplace. The world of finance has become extremely diverse, and describing investment sectors in simple terms can help individuals get up to speed quickly. The book introduces the basics and then gradually moves on to more advanced topics. Some of the information may seem very basic, yet it is necessary for a thorough understanding of the world of foreign currency exchange, FX, or forex.

The book begins with an overview of the general topics and terminology of foreign currency trading. The objective is to make the jargon completely clear. A framework of examples is created to establish a solid base and starting point. Account statements are explained to point out their function in day-to-day operations. Chapter 1 ends with a sampling of the jargon used in forex trading.

Chapter 2 focuses on recent events and their relationship to the interbank market. Emphasis is placed on the risk associated with the interbank market and how the general public and media perceive foreign currency trading. Some myths are explained, and the real risks are brought into focus with recent industry examples.

In Chapter 3, the mechanics of foreign currency trading are explained in spot currency and currency futures terms. The simple concept of buying at a low price and selling at a high price is much more difficult than it sounds. The reader will learn how buying one currency means selling another. The pricing mechanism of spot currency trading is explained, showing how interest rates and arbitrage are integral parts of the equation. This discussion is expanded into the forward and futures currency markets, showing the future relationship between two currencies. The chapter ends with explanations of pricing models such as purchasing price parity and country balance sheet capital flows.

In Chapter 4, the current regulatory environment is examined, with an emphasis on the interpretation of the Treasury Amendment of the Commodity Exchange Act opening the regulatory debate of foreign currency trading. The interpretations of sophisticated institutions and participants are examined in relation to recent case law. In addition, pending cases are examined for their bearing on the possible future regulatory environment.

To follow up the discussion of regulation, the book examines the necessary investigation that investors should conduct before getting involved in forex trading. Readers are given some tools to use to detect investment swindlers.

Chapter 6 explains the rudiments of technical and fundamental analysis. Some of the common techniques of technical analysis for foreign currency trading are explained. Then fundamental analysis is reviewed as a tool for the prediction of future currency prices.

Chapter 7 addresses the difficulties that individual investors find when trading in the volatile currency market. The alternative of trading via a manager is examined, including suggestions to help the investor control the trading manager.

More complex subjects are discussed in Chapter 8. Sophisticated investments such as swaps are broken down into their basic elements. The reader is shown how simple the complex really can be once the basics are understood. The chapter concludes with an explanation of the Euro market and how the money market influences the foreign exchange rates.

Chapter 9 emphasizes the topic of risk. The risk of foreign exchange trading is broken down into counterparty risk, settlement risk, and country risk. Also discussed is the potential exposure investors and counterparties experience when investing in the interbank market. The chapter explains the ways investors can decrease their exposure to these risks. Hedging alternatives are reviewed for managing currency trading risks. Some of the risk-monitoring methods and clearing systems are also reviewed.

Appendix A contains a standard foreign exchange agreement. Appendix B offers cash currency charts. Appendix C contains S.W.I.F.T. currency codes. The book concludes with a glossary of key terms used in foreign exchange.

Russell R. Wasendorf, Sr.
Russell R. Wasendorf, Jr.

ABOUT THE AUTHORS

Russell R. Wasendorf, Sr., is Chairman and Chief Executive Officer of PFG, Inc., a futures commission merchant. He also heads Wasendorf & Associates, Inc., a research firm specializing in managed futures investment, and is President of Wasendorf & Son Company.

He has authored (or co-authored) four books: *Commodity Trading— The Essential Primer* (Dow Jones/Irwin); *All About Futures* (Probus); *All About Options* (Probus); and *All About Commodities* (Probus).

Since 1980 he has written and published the popular market letter *Futures and Options Factors.* He is the past Director of the Commodity Education Institute and founder of the Center for Futures Education.

Russell R. Wasendorf, Jr., is a registered Commodity Trading Advisor (CTA). He began his career in the futures industry in the summer of 1987 conducting branch-office compliance audits for Wasendorf & Son (W&S) Company, an introducing broker. He became a registered associated person in 1988 and a registered principal in 1991 of W&S.

In November 1993, he became an associated person and principal of PFG, Inc. In June 1995, he formed PFX, Inc., a foreign currency trading and brokerage firm.

PROLOGUE

There I was, in Kansas City, Missouri, leading my inaugural, week-long class for candidates studying to take the Commodity Brokers Examination. This was over 20 years ago, and I was Director of the Commodities Education Institute.

K.C. may seem an unlikely location to begin a series of broker training classes, but I had a good reason for this kickoff location. I selected Kansas City as a test site for my new curriculum because I felt it would be best to work out quirks in a location that would draw less attention than a high-profile location like Chicago or New York. Here I could conduct a class that still had some bugs in it.

I expected the class to be filled with midwestern "broker wanna-bes," not unlike the type of people I would expect to meet on the streets of my hometown, Cedar Falls, Iowa. My expectation was generally fulfilled. As individuals arrived and signed in, I was greeted by several young men and a couple of young women who could easily have been my Iowa neighbors. At least I would be comfortable with the audience, if not the roughly hewn instructional materials.

I stood in front of 20 or so bright, shiny, eager commodity market dilettantes, welcoming them to participate in a career in the exciting yet somewhat inexplicable world of commodity trading. The fact was, I barely knew more about the commodity broker exam than they did. My plan was to stay "one chapter ahead" and perhaps muddle through without any apparent disasters.

As I made my introductory remarks, I was interrupted by a pair of rather striking individuals entering the classroom. They were striking in nearly every way. This attractive couple, a man and a woman, were very handsomely dressed, he in a smartly tailored suit, she in furs and fine jewelry. My immediate reaction was to inquire whether they were in the right place. The gentleman responded, to my surprise, in impeccable English and a British accent, "This is the commodities class, is it not?" Yes, I'm afraid, it is, I thought, as I affirmed that they were in the right place.

Fortunately, next on the schedule was my introduction of the guest instructor for the evening. I took a place in the back of the room and wondered what this couple was doing in a Kansas City commodity class.

As the first break was announced, I didn't waste any time in interrogating the late arrivals. "What brings you to a class in Kansas City?"

"Penny and I felt it was high time that we extended our ventures into the commodities futures markets," Peter pronounced.

"And what are your current ventures?" I blurted in an attempt to appear curious rather than completely befuddled.

"I have traded the currency exchange markets for my entire adult life. "Your [meaning the U.S.] currency futures markets could be an appropriate departure from my past procedures."

"Your past procedures?"

"Years ago," Peter continued, "I became aware that European currencies fluctuated with one another. Occasionally the pound will lose ground with the mark, only later to gain some value back, then perhaps remain idle for a bit. Then something would happen, and before long one currency would be proudly in the lead.

"I discovered that I could visit an exchange bank and trade my pounds for marks and profit from the mark's gain against the pound. Provided, of course, that I scheduled my trade for the mark at a proper moment."

This wasn't the first time I had heard of foreign currency trading. My career up to that time had taken me to Europe, Latin America, and the Orient on several occasions. I was acutely aware that currency values change relative to one another. But I had never considered trading currencies as a source of personal income.

Peter went on. "I slowly built my livelihood on the practice of exchanging one currency for another. Now I see the currency exchange market has wedded with the commodity futures market at the Chicago Mercantile Exchange. You may have simplified my occupation. . . . I am here to make that determination."

This was my initiation to the foreign currency exchange markets, a professional trader earning his personal livelihood from trading currencies. Peter's example was the first of many that proved that the opportunities of benefiting in currency value fluctuations were enormous. His early lesson also told me that investors will gravitate to the most convenient marketplace. Convenience of access is essential to the development of an efficient market. Twenty years ago, currency futures markets were burgeoning as the most consistent mechanism to access the opportunities of currency markets.

Currency futures allow the investor to speculate on tomorrow's value of a particular currency in a legitimate, highly regulated marketplace. This book describes interbank foreign currency exchange in plain terms. The interbank market is a trillion-dollar-per-day monster of a market. Interbank and futures alike provide investors with the opportunity to speculate and transfer risk in the currency exchange market. The chapters in this book are intended to help investors to better understand the risks, benefits, and operations of forex and to compare and contrast forex with futures.

1

Understanding the Language of Foreign Currency Trading

INTRODUCTION

The financial world consists of many specialized sectors—stocks, bonds, metals, commodities, options, futures, swaps, derivatives, derivatives of derivatives—each with its own dynamics and vocabulary. Even veterans of the financial battleground do not know all investment venues or nomenclature. That's one reason why there are so many specialized investment advisors. They know the ins and outs of their own bailiwick, but will refer you to another specialist if you ask about an unrelated investment.

The objective of this book is to take one aspect of the investment world, foreign currency trading, and make it understandable to a general audience, even someone who knows little about the complexities of the world of finance. The subject may appear complex on the surface, but if you take it one step at a time, with a solid grounding in the basics, it becomes simple. Remember: Complexity is just a combination of basics creatively arranged.

When you finish this first chapter, you should understand the terminology of foreign currency trading. This in turn will allow you to grasp the larger concepts presented in subsequent chapters.

BASIC CONCEPTS OF FOREIGN EXCHANGE

Foreign exchange, often abbreviated *FX* or *forex*, is a trade of one currency for another at a set rate called the *exchange rate*. This rate, often referred to as a price, can be the result of supply and demand for the currency in the open, unrestricted market or, at the other extreme, a firmly fixed value determined by an edict of a government and/or its monetary authority, usually its central bank.

The Interbank Market

The setting for the interbank market is not a single location; it is virtually everywhere. It can be equated to the Internet—accessible from seemingly infinite locations. The market could be two individuals on the street exchanging U.S. dollars for deutschemarks, enabling a tourist to make a phone call in Germany.

The forex market is located in the complex network of the world's banks. The interbank market—*inter*, meaning "between," and *bank*, which simply is a depository for holding currency—could include a government bank, a public or private bank, a dealing house, a brokerage house, or a cashier desk. In traditional nomenclature, the term *interbank* implies the involvement of a large, international bank.

The balance of payments is the squaring of the account books of one bank with another so that the credit (positive) balances equal the debit (negative) balances. When a corporation buys (imports) or sells (exports) goods or services in two different currencies, the currency flows through the interbank system.

Following is a list of the top ten banks in the interbank foreign exchange market as rated by *Euromoney*'s May 1997 feature, Foreign Exchange:

1. Citibank
2. NatWest
3. Merrill Lynch
4. Deutsche Morgan Greenfell
5. Chase Manhattan
6. SBC Warburg
7. JP Morgan
8. Goldman Sachs
9. HSBC Markets/Midland
10. BZW

Currency Futures Market

Currency futures are a derivative market based on the interbank cash and forward exchange rates. Forward (and futures) exchange rates are directly influenced by the Eurodollar rate, the short-term interest rate of U.S. dollars held in Europe and in locations outside the United States. The Eurodollar rate is considered an unbiased interest rate on the U.S. dollar. The Eurodollar rate is used to calculate, determine, and evaluate the cash forwards and futures prices. In theory, to construct a forward exchange rate, one needs to factor only today's exchange rate for a currency by the interest rate the currency will gain over the given time.

Forward Market

A forward market provides the currency exchange rate for delivery in the future. Typically the interbank market enables traders to determine a forward exchange rate 30, 60, and 90 days into the future. In forex all spot (current cash) markets in practice are forwards, because all the spot currency rates are quoted on a two-day settlement time frame in order to get one currency from a counterparty to another counterparty.

Liquidity and Price

The more accessible a currency is to different countries, traders, and banks, the more it can be traded. The more trading that occurs in a currency, the greater its liquidity and therefore its efficiency.

Liquidity indicates the ease with which buyers and sellers are able to enter and exit the market. The more traders that are buying and selling a currency, the greater the likelihood of a seller wanting to sell at the same price a buyer is willing to pay. A very liquid market has numerous participants buying and selling at the same prices. An extremely liquid market is said to be deep, signifying the large number of buyers and sellers willing to trade at any given price. The efficiency of any market is determined by its liquidity.

Rate of Exchange

Ideally, currency exchange rates are determined by the natural forces of supply and demand in an open market, free of the intervention by monetary authorities. Yet, to ensure their currencies do not depreciate or appreciate excessively, intervention by a nation's monetary authorities (central banks) does occur. The intervention of central banks in currency exchange rates results in a "dirty float."

Rates of exchange on currencies can be truly floating, fixed, or a hybrid of the two. Most major currencies traded in the interbank market are floating-rate currencies. Free-floating currency rates are determined in a free-enterprise market environment where private businesses operate competitively with a minimum of government regulations and intervention.

A currency's price in relation to itself is always 1.00. One dollar can be exchanged freely for one dollar. It can also be exchanged for other free-floating currencies at a rate determined by the interbank market. Non-floating-rate currencies are controlled strictly by their respective governments and therefore are not as accessible for trade or as efficient in their pricing.

FIGURE 1-1

Wall Street Journal, "Currency Trading, Exchange Rates," Wednesday, February 12, 1997 (Reprinted by permission of *The Wall Street Journal,* © 1997 Dow Jones & Company, Inc. All Rights Reserved Worldwide.)

CURRENCY TRADIING

EXCHANGE RATES

Wednesday, February 12, 1997

The New York foreign exchange selling rates below apply to trading among banks in amounts of $1 million and more, as quoted at 4 p.m. Eastern time by Dow Jones Telerate Inc. and other sources. Retail transactions provide fewer units of foreign currency per dollar.

Country	U.S. $ equiv. Wed	Tue	Currency per U.S. $ Wed	Tue
Argentina (Peso)	1.0012	1.0012	.9988	.9988
Australia (Dollar)	.7596	.7583	1.3165	1.3187
Austria (Schilling)	.08415	.08467	11.884	11.810
Bahrain (Dinar)	2.6525	2.6525	.3770	.3770
Belgium (Franc)	.02876	.02899	34.775	34.500
Brazil (Real)	.9551	.9550	1.0471	1.0471
Britain (Pound)	1.6305	1.6372	.6133	.6108
30-Day Forward	1.6296	1.6361	.6136	.6112
90-Day Forward	1.6272	1.6343	.6145	.6119
180-Day Forward	1.6246	1.6312	.6155	.6130
Canada (Dollar)	.7378	.7378	1.3553	1.3553
30-Day Forward	.7392	.7392	1.3529	1.3529
90-Day Forward	.7419	.7421	1.3478	1.3475
180-Day Forward	.7463	.7464	1.3399	1.3398
Chile (Peso)	.002402	.002397	416.25	417.15
China (Renminbi)	.1202	.1202	8.3200	8.3216
Colombia (Peso)	.0009301	.0009309	1075.17	1074.26
Czech. Rep. (Koruna)				
Commercial rate	.03578	.03595	27.946	27.813
Denmark (Krone)	.1557	.1569	6.4233	6.3727
Ecuador (Sucre)				
Floating rate	.0002685	.0002685	3725.00	3725.00
Finland (Markka)	.2018	.2024	4.9550	4.9415
France (Franc)	.1757	.1766	5.6900	5.6610
30-Day Forward	.1760	.1769	5.6809	5.6519
90-Day Forward	.1763	.1776	5.6734	5.6311
180-Day Forward	.1777	.1786	5.6270	5.5981
Germany (Mark)	.5926	.5958	1.6876	1.6785
30-Day Forward	.5935	.5968	1.6848	1.6757
90-Day Forward	.5959	.5991	1.6781	1.6692
180-Day Forward	.5996	.6029	1.6677	1.6586
Greece (Drachma)	.003793	.003832	263.64	260.97
Hong Kong (Dollar)	.1291	.1291	7.7463	7.7450
Hungary (Forint)	.005773	.005805	173.22	172.28
India (Rupee)	.02789	.02787	35.860	35.875
Indonesia (Rupiah)	.0004207	.0004208	2376.95	2376.25
Ireland (Punt)	1.5863	1.6010	.6304	.6246
Israel (Shekel)	.2993	.3001	3.3406	3.3325
Italy (Lira)	.0006050	.0006081	1653.00	1644.50

Country	U.S. $ equiv. Wed	Tue	Currency per U.S. $ Wed	Tue
Japan (Yen)	.008052	.008102	124.20	123.43
30-Day Forward	.008082	.008133	123.73	122.96
90-Day Forward	.008153	.008203	122.66	121.91
180-Day Forward	.008260	.008311	121.07	120.33
Jordan (Dinar)	1.4094	1.4094	.7095	.7095
Kuwait (Dinar)	3.2971	3.3047	.3033	.3026
Lebanon (Pound)	.0006456	.0006455	1549.00	1549.25
Malaysia (Ringgit)	.4020	.4018	2.4873	2.4885
Malta (Lira)	2.6316	2.6316	.3800	.3800
Mexico (Peso)				
Floating rate	.1285	.1284	7.7830	7.7900
Netherland (Guilder)	.5274	.5313	1.8962	1.8822
New Zealand (Dollar)	.6869	.6875	1.4558	1.4545
Norway (Krone)	.1512	.1519	6.6151	6.5848
Pakistan (Rupee)	.02520	.02520	39.680	39.680
Peru (new Sol)	.3811	.3810	2.6238	2.6248
Philippines (Peso)	.03795	.03795	26.347	26.349
Poland (Zloty)	.3311	.3321	3.0200	3.0113
Portugal (Escudo)	.005906	.005962	169.32	167.72
Russia (Ruble) (a)	.0001773	.0001773	5640.00	5640.00
Saudi Arabia (Riyal)	.2666	.2666	3.7505	3.7505
Singapore (Dollar)	.7051	.7065	1.4183	1.4155
Slovak Rep. (Koruna)	.03080	.03080	32.473	32.473
South Africa (Rand)	.2269	.2254	4.4065	4.4375
South Korea (Won)	.001150	.001151	869.35	869.15
Spain (Peseta)	.007010	.007070	142.66	141.45
Sweden (Krona)	.1351	.1349	7.4015	7.4104
Switzerland (Franc)	.6887	.6957	1.4520	1.4375
30-Day Forward	.6907	.6976	1.4479	1.4334
90-Day Forward	.6950	.7021	1.4388	1.4243
180-Day Forward	.7020	.7090	1.4246	1.4105
Taiwan (Dollar)	.03629	.03631	27.557	27.540
Thailand (Baht)	.03848	.03855	25.990	25.937
Turkey (Lira)	.00000839	.00000851	119195.00	117555.00
United Arab (Dirham)	.2723	.2723	3.6720	3.6720
Uruguay (New Peso)				
Financial	.1129	.1129	8.8600	8.8600
Venezuela (Bolivar)	.002113	.002107	473.25	474.53
SDR	1.3820	1.3860	.7236	.7215
ECU	1.1561	1.1612		

Special Drawing Rights (SDR) are based on exchange rates for the U.S., German, British, French, and Japanese currencies. Source: International Monetary Fund.

European Currency Unit (ECU) is based on a basket of community currencies.

a-fixing, Moscow Interbank Currency Exchange.

Figure 1-1, from *The Wall Street Journal,* shows the exchange rates around the world that will be used throughout the book to create exchange rate examples.

Spot Rate

The *spot rate* for a currency is the exchange rate quoted for the closest standard settlement day. This is the current exchange rate for a trade of one currency for another. The spot rate, whether floating freely or fixed, reflects the external value of a currency at the time of trade. The spot rate is also termed the *cash price, cash rate,* or *today's rate.* Most spot interbank rates are actually traded with two-day settlements to allow for a reasonable amount of time to transfer the currencies for the transaction.

Cross Rate

An exchange rate is classified as a *cross rate* when the home currency in the transaction is not a party to the exchange rate traded. A common cross-rate transaction quoted in New York is the deutschemark versus the Japanese yen. In this case, a trader is concerned about the exchange rate changes of the deutschemark relative to the yen. If the trader thinks the mark will increase in value against the yen, then the trader will buy the deutschemark/yen cross.

Although all currencies are crosses, common practice views crosses as non-U.S. dollar transacted trades. Figure 1-2 is a table of cross-currency rates from *The Wall Street Journal.*

Forward Rate

A *forward rate* is the value of a currency relative to another currency at some set time in the future. Swiss francs valued in U.S. dollars 30 days from now will be different from the value of Swiss francs to U.S. dollars today. Forward rates are the exchange rates expected in the future. The forward rate settlement date is the date in the future when one currency will be debited (withdrawn) from the account and the other credited (deposited) into the account. Settlement dates can be 30, 60, or 90 days into the future. The difference between the spot rate and the forward rate is determined by interest rates, speculator expectation, possible government intervention, supply and demand, and other factors. Currency futures prices are very similar to forward prices except that futures contracts are standardized in size, quote mechanism, and settlement dates, and they are executed on a regulated exchange by open outcry.

FIGURE 1-2

Wall Street Journal, "Key Currency Cross Rates," Wednesday, February, 12, 1997 (Reprinted by permission of *The Wall Street Journal,* © 1997 Dow Jones & Company, Inc. All Rights Reserved Worldwide.)

Key Currency Cross Rates Late New York Trading Feb 12, 1997

	Dollar	Pound	SFranc	Guilder	Peso	Yen	Lira	D-Mark	FFranc	CdnDlr
Canada	1.3553	2.2098	.93340	.71475	.17414	.01091	.00082	.80309	.23819	....
France	5.6900	9.2775	3.9187	3.0007	.73108	.04581	.00344	3.3717	....	4.1983
Germany	1.6876	2.7516	1.1623	.88999	.21683	.01359	.00102	....	.29659	1.2452
Italy	1653.0	2695.2	1138.4	871.74	212.39	13.309	....	979.5	290.51	1219.7
Japan	124.2	202.51	85.537	65.499	15.958	....	.07514	73.596	21.828	91.64
Mexico	7.7830	12.69	5.3602	4.1045	....	.06267	.00471	4.6119	1.3678	5.7426
Netherlands ..	1.8962	3.0918	1.3059	....	.24363	.01527	.00115	1.1236	.33325	1.3991
Switzerland ...	1.4520	2.3675	....	.76574	.18656	.01169	.00088	.86039	.25518	1.0713
U.K.	.61331	....	.42239	.32344	.07880	.00494	.00037	.36342	.10779	.45253
U.S.	....	1.6305	.68871	.52737	.12849	.00805	.00060	.59256	.17575	.73784

Source: Dow Jones Telerate Inc.

Swap Rates

The *swap rate* is the short-term interest rate between the spot price and a forward price. In dealing terms, a swap rate is expressed in terms of swap points or forward points. The swap rate is calculated as follows:

Forward points =

$$\frac{\text{Spot rate x difference in interest rate of the two currencies x days until the forward}}{\text{Number of days for which the interest rate applies x 100}}$$

or

$$FP = \frac{S \times (IR1 - IR2) \times N}{YR \times 100}$$

For example, if:

$$S = 1.6875 \text{ DEM/USD}$$
$$IR1 = 1 \text{ year interest on DEM} = 3.15 \% *$$
$$IR2 = 1 \text{ year interest on USD} = 5.50\% *$$
$$N = 90 \text{ days}$$
$$YR = 360 \text{ days in a year}$$
$$FP = \frac{1.6875 \times (3.15 - 5.50) \times 90}{36,000}$$

$$FP = -.00991$$

90-day forward $= 1.6875 - .00991 = 1.67759$

* IR1 & IR2 based on Eurodollar and Euromark rates.

Swap points or forward points are a quick method for dealers, arbitrageurs, pit traders, and speculators to calculate the forward price off the cash price. Swap points are added to the cash (spot) price in order to equal the forward price.

Market Quotations

Currencies are typically quoted in the interbank market to many decimal places smaller than standard currency. For example, the U.S. dollar is expressed in dollars and cents in standard usage, but the U.S. dollar interbank market quote accounts for thousandths of a U.S. cent. The reason is obvious: When dealing in large transactions, a difference of one cent in price may equal thousands of dollars in the interbank. These thousandths of a cent are called *pips*.

Pips are defined as the smallest incremental price movement in the interbank market. Even though price movements and quotes can be less than a pip, for most practical purposes a pip can be considered the smallest increment. In the sometimes hectic action of the interbank market, it is typical to hear traders quote currency exchange rates using only a two-digit price. If the exchange rate is 1.6388, then the trader may quote only what is called the "small figure," the last two digits; i.e., 88. In this case the "big figure" is 63.

Dealing in currencies, the price (rate) is equal to a ratio of one currency to another currency. For example, if $/DEM "dollar-mark" is at 1.6388, then one dollar buys 1.6388 deutschemarks. If you invert the price (meaning "divide the price into 1"), you will get the price in terms of the other currency. For example, the price of dollars in terms of deutschemarks is DEM/$, or 1/1.6388 = .6102 (61.02 cents = one deutschemark).

Direct Quotations

A direct exchange-rate quotation is always quoted in terms of the host currency; if you are in Germany, a direct quote will be all other currency in terms of deutschemarks. This type of exchange rate is commonly quoted when a tourist walks into a country's local bank to exchange money. The exchange rates quoted for the currency futures market at the Chicago Mercantile Exchange (CME) are direct quotations. All currency prices are quoted in terms of U.S. dollars, since the U.S. dollar is the host currency. The profit and loss from a trade executed "in the currency" is computed in the host currency (for example, buying one deutschemark at $.65 and selling of the same deutschemark at $.67 yields a profit of $.02). In the interbank market, most quoting of currency prices in the United States is done on an indirect basis with foreign countries.

Indirect Quotations

Indirect quotations are the opposite of direct quotations. An example of an indirect quote in the United States for the Swiss franc is that it takes 1.23 Swiss francs to buy one U.S. dollar. If a trader bought one U.S. dollar for 1.23 Swiss francs and later sold that U.S. dollar back for 1.21 Swiss francs, he or she would lose .02 Swiss francs. Notice the loss from the transaction is in francs. To figure your loss in U.S. dollars you would have to convert the .02 Swiss francs to U.S. dollars at the current exchange rate for CHF/USD. (USD is the common code in the interbank market for U.S. dollars, and CHF is the common code for Swiss franc. Refer to Appendix C for a complete list of currency codes.)

Standard Quotations

The interbank market quotes all currencies except the British pound sterling as U.S. dollar-based. Pound sterling quotes are usually currency-based in the interbank world.

Margins and Lines of Credit

Currency transactions are executed under various conditions based on the creditworthiness of the counterparties.

Lines of credit are the main mechanisms for executing forex transactions. Less creditworthy traders (lower than AAA-rated) usually trade on a margined basis. Margin trading also is the cornerstone of futures trading.

The interbank market uses margin trading for less creditworthy customers in order to maintain the integrity of the interbank transactions. Margins are, in effect, performance bonds. Futures exchanges have created elaborate systems to calculate margins, taking into account the historical volatility of a currency and the total value of the standardized futures contract. The interbank market takes its lead from the futures exchanges' calculations and also uses margin amounts as a lever to control the volume a customer may trade at any one time.

Currency Symbols

Figure 1-3 is a partial list of common quote symbols used in the interbank and futures markets (refer to Appendix C for a complete list of currency symbols or codes).

FIGURE 1-3

Currency Symbols

Spot:		Futures:*
ARP	ARGENTINE PESO	Not Available
ATS	AUSTRIAN SCHILLING	Not Available
AUD	AUSTRALIAN DOLLAR	AD
BEF	BELGIAN FRANC	Not Available
GBP	BRITISH POUND	BP
CAD	CANADIAN DOLLAR	CD
CHF	SWISS FRANC	SF
DEM	DEUTSCHEMARK	DM
DKK	DANISH KRONER	Not Available
ECU	EUROPEAN CURRENCY UNIT	EC
FRF	FRENCH FRANC	FF
GRD	GREEK DRACHMA	Not Available
HUF	HUNGARIAN FORINT	Not Available
IEP	IRISH PUNT	Not Available
ITL	ITALIAN LIRA	Not Available
JPY	JAPANESE YEN	JY
MYR	MALAYSIAN RINGGITT	Not Available
MXP	MEXICAN PESO	Not Available
NGL	NETHERLANDS GUILDER	Not Available
NZD	NEW ZEALAND DOLLAR	Not Available
NOK	NORWEGIAN KRONER	Not Available
PTE	PORTUGUESE ESCUDO	Not Available
RUR	RUSSIAN RUBLE	Not Available
SEK	SWEDISH KRONA	Not Available

*Futures symbols are those used at the Chicago Mercantile Exchange, International Monetary Market Division. The contract month symbols for currency futures are H = March, M = June, U = September, and Z = December.

ACCOUNT STATEMENTS—HOW TO UNDERSTAND THEM

Customer account statements in any field of finance can be confusing and even a little scary. Unfortunately, forex statements are frustrating nearly all the time. FX statements are very user-unfriendly and should be viewed as "armed and dangerous." Each firm's statement looks different from those of other firms depending on the back-office computer platform used.

Most customer account statements are never seen or reviewed by a regulatory agency and may have many inaccuracies, so the trader's ability to accurately analyze the statements is extremely important.

There are basically three types of systems for producing statements: proprietary systems, standardized systems, and homemade systems.

Proprietary Systems

Proprietary systems usually have many "bells and whistles" and are customized for a major banking institution with millions of dollars to budget for back-office systems. They can often offer information tailored to the customers. The statements might provide a combination of different types of accounts offered by the institution such as futures, spot currencies, forwards, equities, and fixed income. These statements might eliminate some confusion by showing only the information needed by the institution's specific customers.

The flip side of the coin is that custom-made proprietary systems may have glitches that need to be worked out. Formulas or calculations might not have been reviewed by outside regulators for accuracy, and the system might not have enough fail-safe backups. In other words, any system that is created for only one institution does not have to go through the rigors of competition that a standardized system does.

Standardized Systems

A standardized system for producing statements is a generic one purchased "off the shelf" and ready for any institution to use for internal or customer use. Standardized systems for the forex industry are fairly expensive and involve a monthly fee for support, upgrades, training, and special requests. The companies selling standardized systems are usually put through intensive testing and review by regulatory authorities, testing the limits and security of the system before using it to service their customers. Standardized systems are usually backed up and well protected from system failures.

Problems associated with standardized systems are that they are often confusing due to extraneous information built into a "one size fits all" system. The standardized systems usually are very generic and therefore not as sophisticated as the customized proprietary systems. The standardized systems also are usually somewhat clumsy and difficult to read and understand.

Systems that have been subject to regulatory scrutiny are likely to produce statements that will show if a trade was improperly entered to the account and then corrected. The firm is unable to make any change in the account without the change showing up on the customer's statement. There is a side benefit in all the red tape of a standard system in that the trader can sleep comfortably knowing that no one can modify the calculations in his or her account without the modifications being apparent.

Homemade Systems

The lowest form of proprietary system is one home-made on a personal computer spreadsheet program. These "customized" systems have a serious lack of controls, checks, and balances and are ripe for abuse. Traders receiving spreadsheet-style customer statements should be on the alert that they may be dealing with a less than desirable counterparty. In addition, home-made systems usually do not account for regulatory or tax reporting.

The Basic Statement

Customers should expect to see the account name, counterparty, date, account number (if any), daily account activity, open positions, and currency account balance summaries on the forex statement. Figure 1-4 is a sample statement produced from a standard statement provider. (The names and transactions are fictitious and have no relationship to any person or corporation. Any similarities are purely coincidental.) In this statement, the daily account activity is divided into three sections: 1. Trades made "as of the date indicated"; 2. Trades made "today for your account and risk"; and 3. Trades that "have been delivered" (or settled). In addition to these there may also be a section for "trades that have been confirmed in error and canceled."

The open positions section of this statement (Figure 1-5) shows the "open positions," "currency recap for open positions," and the "net exposure by currency combination."

The currency account balance section of the statement (Figure 1-6) should break down any currency that has a balance, either credit or debit. Most statements also provide a combined currency section converting all the currency balances to one currency for ease of use. Figure 1-7 is a copy of a combined currency summary that converts all the previous currency balances to U.S. dollars, based on the closing currency prices.

FIGURE 1-4

Daily Account Activity

PFX, INC.
30 SOUTH WACKER DRIVE STE 2015
CHICAGO IL 60606

ACCOUNT NUMBER : B   11111
STATEMENT DATE : 19 FEB 1997

FX MULTI-NATIONAL CO

DELIVER TO RUSS JR.

* * * * * * * * * * * * * A C C O U N T   A C T I V I T Y * * * * * * * * * * * *

THE FOLLOWING TRADES HAVE BEEN MADE AS OF THE DATE INDICATED

DOCKET NUMBER	ORIGINAL TRD DATE	VALUE DATE	B/S	DEALT CCY	QUANTITY	RATE	CONTR CCY	TRANSACTION FEE IN CONTRA CCY	NET AMOUNT
	02/18/97	02/18/97	BUY	FRF	500,000.00	5.72032	USD		87,407.70-
	02/18/97	02/19/97	SELL	FRF	500,000.00-	5.72032	USD		87,407.70
					.00 *				

TOTAL FOR CONTRA USD

THE FOLLOWING TRADES HAVE BEEN MADE TODAY FOR YOUR ACCOUNT AND RISK

DOCKET NUMBER	ORIGINAL TRD DATE	VALUE DATE	B/S	DEALT CCY	QUANTITY	RATE	CONTR CCY	TRANSACTION FEE IN CONTRA CCY	NET AMOUNT
ROLL	02/19/97	02/21/97	BUY	USD	1,000,000.00	1.466	CHF		1,466,000.00-
ROLL	02/19/97	02/20/97	SELL	USD	1,000,000.00-	1.46614	CHF		1,466,140.00
					.00 *				140.00

TOTAL FOR CONTRA CHF   140.00

```
ROLL   02/19/97 02/21/97 BUY  FRF  500,000.00   5.743   USD      87,062.51-

ROLL   02/19/97 02/20/97 SELL FRF  500,000.00-  5.7433  USD      87,057.96
                                        .00 *                         4.55-

       TOTAL FOR CONTRA USD                                          4.55-
```

THE FOLLOWING TRADES HAVE BEEN DELIVERED

DOCKET NUMBER	ORIGINAL TRD DATE	VALUE DATE	B/S	DEALT CCY	QUANTITY	RATE	CONTR CCY	TRANSACTION FEE IN CONTRA CCY	NET AMOUNT
	02/18/97	02/19/97	SELL	USD	1,000,000.00-	1.47295	CHF		1,472,950.00
	02/18/97	02/19/97	BUY	USD	1,000,000.00	1.482	CHF		1,482,000.00-
					.00 *				9,050.00-
	TOTAL FOR CONTRA CHF								9,050.00-
	02/18/97	02/19/97	BUY	FRF	500,000.00	5.698	USD		87,750.09-
	02/18/97	02/18/97	BUY	FRF	500,000.00	5.72032	USD		87,407.70-
	02/18/97	02/19/97	SELL	FRF	500,000.00-	5.72032	USD		87,407.70
					500,000.00 *				87,750.09-
	TOTAL FOR CONTRA USD								87,750.09-

FIGURE 1-5
Open Positions

PAGE-   2

FX MULTI-NATIONAL CO

DELIVER TO RUSS JR.

```
                              PFX, INC.
                       30 SOUTH WACKER DRIVE STE 2015
                            CHICAGO IL 60606
```

ACCOUNT NUMBER : B   11111
STATEMENT DATE : 19 FEB 1997

* * * * * * * * * * * * * O P E N   P O S I T I O N S * * * * * * * * * * * * *

OPEN POSITIONS

DOCKET NUMBER	ORIGINAL TRD DATE	VALUE DATE	B/S	DEALT CCY	QUANTITY	RATE	CONTR CCY	MARGIN RATE	UNREALIZED P/L	NET AMOUNT
	02/18/97	02/20/97	BUY	USD	1,000,000.00	1.4728	CHF	1.4845500	11,750.00	1,472,800.00-
	02/19/97	02/21/97	BUY	USD	1,000,000.00	1.466	CHF	1.4845500	18,550.00	1,466,000.00-
	02/19/97	02/20/97	SELL	USD	1,000,000.00-	1.46614	CHF	1.4845500	18,410.00-	1,466,140.00
					1,000,000.00 *				11,890.00 *	1,472,660.00-

TOTAL FOR CONTRA CHF

DOCKET NUMBER	ORIGINAL TRD DATE	VALUE DATE	B/S	DEALT CCY	QUANTITY	RATE	CONTR CCY	MARGIN RATE	UNREALIZED P/L	NET AMOUNT
	02/18/97	02/20/97	BUY	FRF	500,000.00	5.72	USD	5.7270000	106.85-	87,412.59-
	02/19/97	02/21/97	BUY	FRF	500,000.00	5.743	USD	5.7270000	243.23	87,062.51-
	02/19/97	02/20/97	SELL	FRF	500,000.00-	5.7433	USD	5.7270000	247.78-	87,057.96
					500,000.00 *				111.40-*	87,417.14-

TOTAL FOR CONTRA USD   87,417.14-

14

```
CURRENCY RECAP FOR OPEN POSITIONS
CCY      DEALT AMOUNT              CONTRA AMOUNT              NET AMOUNT
---      ------------              -------------              ----------
USD      1,000,000.00                 87,417.14-            912,582.86
CHF              .00              1,472,660.00-           1,472,660.00-
FRF        500,000.00                      .00             500,000.00


NET EXPOSURE BY CURRENCY COMBINATION
            USD                        CHF                       FRF
         --------------             --------------             --------------
USD                                  1,000,000.00               87,417.14-

CHF      1,472,660.00-

FRF        500,000.00
```

FIGURE 1.6
Currency Account Balances

PFX, INC.
30 SOUTH WACKER DRIVE STE 2015
CHICAGO IL 60606

ACCOUNT NUMBER : B   11111
STATEMENT DATE : 19 FEB 1997

FX MULTI-NATIONAL CO

DELIVER TO RUSS JR.

DEM

PREVIOUS BALANCE	4,700.00
MATCHOUT PROCEEDS	.00
DELIVERY PROCEEDS	.00
ROLLOVER PROCEEDS	.00
JOURNAL POSTINGS	.00
ENDING BALANCE	4,700.00
UNREALIZED P & L	.00
DEPOSIT REQUIREMENTS	.00
SECURITIES ON DEPOSIT	.00
EXCHANGE RATE TO USD	1.69665

FRF

PREVIOUS BALANCE	500,000.00-
MATCHOUT PROCEEDS	.00
DELIVERY PROCEEDS	500,000.00
ROLLOVER PROCEEDS	.00
JOURNAL POSTINGS	.00
ENDING BALANCE	.00
UNREALIZED P & L	.00
DEPOSIT REQUIREMENTS	.00
SECURITIES ON DEPOSIT	.00
EXCHANGE RATE TO USD	5.72700

CHF

PREVIOUS BALANCE	32,760.00
MATCHOUT PROCEEDS	.00
DELIVERY PROCEEDS	9,050.00-
ROLLOVER PROCEEDS	.00
JOURNAL POSTINGS	.00
ENDING BALANCE	23,710.00
UNREALIZED P & L	11,890.00
DEPOSIT REQUIREMENTS	.00
SECURITIES ON DEPOSIT	.00
EXCHANGE RATE TO USD	1.48455

USD

PREVIOUS BALANCE	335,131.65
MATCHOUT PROCEEDS	.00
DELIVERY PROCEEDS	87,750.09-
ROLLOVER PROCEEDS	.00
JOURNAL POSTINGS	.00
ENDING BALANCE	247,381.56
UNREALIZED P & L	111.40-
DEPOSIT REQUIREMENTS	.00
SECURITIES ON DEPOSIT	.00
EXCHANGE RATE TO USD	1.00000

FIGURE 1-7

Equivalent U.S. Dollar Account Balance

```
PAGE-    4

FX MULTI-NATIONAL CO

DELIVER TO RUSS JR.


                              PFX, INC.
                    30 SOUTH WACKER DRIVE STE 2015
                            CHICAGO IL 60606

                                          ACCOUNT NUMBER : B    11111
                                          STATEMENT DATE : 19 FEB 1997

EQUIVALENT
U.S. DOLLARS

PREVIOUS BALANCE              272,663.36
MATCHOUT PROCEEDS                    .00
DELIVERY PROCEEDS               6,540.47-
ROLLOVER PROCEEDS                    .00
JOURNAL POSTINGS                     .00
ENDING BALANCE                266,122.88
UNREALIZED P & L                7,897.76
DEPOSIT REQUIREMENTS                 .00
SECURITIES ON DEPOSIT                .00
ACCOUNT EXCESS/DEFICIT        266,122.88
LIQUIDATING A/C VALUE         274,020.64
WITHDRAWABLE FUNDS            266,122.88
```

CHAPTER 2

What You Don't Know May Hurt You

INTRODUCTION

When it comes to the design of regulatory systems, disaster can teach some powerful lessons. California's building codes are based on that state's experience with earthquakes. Florida's standards owe their structure to hurricanes. The same principle holds true in the world of finance, where disasters are usually caused by human beings. Coordinated circuit breakers in the securities and stock index futures markets (as well as many other reforms) are an outgrowth of the October 1987 stock market break. The very existence of an independent CFTC, with jurisdiction over futures trading in all commodities, owes a great deal to the early 1970s Goldstein-Samuelson options fraud and the $70 million in customer losses it entailed.

The most recent fiscal "earthquake" to shake global financial markets involved trading in a foreign office of a British merchant bank.* The losses topped $1 billion and ultimately leveled an institution that traced its origins back to the Napoleonic Wars.

LEVERAGE: A WAY OF LIFE IN FOREX TRADING

Now for the real kicker: News about the foreign exchange world may not be as bad as the real danger. Foreign currency trading is a sector of the

---

*Introduction to the "Status Report on Regulatory and Self-Regulatory Responses to the Barings Bankruptcy," Joseph B. Dial, Commissioner of the Commodity Futures Trading Commission, 18th Annual Commodities Law Institute and 4th Annual Financial Services Law Institute, October 19, 1995, Chicago, Illinois.

financial industry based upon credit, interest rates, and leverage. Enough leverage can lift the pyramids, but it can also kill pharaohs!

Leverage is the use of a small deposit of capital to secure a larger position. In the case of foreign currency trading, a bank often does not have to put any money with a counterparty to make a transaction. The volume and past performance of the bank have created a relationship of trust and reliability. Yet, as all traders understand all too well, past performance is not necessarily indicative of future results. Therefore, a bank on the long road to decline may maintain foreign currency operations even though the bank maintains little to zero cash reserves. Even a slight market hiccup may surpass the capital backing of the transaction and push the bank into insolvency. This hiccup, if passed on to another relatively unprotected bank, can cause a devastating chain reaction: One bank's default is another bank's default and so on.

NONSEGREGATED FUNDS

To make matters worse, the banking world does not normally segregate customer funds for foreign currency trading. The concept of segregation of customer funds came from abuses in the brokerage industry. Their practices started to follow the path of a Ponzi scheme, whereby customers' funds were commingled with the funds of the investment bank or broker. The end result would inevitably be the loss of the customers' funds.

For example, say Joe Investor went to his reputable local brokerage firm and invested $10,000. Half of the investment would be tied up in some financial asset, such as the corporate stock of the brokerage firm, and the other half would sit in the brokerage firm's cash reserves. Because interest can be made on those available funds, the brokerage would invest them in short-term, reliable instruments. The funds would be secure, and the investor would get the cash reserves back upon request.

The problem arises when brokers realize they could make a slightly higher return in higher-risk investments. The cash reserves would be invested into low-capital corporate stocks, junk bonds, and other higher-yielding assets. When a loss occurred, the firm would have to borrow cash from a bank to pay back the loss in the customer's cash reserves. The brokerages then take the procedure one step further by borrowing from the cheapest lender—the customer. The reserves of one customer would be used to meet the firm's obligations to other customers. In the end, a deficit would occur if the customers overall lost money. The remaining customers would request funds more actively, as they sensed financial instability in the brokerage. The brokerage firm would then collapse in bankruptcy, with little recourse for the unpaid investors.

One solution would be to segregate the customer funds from the firm's operating capital. Customer funds would be held in customer-segregated accounts at different banks and depositories, and cash accounts would be audited by a regulatory agency and/or a certified public accountant.

An example of the system gone awry is the Barings disaster. Even though it was not a direct result of foreign currency trading in the interbank community, the bankruptcy was a result of transactions in the futures and the over-the-counter (OTC) market. The over-the-counter market deals in products that are not listed on an officially recognized stock exchange but rather are traded in direct negotiation between buyers and sellers.

COUNTERPARTY RISK

The least visible risk of the interbank or OTC markets is counterparty risk. Interbank transactions consist of at least two parties, or counterparties, per transaction. Each party to the transaction is responsible for fulfilling the agreed-upon terms. If one counterparty to the transaction doesn't fulfill the terms, the entire transaction can be considered in default. Any default or risk of default is considered counterparty risk. Counterparty risk may not have anything to do with a trader's direct counterparty. Perhaps it is the counterparty's counterparty. There can be many counterparties to a single transaction, any one of which can cause a default.

For example, assume that ABC Bank is buying deutschemarks and XYZ Bank is selling deutschemarks and together they execute the contract at a given exchange rate. XYZ Bank decides that it doesn't want to hold onto the position, so it lays off the risk to DEF Bank. If DEF Bank defaults on the transaction, XYZ Bank won't get the money from DEF Bank and won't be able to meet its agreement with ABC Bank. So it goes, the chain reaction, with each bank defaulting on promises to the next bank.

Risk Transfer—Exchanges and Clearinghouses

Regulated exchanges were created, in part, to address the issue of counterparty risk. Exchanges are locations where different counterparties meet to execute transactions. Transactions are made at and with the exchange, and at the end of the day all transactions are cleared by the exchange clearinghouse. The losses on one side of the transaction are debited from one customer's account, and the profits are added to the other customer's account. Clearinghouses become the buyer to every seller and the seller to every buyer. In that way, they are able to balance the books of each customer so both sides are protected. When a trader makes a transaction through a regulated exchange, the risk is not the risk of default from any one counterparty but the risk of the exchange or the clearinghouse defaulting, which is far more remote. Your counterparty is the exchange, not any one corporation or individual.

Exchange clearinghouses require a certain margin or performance bond, usually based on market volatility. It is the responsibility of clearinghouses to make sure that enough of a margin is specified for each transaction They closely monitor margin levels and market fluctuations to reduce the risk of loss due to counterparty risk. An exchange such as the Chicago Mercantile Exchange is considered "good to the last drop," meaning the combined capital of all clearing members is security for transactions on the exchange, protecting the integrity of the marketplace.

Margined and Credit-Based Trading

There is no clearinghouse in the over-the-counter market or the foreign currency market. The transactions are primarily bank to bank, principal to principal, counterparty to counterparty. Many transactions are based on credit lines alone, with no margin requirement.

There are different levels of credit: the central bank level, the AAA-rated banks that can transact solely on credit, and the margined currency transactions. Margined currency transactions require a percentage of margin to be placed with each counterparty in order to meet any market movement that may occur between the time the transaction is initiated and the time it is actually delivered or settled.

Transactions in the spot currency markets normally settle in two days. Between the time when the transaction is executed and settlement occurs, there is a risk of market movement in case one party defaults on the transaction. For example, if a customer buys deutschemarks from a bank and then fails to put up the full value of the money to take delivery, the bank can close the transaction by buying deutschemarks from another bank. Remember, the bank originally sold the deutschemarks to the customer, which left the bank with an open sell position. In buying deutschemarks from another bank, it offsets the transaction. Hopefully the bank can cover the difference of the market movement from the time the customer bought to the time the settlement is to occur, with the margin on deposit from the customer. That's counterparty risk.

Banks or counterparties usually have their own compliance departments performing due diligence to evaluate customers' net worth and cred-itworthiness. Their main priority is to limit their liability with each counterparty. The margin is employed in the event of a default, to offset the risk of any transaction the customer might make. For example, assume a customer puts up $1 million with a bank and executes a transaction repre-senting a total value of $100 million. If the $100 million transaction ends up losing $1.5 million, and the customer is not able to meet the terms of the transaction, the bank has only $1 million to cover a $1.5 million loss.

For customers trading on a credit basis, the bank's due diligence usu-ally reduces the risk by limiting the customer's transaction size. If the cus-tomer is trading on margin, the transactions are normally based solely on how much money the customer has in the account or the liquidating value of the account—the value of the customer's account if closed out of the market at the current price. A customer who has $100,000 in his or her account and an allowance to trade on 5% margin will be able to execute transactions up to $2 million. And if the margin requirement is lowered from 5% to 1%, the $100,000 would enable the customer to execute a $10 million position. With a position that size, it becomes much easier to lose $100,000. The counterparty is at risk from the time the customer loses $100,000 or more.

A more extreme credit department stance may require full margin, meaning that if a customer executes a $1 million position, the customer must place $1 million on margin or on deposit. That leaves the counterparty virtually risk-free.

In the absence of full margin, the best risk-stance margin is one in which a counterparty has a credit customer—a customer trading on a credit line. The customer does not have to put up any money but promises to pay any losses in the underlying position. All transactions are protected with a letter of credit from a qualified bank.

A final example of a credit stance is one in which the customer is allowed to trade any size contract and lose any amount based on the customer's ability to meet any liabilities to counterparties. The stance is only for central banks, governments, and for AAA-credit rated banks. The risk of default is extremely unlikely. Unfortunately, it is not as unlikely as most people think it is. A counterparty default on an AAA credit rating level is enough to put the financial world in turmoil, as was the case with the Barings Bank default.

The trillion-dollar-per-day foreign exchange industry is constantly looking at ways to protect against counterparty risks and losses that could devastate the entire financial world.

Counterparty Jurisdiction Risk

Another consideration is whether a counterparty is in the same jurisdiction and whether or not the counterparty is regulated. When a customer enters an agreement with a counterparty, the customer is normally required to complete a contract that specifies the provisions of that agreement. The agreement is likely to include provisions for the remedy of disputes between the counterparty and the customer and the responsibilities of the customer.

These contracts will normally specify the legal jurisdiction of the transactions, the court where any dispute of a transaction may be resolved, and what laws will be applicable. A U.S. customer might feel just as comfortable executing a transaction with a counterparty in Hong Kong as with one located inside the United States, until there is a dispute in a transaction. It may be much more difficult for the U.S. customer to resolve the dispute in Hong Kong courts.

A DAY IN THE LIFE OF FOREX

Forex news stories are almost as large and interesting as the industry itself. What central bank is going to cut rates? Who's going to intervene? Who are the major speculators? And who actually knows which direction the currencies are going? Who has control?

Despite all the powerful governments, central banks, large speculators, and private banks in the world, no one has control of foreign currencies. Governments have tried to control their currencies, but the size and depth of the interbank are so great that a country which tries to stifle the volatility of its currency by fixing exchange rates finds its currency floating in the black market.

To get a better perspective of a day in the foreign exchange industry, consider February 12, 1997. The news article reprinted in Figure 2-1 illustrates the impact of foreign exchange on world events. The article discusses how the exchange rate of the yen versus the U.S. dollar has affected trade surpluses and deficits between the United States and Japan. The yen had just reached its four-year low against the U.S. dollar, making foreign goods more expensive in Japan and Japanese products cheaper overseas. In keeping with the buy low, sell high theory, the article predicts an increase in Japan's trade surplus due to the low cost of Japanese products and the high cost of U.S. exports. This would certainly affect the balance of trade between the two countries.

FIGURE 2-1

Wall Street Journal, "Economy, Japan's Exporters Grow Bolder, Stronger, Trade Surplus Is Poised to Rise, Which Worries Some," February, 12, 1997. (Reprinted by permission of *The Wall Street Journal,* © 1997 Dow Jones & Company, Inc. All Rights Reserved Worldwide.)

ECONOMY

Japan's Exporters Grow Bolder, Stronger
Trade Surplus Is Poised to Rise, Which Worries Some

By DAVID P. HAMILTON
Staff Reporter of THE WALL STREET JOURNAL

TOKYO — Maybe Japan is going to export its way out of its economic doldrums after all.

The yen is at a four-year low against the dollar, making foreign goods more

Double Whammy

Already shaken by a spate of bad loans, Japan's banks are under siege on another front: the strong dollar, which makes their balance sheets look riskier and makes it tougher to meet international standards. Article on page A12.

expensive in Japan and Japanese products cheaper overseas. Largely as a result, imports are starting to sag after a long boom, while exports are once again rising. The upshot: Japan's trade surplus, which has fallen for four straight years, is all but certain to head back up this year, buoying the economy and annoying Japan's trading partners.

Measured in terms of the volume or amount of goods shipped, imports to Japan fell in four of the last seven months of 1996 and increased only 1.6% for the whole year — a poor showing compared with gains of 14% in 1994 and 13% in 1995. Exports rose 6% in volume over the last three months of 1996, their strongest performance in a year and a half. The effects of both trends are strongest where the U.S. is concerned; imports from the U.S. were down 4% over the last quarter of 1996 compared with a year earlier, while exports to the U.S. were up 7%.

Welcome News

The trade surplus, measured in yen, hasn't started rising yet, but the underlying trends in trade volume — pushed by the weak yen — suggest it is only a matter of time.

Peter Morgan, an economist in Tokyo with James Capel Pacific Ltd., expects Japan's overall current-account surplus to jump 26% this year, to 9.2 trillion yen ($74.54 billion), and to rise 17% next year. For Japan, a rising trade surplus is welcome news. Any increase in the nation's still-huge trade advantage—which amounted to 6.744 trillion yen in 1996 — adds directly to economic growth as "net exports," since it means more goods from Japanese factories are being sold overseas. And a rising surplus may be about the only hope for the Japanese economy this year, now that the govern-

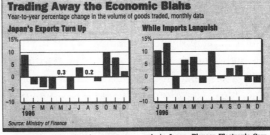

Trading Away the Economic Blahs
Year-to-year percentage change in the volume of goods traded, monthly data

Japan's Exports Turn Up

While Imports Languish

Source: Ministry of Finance

ment appears determined to attack its rising budget deficit by raising sales taxes and cutting public-works spending, steps that will probably suppress household spending.

"Japan hasn't got anywhere else to go," says Russell Jones, an economist with Lehman Brothers Japan Inc. who thinks net exports will contribute half a percentage point to what he estimates will be 2% economic growth in 1997. Some economists go even further; Jesper Koll of J.P. Morgan Securities Asia Ltd. expects 2.1% growth in 1997 and says net exports will account for 0.9 percentage point of that.

That's a turnabout from the past several years, when weak exports and an import surge held down economic growth. In 1996, the falling trade surplus is estimated to have cut roughly a full percentage point off Japan's growth rate.

Made (Only) in Japan

Exporters are growing bolder, tempted by the weak yen and fresh demand for products made only in Japan. Toyota Motor Corp. has expanded exports to the U.S. of its Lexus luxury sedans and its hot RAV4 and 4-Runner sport-utility vehicles, which it makes only in Japan. Honda Motor Co. plans to boost exports to the U.S. in 1997 by 24%, to 460,000 vehicles, mostly to meet demand for its CR-V sport-utility vehicle. Overall auto exports from Japan surged almost 13% in the last quarter of 1996, mostly representing vehicles shipped to the U.S.

Cars aren't the only popular exports these days. Many Japanese electronics companies are starting to turn out new generations of digital consumer-electronics and office-equipment products, many of which also are currently made

only in Japan. Pioneer Electronic Corp., for instance, says that by March, its ratio of overseas production will have declined to 49% from 51% a year ago, largely because only its factories in Japan make its new digital-videodisk players and large, flat-panel "plasma display" televisions. Exports of **Ricoh** Co.'s digital photocopiers have jumped to 28% of total sales from 26% a year ago.

The resurgence in exports isn't unalloyed good news for Japan. It could stall or reverse many of the important structural changes to Japan's economy wrought by hard times the past four years. Although many big exporters insist they will continue manufacturing their products overseas, some, like **Sanyo Electric** Co., say they have started thinking about "rebalancing" production by shifting some back to Japan. Strapped exporters that a year ago faced the choice of restructuring or bankruptcy now can enjoy profits from the weak yen. Domestic cartels that were pressured by cheap imports can take a breather.

A bigger trade surplus would cause political problems abroad, too. To Japan's trading partners, the specter of an export-led economy could revive the image of Japan Inc. as a mercantilist power bent on prospering at others' expense. Japan's economy today in some respects resembles that of almost 15 years ago, when the Japanese government raised taxes and clamped down on spending in order to bring down a stubborn deficit. Back then, the resulting export boom created so much trade friction that the world's industrial powers eventually agreed to slow Japan down by boosting the yen in the 1985 Plaza Accord.

The U.S. auto industry has already resurrected that rhetoric. "After five years of slow growth, Japan's Ministry of Finance is reverting to its old tricks," Richard Wagoner, head of **General Motors** Corp.'s North American operations, said last week. "It's a mystery to me why the U.S. continues to accept Japan's attempts to export its problems." Wary of being made political scapegoats, Japanese auto

Please Turn to Page A5, Column 1

Balance of trade is the net of imports minus exports. Imports are the products a country buys for its internal consumption. Exports are the items it produces to sell to other countries. A car that is produced in Japan to be sold to a consumer in the United States is an export of Japan and an import of the United States. The car would be valued in yen because its production costs are generated from yen-based natural resources. The labor, the factory, and the metals, plastics, and products that were used in the production of the car are all yen-based. If the yen is cheap, the cost of the car will also be cheap.

The expected increase in Japan's trade surplus should spell economic growth for Japan, and the timing couldn't be better. The Japanese government was planning to implement some fairly drastic measures to decrease its growing budget deficit, such as increasing its sales taxes and decreasing public work spending. Japanese exporters, particularly electronics and car companies, were looking to take advantage of the yen's low cost by increasing exports to the United States.

This spells trouble for Japanese politicians because the United States is not going to be happy with the Japanese government decreasing its investment in the United States while the United States will be increasing its investment in Japan.

In 1985, the industrial world leaders agreed to slow Japanese exports by boosting the value of the yen.

If Japan wants the United States to continue buying Japanese products, it must maintain the image of increasing its investments in the United States. In fact, Japan has been talking about increasing investments in overseas (U.S.) factories, but that may just be rhetoric in light of the recent decrease in imports of U.S. products into Japan.

Finally, the article points out that Japan will eventually fall back in line with the rest of the world's economic powers, as the cycles of currency balance each other out. Japan's expected trade surplus means an expected increase in political pressure from the United States, which means decreasing profitability of exports due to U.S. import taxes and tariffs. Imports into Japan also will become more expensive for the Japanese, which means there will be an increase in the cost of goods and hence higher inflation.

Reserve Requirements: The Lessons of Barings

The article in Figure 2-2 focuses on how the value of the U.S. dollar versus the Japanese yen has had a dramatic effect on Tokyo banks in the last few years. Japanese banks were already under a lot of pressure from the financial world, and the Barings disaster led to stricter international banking standards to avoid major financial disaster. International standards require international banks to maintain a level of reserves, usually around 12% of the assets they have on deposit. The reserves may be held in either securities or cash. Reserves are used to cover the loans offered to different corporations and countries.

Unfortunately, Japanese banks loaned large sums of money to Japanese corporations for U.S. development. Because these loans are U.S. dollar-based, their value is that much greater on their books, due to their strength, so they must maintain a higher reserve for those loans. The value of the loan on the Japanese books has to be expressed in yen, and since a stronger dollar represents more yen, it swells the value of the outstanding loans. Thus, Japanese banks need more reserves. Unfortunately, security reserves of the major Tokyo banks have decreased dramatically due to declines in the Tokyo stock market. Many major Japanese banks have unrealized paper losses on their balance sheet, and their reserves have decreased with the declining value of the Tokyo stock market. Banks become more risky when they fall below international banking standards. The Tokyo banks breathed a sigh of relief when the stock market gained 1.3% on February 12 due to news that the Japanese government was going to support its troubled banks (see Figure 2-3).

Strong versus Weak Currencies

The article in Figure 2-4 examines how a strong U.S. dollar and a weak foreign currency will produce higher stock values for foreign markets. The stocks of foreign companies will become more valuable when they are priced in a weak currency and therefore more in demand by international investors.

The article in Figure 2-5 describes a classic "game of chicken" between market speculators and central banks. Who's going to flinch first? Interbank traders ignored calls by finance ministers and central banks to slow the rise of the dollar, which was then valued at 1.6932 deutschemarks per dollar. Until the central banks intervene, the market will challenge their authority. This potentially increases the probability of intervention.

The same economic forces discussed in the previous articles apply here as well. Trade surplus increases economic growth. Economic growth increases inflation. Inflation increases interest rates. As interest rates increase, so does the value of the currency. This article also suggests that the European countries would actually prefer to see their currencies weaker

FIGURE 2-2

Wall Street Journal, "Japan's Trade Surplus Looks Poised to Rise, Thanks to Weak Yen," February 12, 1997. (Reprinted by permission of *The Wall Street Journal,* © 1997 Dow Jones & Company, Inc. All Rights Reserved Worldwide.)

Japan's Trade Surplus Looks Poised to Rise, Thanks to Weak Yen

Continued From Page A2

executives insist that they intend to continue investing in overseas factories and say they don't expect the surge in auto exports to last.

Japan would probably be less sensitive to such attacks if imports continued to grow steadily. Import growth has slowed sharply, and imports might even start shrinking later this year. Again, the U.S. is bearing the brunt of this shift. Japan's auto makers, for instance, are scaling back "reverse imports" of their U.S.-made cars to Japan, contributing to a roughly 6% fall in auto imports over the October-December quarter from a year earlier. Steel imports are down almost 10% over the same period.

Japan's increasing propensity to import manufacturing goods—one of the most notable economic trends here of the past few years—may also be reversing itself. In September, manufactured goods as a percentage of total imports reached a record high of 62%. Since then, however, that percentage has steadily fallen, to 56% in December.

Any growth in Japan's trade surplus, of course, may eventually temper itself. A sharp rise in the trade balance would very likely push the yen upward as currency markets bet on political pressure from the U.S., thus cutting the profitability of exports. The weak yen is also slowly forcing up the prices of imported goods, which could eventually fuel domestic inflation, resulting in higher interest rates and again a stronger yen.

Yet even if the yen does suddenly strengthen, it probably won't change the trade picture much in the near term. Mr. Jones of Lehman Brothers argues that trade flows tend to lag behind exchange-rate shifts by three to five quarters, suggesting that the recent export surge and import slowdown is actually the result of the yen falling to 106 to the dollar almost a year ago. "This trend," he says, "is likely to deepen over the year."

FIGURE 2-3

Wall Street Journal, "Raging Dollar Threatens Tokyo's Banks, Balance Sheets Look Riskier, Global Mandates Tougher," February, 12, 1997 (Reprinted by permission of *The Wall Street Journal,* © 1997 Dow Jones & Company, Inc. All Rights Reserved Worldwide.)

Raging Dollar Threatens Tokyo's Banks
Balance Sheets Look Riskier, Global Mandates Tougher

By ROBERT STEINER
Staff Reporter of THE WALL STREET JOURNAL

TOKYO — Japan's troubled banks now have another headache: The strong dollar may make it harder for them to meet international banking standards.

The rising dollar in essence makes their balance sheets look riskier. Japanese banks lend lots of money in dollars, but their ledgers account for those loans in yen. As those lent-out dollars strengthen, they represent more yen and swell the value of the banks' loans outstanding.

The upshot: Bigger loans on the books mean the banks need more capital in mandatory reserves. Some major Japanese banks now have barely enough in reserve to meet standards set by the Bank for International Settlements, the Switzerland-based watchdog of global banking. The BIS requires minimum reserves equal to 8% of loans by international banks.

Daiwa Bank, for example, has reserves equal to 9% of assets, compared with about 12% at most big U.S. banks. But "if the yen is depreciating, the size of our risk assets gets bigger," says a Daiwa spokesman in Osaka. "So meeting the ratio is a little difficult."

The low-yen woes are a double-whammy for Japan's banks. The tumbling Tokyo stock market has already dealt a blow by shrinking paper profits on banks' stock portfolios—paper profits they used to help meet BIS standards. With the Nikkei 225 average at just over 18,400, down 12% since Dec. 5, Goldman, Sachs & Co. calculates that some big banks, such as Yasuda Trust & Banking Co., are near their danger zones: If the Nikkei falls below 18,200, Yasuda will lose all its hidden profits on stocks, Goldman says.

The U.S. dollar, meanwhile, continued its bull run in Tokyo yesterday, trading for as much as 124.22 yen, a four-year high. Investors appeared to ignore hints from the Group of Seven finance ministers over the weekend that the dollar had risen too far. Economists note that the dollar won't stop rising until relative economic conditions in the industrialized economies change.

Foreign loans and other assets account for an average 22% of the assets at Japan's top 20 banks, says Paul Heaton, an analyst at Deutsche Bank Capital Markets (Asia) Ltd.; most of that is pegged to the dollar.

As a result, every time the dollar jumps 10 yen, a big Japanese bank's reserves on average covers 0.4 percentage point less of its loans, according to IBCA Ltd., a London credit rating agency. To make up for that, the bank would have to shovel six months' operating profits into reserves, money Japanese banks badly need to get new business and write off bad loans, says

Sitting on the Edge
Estimated capital-adequacy ratios at major Japanese banks, under different market conditions

NIKKEI 225	18000	17000
YEN PER DOLLAR	120	130
Ind. Bank of Japan	8.39%	8.10%
Sakura Bank	8.68	7.77
Fuji Bank	8.22	7.16
Daiwa Bank	9.54	7.94
Tokai Bank	8.79	7.51
Chuo Trust	9.71	7.85

Source: Deutsche Bank Capital Markets Ltd.

Koyo Ozeki, a director for IBCA in Tokyo.

Another option for banks is to raise capital by selling off stock holdings — not an attractive notion in today's market. Meanwhile, Merrill Lynch expects the dollar to rise to 130 yen this year, and many Japanese securities firms say the Nikkei stock average could slip to 17,000.

The combination would drive at least five banks below the 8% minimum, says Deutsche Bank's Mr. Heaton: Sakura Bank, Fuji Bank, Tokai Bank, Daiwa Bank and Chuo Trust & Banking Corp. He concedes his calculations don't account for money banks may have raised through private bond offerings in recent months.

Still, "we are talking about skating a little closer to the edge," he says. "That is not good."

Sakura won't comment on Mr. Heaton's calculations. But other banks say they could keep reserves above 8% by selling loans or issuing bonds. A Fuji Bank spokesman says it can sell off one trillion yen ($8.1 billion) of loans every six months.

But selling loans "can't be done rapidly," Mr. Heaton says. It would amount to "a fire sale" of the real estate that banks hold as collateral, he says, "and the losses involved would be substantial." Banks have been selling loans for some time, IBCA's Mr. Ozeki adds, and still, "some negative pressures remain" on them. And analysts note that issuing bonds is a costly way to add to reserves.

To have foreign lending boomerang as a liability is a cruel twist for Japanese banks. In recent years, they pinned their hopes on global banking because Japan's economy is growing so slowly. As a first step, they followed their Japanese clients overseas, financing factories everywhere from Southeast Asia to the U.S.

But the dollar's rise could force them back to basics. "Unless banks build up a reasonable reserve," Mr. Ozeki warns, "their capacity as financial intermediaries will diminish greatly."

FIGURE 2-4

WORLD MARKETS

Tokyo Prices Surge, Bolstered by Strong Dollar; Several Bourses Extend Record-Setting Streaks

A WALL STREET JOURNAL News Roundup

Tokyo stocks racked up a 1.3% gain Wednesday, bolstered by a stronger U.S. dollar against the yen and more indications that the Japanese government will support ailing banks. The London market ended mixed, its early gains erased by a sharp drop in British unemployment. Frankfurt equities jumped to their eighth consecutive record. Amsterdam, Mexico City and Sydney shares all extended their record-setting streaks.

World-wide, stock prices rose in dollar terms. The Dow Jones World Stock Index was at 150.34, up 1.32, reflecting higher markets in the Americas and Asia/Pacific and declines in Europe/Africa.

Semiconductor stocks were the top gainers in the Dow Jones Global Industry Groups, closing at 555.54, up 22.38, or 4.20%, with Applied Materials of the U.S. posting a 15.51% gain. Trucking stocks trailed at 82.40, down 1.07, or 1.28%, with Arnold Industries of the U.S. sliding 9.84%.

In Tokyo, the Nikkei 225-stock index climbed 228.79 points to 18409.96, after advancing 314.13 points Monday; the market was closed Tuesday for a national holiday. On Thursday, the Nikkei surged 343.18 points to close the morning session at 18753.14. Wednesday's first-section volume was estimated at 457 million shares, up from 340.5 million shares on Monday. Losers narrowly topped gainers, 552-523. The Tokyo Stock Price Index, or Topix,

of all first-section issues gained 13.54 points, or 1%, to 1368.43.

The head of Japan's ruling Liberal Democratic Party said the government was prepared to use tax funds to help commercial banks in an emergency; this followed the finance minister's Monday remarks, also suggesting government support for the banks. Positive sentiment prompted buying to cut losses in short sales of stock that had been borrowed in hopes of a price drop that would allow its replacement at a profit. With the dollar up against the yen in Tokyo, Japanese public pension funds bought export-oriented real estate issues, which soared 2.1%, while foreign investors snapped up high-technology blue chips; the electronics sector zipped up 1.9%.

In London, the Financial Times-Stock Exchange 100-share index slipped 0.1 point to 4304.3 after moving between an intraday low of 4293.6 and high of 4324.3. The FT 250-stock index fell 12.1 points to 4574.5. Provisional volume was 915.6 million shares, compared with 868.7 million shares a day earlier.

DOW JONES GLOBAL INDEXES

5:30 p.m., Wednesday, February 12, 1997

REGION/ COUNTRY	DJ GLOBAL INDEXES, LOCAL CURRENCY	PCT. CHG.	IN U.S. DOLLARS 5:30 P.M. INDEX	CHG.	PCT. CHG.	12-MO HIGH	12-MO LOW	12-MO CHG.	PCT. CHG.	FROM 12/31	PCT. CHG.
Americas			187.39 +	2.92 +	1.58	187.39	146.19 +	34.73 +	22.75	+14.00 +	8.07
Canada	167.33 +	0.59	142.61 +	0.86 +	0.61	143.22	110.46 +	28.15 +	24.60 +	7.20 +	5.32
Mexico	271.82 +	1.62	107.20 +	1.81 +	1.72	107.20	78.44 +	21.71 +	25.40	+12.89	+13.66
U.S.	757.74 +	1.64	757.74	+12.19 +	1.64	757.74	591.10	+139.71 +	22.61	+57.19 +	8.16
Europe/Africa			162.80 −	0.25 −	0.15	164.30	137.76 +	22.91 +	16.38 +	2.50 +	1.56
Austria	118.43 +	0.51	106.49 −	0.09 −	0.08	114.62	102.06 +	0.31 +	0.29 −	3.51 −	3.19
Belgium	176.36 +	0.42	159.00 −	0.67 −	0.42	162.27	139.85 +	14.82 +	10.28 +	0.36 +	0.23
Denmark	156.15 +	1.13	143.87 +	0.49 +	0.34	145.81	113.59 +	24.98 +	21.01 +	6.61 +	4.82
Finland	358.54 −	0.10	299.90 −	1.19 −	0.40	303.18	191.46 +	99.97 +	50.01	+19.18 +	6.83
France	159.36 +	0.77	144.77 +	0.04 +	0.03	147.77	123.13 +	21.36 +	17.31 +	2.40 +	1.68
Germany	183.04 +	1.05	164.19 +	0.86 +	0.53	165.15	139.31 +	18.96 +	13.05 +	2.78 +	1.72
Ireland	229.90 −	0.88	200.74 −	2.38 −	1.17	203.91	152.37 +	46.68 +	30.30 +	4.74 +	2.42
Italy	166.21 −	0.59	124.10 −	1.41 −	1.12	130.10	97.44 +	17.21 +	16.10	+10.48 +	9.22
Netherlands	237.49 +	1.10	211.00 +	0.88 +	0.42	211.28	168.43 +	36.89 +	21.18 +	3.42 +	1.65
Norway	186.00 +	0.61	168.29 +	0.25 +	0.15	173.00	128.44 +	38.50 +	29.67 +	8.32 +	5.20
South Africa	213.45 −	0.21	132.83 +	0.11 +	0.08	156.03	112.45 −	22.23 −	14.34	+14.19	+11.96
Spain	213.90 +	0.27	145.63 −	0.86 −	0.59	155.35	113.09 +	29.52 +	25.42 −	3.81 −	2.55
Sweden	291.91 +	0.11	218.93 +	0.48 +	0.22	220.59	163.86 +	53.67 +	32.47 +	5.06 +	2.36
Switzerland	264.12 +	0.78	246.38 −	0.80 −	0.32	251.52	223.57 +	22.81 +	10.20	+10.35 +	4.39
United Kingdom	171.43 −	0.14	149.69 −	0.65 −	0.43	152.02	122.11 +	23.67 +	18.78 −	2.34 −	1.54
Europe/Africa (ex. South Africa)			164.24 −	0.27 −	0.16	165.80	137.50 +	25.34 +	18.25 +	1.83 +	1.13
Europe/Africa (ex. U.K. & S. Africa)			175.97 −	0.04 −	0.02	177.93	147.98 +	26.83 +	17.99 +	4.41 +	2.57
Asia/Pacific			99.03 +	0.62 +	0.63	128.30	97.95 −	22.39 −	18.44 −	9.90 −	9.09
Australia	145.75 +	1.15	145.60 +	1.99 +	1.39	150.27	126.73 +	10.66 +	7.90 −	3.18 −	2.14
Hong Kong	296.84 +	0.04	297.77 +	0.07 +	0.02	307.52	231.00 +	42.86 +	16.81 −	1.73 −	0.58
Indonesia	241.75 +	0.81	202.61 +	1.56 +	0.78	202.61	156.38 +	10.42 +	5.42	+15.19 +	8.10
Japan	82.60 +	1.23	83.04 +	0.50 +	0.61	121.16	81.75 −	30.24 −	26.70	−12.59	−13.17
Malaysia	252.81 +	1.23	276.61 +	3.47 +	1.27	276.61	230.46 +	40.51 +	17.16	+11.11 +	4.19
New Zealand	153.88 +	0.83	195.50 +	1.77 +	0.91	211.01	165.69 +	20.16 +	11.50 −	7.85 −	3.86
Philippines	367.71 −	0.46	362.64 −	1.67 −	0.46	371.03	301.69 +	39.47 +	12.21	+20.28 +	5.92
Singapore	181.06 +	1.54	206.92 +	2.93 +	1.44	223.07	180.30 −	10.12 −	4.66 +	7.08 +	3.54
South Korea	111.43 −	0.22	97.23 −	0.20 −	0.21	158.55	86.88 −	45.50 −	31.88 +	6.24 +	6.86
Taiwan	180.78 −	0.09	169.38 −	0.26 −	0.15	169.64	108.62 +	57.79 +	51.79 +	8.61 +	5.36
Thailand	118.79 −	1.65	107.81 −	2.04 −	1.86	216.55	107.81	−107.66 −	49.96	−18.85	−14.88
Asia/Pacific (ex. Japan)			202.91 +	1.43 +	0.71	205.51	175.15 +	13.55 +	7.16 +	1.66 +	0.82
World (ex. U.S.)			125.72 +	0.30 +	0.24	133.02	122.95 −	1.71 −	1.35 −	3.98 −	3.07
DJ WORLD STOCK INDEX			150.34 +	1.32 +	0.89	150.84	133.22 +	11.98 +	8.66 +	2.77 +	1.88

Indexes based on 6/30/82=100 for U.S., 12/31/91=100 for World.

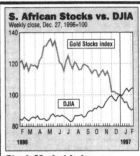

S. African Stocks vs. DJIA
Weekly close, Dec. 27, 1996=100

Gold Stocks index

DJIA

1996   1997

Stock Market Indexes

EXCHANGE	02/12/97 CLOSE	NET CHG	PCT CHG
Amsterdam AEX Index	705.58 +	6.86 +	0.98
Argentina Merval Index	718.42 +	10.4 +	1.47
Australia All Ordinaries	2473.6 +	25.5 +	1.04
Bombay Sensex	3483.48 −	18.79 −	0.54
Brazil Sao Paulo Bovespa	86706 +	3541 +	4.26
Brussels Bel-20 Index	2087.63 +	6.69 +	0.32
Dow Jones China 88	closed	...	...
Dow Jones Shanghai	closed	...	...
Dow Jones Shenzhen	closed	...	...
Euro, Aust, Far East MSCI-p	1148 +	1.6 +	0.14
Frankfurt DAX	3216.14 +	28.56 +	0.90
Frankfurt IBIS DAX	3211.01 +	19.56 +	0.61
Hong Kong Hang Seng	13462.61 +	8.4 +	0.06
Johannesburg J'burg Gold	1350 −	8 −	0.59
London FT 100-share	4304.3 −	0.1 −	0.00
London FT 250-share	4574.5 −	12.1 −	0.26
Madrid General Index	475.01 +	1.77 +	0.37
Mexico I.P.C.	3802.63 +	52.60 +	1.40
Milan MIBtel Index	12490 −	85 −	0.68
Paris CAC 40	2599.33 +	17.24 +	0.67
Singapore Straits Times	2224.64 +	27.59 +	1.26
S. Korea Composite	712.5 −	0.93 −	0.13
Stockholm Affaersvaerlden	2649.67 +	5.2 +	0.20
Taiwan Weighted	7424.1 +	13.63 +	0.18
Tokyo Nikkei 225 Average	18409.96 +·	228.79 +	1.26
Tokyo Nikkei 300 Index	262.24 +	3.38 +	1.31
Tokyo Topix Index	1368.43 +	13.54 +	1.00
Toronto 300 Composite	6165.38 +	38.46 +	0.63
Zurich Swiss Market	4444.1 +	35.7 +	0.81

p-Preliminary
na-Not available

FIGURE 2-5

Wall Street Journal, "Foreign Exchange, Dollar Exceeds Most Major Currencies As Traders Put Upper Limits to the Test," February 12, 1997 (Reprinted by permission of *The Wall Street Journal,* © 1997 Dow Jones & Company, Inc. All Rights Reserved Worldwide.)

C22   THE WALL STREET JOURNAL THURSDAY, FEBRUARY 13, 1997

FOREIGN EXCHANGE

Dollar Exceeds Most Major Currencies As Traders Put Upper Limits to the Test

By MOLLY SCHUETZ
AP-Dow Jones News Service

NEW YORK — The dollar ended global trading yesterday higher against most major currencies as traders nervously tested central bankers' threshold of pain.

The dollar rallied to an intraday high of 1.6932 marks and 1.4522 Swiss francs, levels unseen since April 1994 when the U.S. currency traded at 1.6935 marks and at 1.4525 Swiss francs, as traders sought to discern just how high central banks would be comfortable with the dollar trading.

After being knocked off a 34-month high against the mark when the Bundesbank denied that it wants the dollar to move higher, the U.S. currency later claimed a 34-month high against the Swiss franc when the Swiss government said it considers a weak Swiss franc as one way to help cure "untenable" unemployment.

The dollar gave up one yen and two pfennigs when the Bundesbank sharply denied a news service report Tuesday citing unnamed sources as saying the central bank would welcome a dollar advance to 1.7000-1.7100 marks over time.

"There is definitely no such opinion on the wish for a higher dollar," a Bundesbank spokesman said.

Late yesterday in New York, the dollar was quoted at 1.6876 marks, up from 1.6785 marks late Tuesday in New York. The U.S. currency also was quoted at 124.20 yen, up from 123.43 yen. Sterling fell to $1.6305 from $1.6372. In Tokyo early Thursday, the dollar was trading at 1.6871 marks, and at 124.24 yen; sterling was at $1.6325.

The dollar's trading ranges this week indicate that traders aren't heeding last weekend's call by finance ministers and central bankers of the seven most industrialized countries to slow the dollar's rise and keep trading volatility at a minimum.

"The thing to keep in mind is that the market is very long dollars, but bold and suicidal enough to want to take on the central banks," said Robert Nelson, managing director of foreign-exchange sales, at WestLB in New York.

"Until the central banks intervene, the market will attempt to challenge their authority. The market has insulted the G-7 in the past two days, and that increases the probability of intervention." The G-7 member countries are: the U.S., Canada, France, Germany, Italy, Japan, and the U.K.

Until global economic fundamentals and interest-rate differentials shift from their overwhelming bias toward the U.S., the dollar will continue to press higher, traders said.

And concerns voiced by the Swiss only magnified the divide.

With the jobless rate in Switzerland having risen to 5.7% in January from 5.3% in December and unemployment at a record 205,000, a government spokesman praised the "value of the Swiss franc and the low level of interest rates." He said they are among the factors on which the government relies to enhance job creation.

"It's just another factor pointing to lower rates," in Switzerland, said Brian Arabia, assistant vice president of foreign exchange at ABN-Amro Bank in Chicago.

Most European countries in fact would "prefer to see their currencies on the weaker side, even if they can't publicly say it," said Seth Garrett, chief dealer at Credit Suisse First Boston in New York.

Meanwhile, sterling ended lower on the day as the gulf between the British Treasury and the Bank of England over monetary policy continued to widen.

because it would stimulate much-needed economic growth in many circumstances.

The world wire in Figure 2-6 is a good snapshot of a day in the life of the FX market.

The first article on the British jobless rate suggests that decreases in the value of the pound to the U.S. dollar will fuel more investment in British companies, which in turn will create jobs.

The next article is on British Aerospace and the French Lagadere Group developing weapons systems for the British Royal Air Force. Again, additional investment in the European currencies due to their cheap cost, relative to the U.S. dollar.

In the item on France's budget gap, the French government reached its goal in decreasing its budget deficit—decreases most likely attributable to expectations of increased economic growth due to the weakness of the French franc relative to the value of the U.S. dollar.

As an addendum to the previous articles, Canon Inc. of Japan, maker of office automation and precision optical equipment, increased its pretax profit, mostly due to the yen's weakness against the U.S. dollar, which boosted sales. Exports helped to increase their profit margin.

These articles illustrate how foreign currencies play a dramatic role in the world economy. Currency values affect budget deficits, interest rates, inflation, unemployment, bank stability, and political fortunes. The U.S. dollar is a closely watched currency, especially as it increases in value. A dominant currency in the world economy can affect the ebb and flow of trade balances.

FIGURE 2-6

Wall Street Journal, "World Wire," February, 12, 1997 (Reprinted by permission of *The Wall Street Journal,* © 1997 Dow Jones & Company, Inc. All Rights Reserved Worldwide.)

WORLD WIRE

BRITISH JOBLESS RATE DROPS

Britain's unemployment rate fell to 6.5% in January from 6.7% in December, the 11th monthly drop in a row. This underscored the economy's buoyancy but added to uncertainty about inflation and interest rates. The Conservative government hailed the lower-than-expected rate as fresh evidence of economic recovery. But economists said job losses affect 20% of British families; poverty and wage inequality are greater than in many other European countries, and a tightening British labor market could boost prices.

BRITAIN LAUNCHES FIGHTER-JET JOB

The Matra BAe Dynamics joint venture of **British Aerospace** PLC and the Matra unit of **Lagardere Groupe** of France signed a £700 million ($1.15 billion) contract with the British government to develop and produce the Storm Shadow weapons-guidance system for Royal Air Force fighter planes. The contract will help secure jobs at three venture sites in Britain and at more than 80 subcontractors. The system will enable RAF Tornados, Eurofighters and Harrier GR7 jets to attack targets without entering enemy airspace.

FRENCH TELECOM GROUP TO EXPAND

Societe Nationale des Chemins de Fer, the French national railway company, picked Cie. **Generale des Eaux** as its telecommunications partner, which could aid its efforts to become the main rival to France Telecom SA. Generale des Eaux and its telecom partners, **British Telecommunications** PLC and **Mannesmann** AG of Germany, will have exclusive rights to develop with SNCF the railroad's 5,580-mile fiber-optic network, the country's second-largest after France Telecom's.

FRANCE'S BUDGET GAP NEARS GOAL

The French government said its budget deficit for 1996 totaled 295 billion francs ($52.1 billion), slightly exceeding the target of 288 billion francs but narrowing from the 1995 gap of 323 billion francs. Last year's deficit represented 4.1% of gross domestic product, which expanded 1.3%. To participate in the European Union's single currency planned for 1999, France must cut its deficit to 3% of GDP. But France said its rising debt means the deficit must fall below 2% of GDP.

CANON LOGS RECORD ANNUAL PROFIT

Canon Inc. of Japan, a maker of office-automation and precision optical equipment, said unconsolidated pretax profit for 1996 surged 56% to a record 125.23 billion yen ($1.01 billion) from 1995. Sales grew 13% to 1.396 trillion yen. Canon said the yen's weakening against the U.S. dollar boosted sales and helped fatten profit margins. Printer sales were strong. Operating profit surged 44% to 151.69 billion yen. Net income jumped 33% to 59.01 billion yen.

POSTSCRIPTS . . .

Israel said its gross domestic product increased an estimated 4.4% in 1996, slowing from an average annual rate of 6% from 1990 through 1995; the government predicted a 4% expansion this year, but economists forecast 3%. . . . Indonesian President Suharto decreed that hard liquor may be sold only at hotels, bars and other licensed locations, and prohibited sales at roadside stalls and supermarkets; the country is largely Muslim, and Islamic teaching bans liquor.

— Compiled by Richard L. Holman

DRYPERS CORP.

Drypers Corp. said it acquired the Puppet disposable-diaper brand in Brazil from **Chansommes do Brasil** in transactions valued at about $12 million in cash and stock. Drypers said it formed a joint venture with Brazilian financial investors to market and distribute Puppet diapers, which will be made for Drypers by closely held Chansommes do Brasil. Drypers said it holds a 51% interest in the venture and has an option to acquire the remaining stake. Drypers, a Houston maker of branded and private-label diapers, said Puppet has annual sales of about $40 million.

CHAPTER **3**

Buy Low, Sell High— It's That Easy

INTRODUCTION

Buy low and sell high—foreign currency trading is that easy. Or is it? As with any other investment, traders barter one item for another at a negotiated value. The economic jargon used in foreign currency trading can seem intimidating, but consider your first experience with the free market system. The dime you received from the tooth fairy was your property. You put it into your pocket and trotted off to the grocery store. You may have watched older kids deposit their coins into the colorful gumball machines. Their faces lit up when they turned the crank and out rolled a mouth-sized gumball. Now it was your turn. Timidly you stepped up to the machine, slid the dime in the slot, and turned the crank. Presto! Out came your reward, and you enjoyed the benefits of free market purchasing power.

In this simple transaction you took your property and sold it, or exchanged it to buy something of value. The value was the price of one dime. In simple terms, you not only bought an asset of one gumball, you sold a currency of one tenth of one U.S. dollar. The exchange rate of your transaction in U.S. dollar terms is .10 USD/gumball or in gumball terms, it is ten gumballs/USD.

If you were Tom Sawyer, you most likely would have continued the process by exchanging the gumball for something of greater profit. By exchanging the gumball for an apple, and the apple for a dime, plus a Band-Aid still in the wrapper. Your profit on this transaction would have been a Band Aid still in the wrapper plus the ability to make another investment in gumballs.

The art of foreign currency trading could be no more complex than this series of exchanges, except for the additional consideration of interest rate. Adding the effect of interest rate to the scenario, imagine Tom Sawyer letting his buddy Huck Finn borrow the apple to impress the local school girls for one day. In return, Tom gets the apple back *and* a plump night crawler—principle, *and* interest.

THE MECHANICS OF FOREX INVESTING

The mechanics of FX trading take into account four simple variables and one basic rule. The variables are currencies, exchange rate, time, and interest rate. These variables are expressed in formulas for forex trading.

The basic rule is that when you are buying one currency, you are also selling another. It is easy to understand and simple to do if you have the currency to sell. It is not so simple if you are speculating that the price is going to move favorably and you are buying a currency without actually having the currency you are selling (called the *contracurrency*). That situation doesn't seem to make much sense for the beginning trader, who will ask the obvious question: How can you buy something you don't have in exchange for selling something you don't have? It might help to reword the rule precisely to address the trader's circumstances: When you buy a currency, you are actually borrowing one currency and loaning another currency until the value date; when you sell a currency, you are actually loaning one currency and borrowing another currency. To refer to the borrowing and loaning of currencies, however, makes the discussion of forex trading more complex, so for now let us focus just on currency conventions and exchange rates, assuming that you actually own the contracurrency. Interest rates and time variables will be discussed later in the chapter.

Currency Conventions and Exchange Rates

The following cross rates (Figure 3-1) are reintroduced from Chapter 1 for use in calculating the examples and problems discussed throughout this chapter.

As explained in Chapter 1, currencies can be quoted on either a direct or an indirect basis. The currency convention specifies the exchange rate. In U.S. dollar terms, the DEM/USD exchange rate from the cross-rate table is 1.6876 deutschemarks for every one U.S. dollar. In other words one U.S. dollar is equivalent to 1.6876 German deutschemarks.

In deutschemark terms, the same exchange rate equals approximately .5926 U.S. dollar for every one deutschemark. This means that one

FIGURE 3-1

Wall Street Journal, "Key Currency Cross Rates," February, 12, 1997 (Reprinted by permission of *The Wall Street Journal,* © 1997 Dow Jones & Company, Inc. All Rights Reserved Worldwide.)

Key Currency Cross Rates Late New York Trading Feb 12, 1997

	Dollar	Pound	SFranc	Guilder	Peso	Yen	Lira	D-Mark	FFranc	CdnDlr
Canada	1.3553	2.2098	.93340	.71475	.17414	.01091	.00082	.80309	.23819	....
France	5.6900	9.2775	3.9187	3.0007	.73108	.04581	.00344	3.3717	....	4.1983
Germany	1.6876	2.7516	1.1623	.88999	.21683	.01359	.00102	....	.29659	1.2452
Italy	1653.0	2695.2	1138.4	871.74	212.39	13.309	....	979.5	290.51	1219.7
Japan	124.2	202.51	85.537	65.499	15.958	....	.07514	73.596	21.828	91.64
Mexico	7.7830	12.69	5.3602	4.1045	....	.06267	.00471	4.6119	1.3678	5.7426
Netherlands ..	1.8962	3.0918	1.3059	....	.24363	.01527	.00115	1.1236	.33325	1.3991
Switzerland ...	1.4520	2.3675	....	.76574	.18656	.01169	.00088	.86039	.25518	1.0713
U.K.	.61331	....	.42239	.32344	.07880	.00494	.00037	.36342	.10779	.45253
U.S.	....	1.6305	.68871	.52737	.12849	.00805	.00060	.59256	.17575	.73784

Source: Dow Jones Telerate Inc.

deutschemark buys .5926 U.S. dollar. Note that in day-to-day commerce the smallest currency unit is only one cent in U.S. dollars and one pfennig in deutschemarks, yet the interbank quotes in one-hundredths of a cent and of pfennig. These are the smallest standard quotations, referred to as *pips*.

A second aspect of currency convention is the currency itself. When an interbank market participant requests a market quotation, they must also specify the size of the transaction. If one bank calls another bank and says, "Make me a market in one dollar/mark," the bank is looking to either buy or sell $1,000,000 (one million U.S. dollars) against deutschemarks at the exchange rate the counterparty bank is willing to offer. The size of the transaction is an important element of the quotation, because certain sizes are more commonly transacted than others in the interbank market. For example, it isn't very common to transact an odd size like $58,973 (fifty-eight thousand nine hundred seventy-three U.S. dollars) in the interbank market. A quote offered on the two amounts would be quite different.

One of the most common mistakes in forex trading and calculations is for a trader to forget the currency convention and the differences in exchange rates. Many times a forex "rookie" will think that trading U.S. $1,000,000 (USD) is the same as trading 1,000,000 deutschemarks (DEM). The following illustrates how great the difference is between these two trades.

Using the previous exchange rate of 1.6876 DEM/1 USD, 1 million USD buys 1,687,600 DEM. Conversely, 1 million DEM buys 592,557.48

USD at the same exchange rate. The difference is $1,000,000 USD - $592,557.40 USD = $407,442.60 USD.

Currency Convention Differences

Selling 1,000,000 USD @ 1.6876 DEM/USD = 1,687,600 DEM

Selling 1,000,000 DEM @ 1.6876 DEM/USD = 592,557.48 USD

Obviously, the profit or loss is much different on a 100-pip move trading 1 million USD versus trading 1 million DEM (or approximately 592,557.48 USD).

To show the exact difference between the two, let's say that we bought $1,000,000 (one million USD) in one transaction, and in a different transaction we bought 1,000,000 DEM (one million DEM). Then the market moved from 1.6876 to 1.6976 DEM/USD, a 100-pip move in DEM/USD rate. Remember that when you are buying one currency you are also selling another currency. In accounting terms, when you buy you are receiving or crediting your account, and when you sell you are debiting your account.

Currency Convention Profit/Loss Differences

1,000,000 USD
Buy (+) 1,000,000 USD @ 1.6876 DEM/USD = sell (–) 1,687,600 DEM
Sell (–) 1,000,000 USD @ 1.6976 DEM/USD = buy (+) 1,697,600 DEM
Profit = 10,000 DEM
10,000 DEM @ 1.6976 DEM/USD = 5,890.67 USD

1,000,000 DEM
Buy (+) 1,000,000 DEM @ 1.6876 DEM/USD = sell (–) 592,557.48 USD
Sell (–) 1,000,000 DEM @ 1.6976 DEM/USD = buy (+) 589,066.92 USD
Loss = -3,490.56 USD

The profit and loss is in DEM for the 1 million USD trade and USD for the 1 million DEM trade. It is also important to note that the 1 million USD trade made money (10,000 DEM or $5890.67 @ 1.6976 DEM/USD), and the 1 million DEM trade lost money (-$3,490).

REAL-WORLD EXAMPLES

In the following examples we will assume the most common interbank quotation system for a given currency. The indirect quotation method will be used for the exchange rate, except for British pound sterling (GBP), Irish punt (IEP), Australian dollar (AUD), New Zealand dollar (NZD), and the European currency unit (ECU). That means that the profit or loss will be given in non-U.S. dollars for all transactions besides the GBP, IEP, AUD, NZD, and ECU, which will have a U.S. dollar profit and loss.

DEM and the Paper Importer

A U.S. importer/exporter of paper just entered into a contract to purchase (import) 2,000,000 DEM worth of printing paper from a company in Frankfurt, Germany, with payment due in 60 days. The exporter (seller) in Frankfurt of the printing paper expects the payment in 60 days in deutschemarks. The importer (buyer), believing that today's exchange rate is better than what the rate will be in two months, calls his bank in the United States and asks for a rate to buy 2,000,000 deutschemarks with U.S. dollars. The bank quotes (gives an exchange rate) 1.6876 DEM/USD to the U.S. importer (buyer). This means the U.S. importer must pay (or sell) $1,185,115 for the receipt (or buying) of 2,000,000 deutschemarks.

The example in mathematical terms is:

2,000,000 DEM bought for 1.6876 DEM/USD.

X amount of U.S. dollars multiplied by 1.6876 DEM/USD
must equal 2,000,000 DEM

$$X * 1.6876 \text{ DEM/USD} = 2,000,000 \text{ DEM}$$

$$X = 2,000,000 \text{ DEM}/1.6876 \text{ (DEM/USD)}$$

X = 1,185,115.00 USD [the answer was rounded to the nearest dollar]

Or the reciprocal of the rate may be used to determine the number of USD that would be bought by 2,000,000 DEM. The example again in mathematical terms is:

Reciprocal of 1.6876 DEM/USD = 1/1.6876
1/1.6876 = 0.5926 [rounded]
2,000,000 DEM multiplied by .5926 USD/DEM
2,000,000 DEM .6431 USD/DEM = 1,185,200.

The U.S. $85 difference ($1,185,115 - $1,185,200 = $85 USD) can be accounted for in the rounding of the exchange rate. This example illustrates why currencies are often quoted in the interbank market to many decimal points smaller than standard currency. A difference of one cent in price may equal many thousands of dollars in the interbank market.

The 2,000,000 DEM, or $1,185,115, from the paper importer has just utilized the interbank market. The question for the importer is: When is the best time to exchange the USD for DEM? The exchange rate in DEM/USD may be dramatically different at the end of the 60-day period during which the importer has to pay for the printing paper. If, at the time of the contract, the importer assumed a rate of 1.6876 for the DEM/USD and waited until the 60-day period passed to exchange the currencies, the importer (buyer) may have to pay much more than originally anticipated for the paper. Assume at the end of the 60-day period the DEM/USD rate is 1.6725. The U.S. importer must now exchange $1,195,815 for the 2,000,000 DEM. That means that those same 2,000,000 DEM that were worth $1,185,115 sixty days ago now cost $1,195,815. The bottom line difference is $10,700 more for the same printing paper than when the contract was first entered.

The example is calculated as follows:

$$2,000,000 \text{ DEM}/1.6876 \text{ USD} = \$1,185,115$$
$$2,000,000 \text{ DEM}/1.6725 \text{ USD} = \$1,195,815$$
$$\$1,185,115 - \$1,195,815 = -\$10,700$$

Thus, the U.S. paper importer lost $10,700 by waiting 60 days, which could eliminate some or all of the profit from the transaction. Importers can protect themselves by employing forward markets, as discussed in later chapters.

British Pound Sterling and the U.S. Stock Market

The paper importer's experience is a fairly simple and common example of situations in the real financial world. Another common exchange that adds new complexity to a forex transaction is the purchase and sale of a financial asset, such as buying or selling shares of stock, between two different currencies.

The story begins with a British investor who wants to buy Microsoft stock, which is traded in the United States in U.S. dollars (USD). The stock must be bought with U.S. dollars and sold in return for U.S. dollars, and the profit or loss from the transaction will also be in U.S. dollars. The transaction is complicated for this investor, because his/her money is in the form of British pound sterling (GBP). Therefore, the investor must start with a transaction in the interbank market. Furthermore, a possible change in the rate of exchange from the time he/she buys the stock and sells the stock could add a new risk of investment.

For the fun of it, let us assume that the British investor is the Queen of England herself. The Queen, after having tea and biscuits with Bill Gates, becomes convinced that Microsoft is the best stock in the world to buy. Bill says that his new Microsoft Office Product, which is to be released within the next five months, will be a great success, with no possible glitches or software conflicts. Bill hints that the release itself, "unofficially," could send Microsoft US $10 higher almost immediately.

The Queen, wanting to keep her personal speculation secret from the London tabloids, calls her broker in the Bahamas on a secured line. The Queen tells her broker to buy U.S. dollars with 5,000,000 pounds in her personal account and then to buy as many shares of Bill's Microsoft stock as possible. Her loyal servant, the Bahamian broker, converts GBP to USD at the rate of 1.6305 USD/GBP in the interbank market. The 5,000,000 GBP buys 8,152,500 USD (notice the exchange rate is in U.S. dollars to the British pound sterling, or direct method in the United States). The Bahamian broker then buys Microsoft stock at an average price of 100 ¼. The Bahamian broker is able to buy 81,320 shares, leaving $170 to pay for commission and fees.

The share purchase in mathematical terms is:

5,000,000 GBP @ 1.6305 USD/GBP = 8,152,500 USD.
8,152,500 USD @ 100.25 per share of MSFT = 81,320 shares of MSFT
81,320 shares MSFT @ 100.25 USD per share = 8,152,330 USD
8,152,330 USD cost of MSFT shares + 170 USD commissions =
8,152,500 USD paid

Three months later, Microsoft launches the new Microsoft Office Product with great fanfare. The only glitch in the new product is a minor compatibility problem, but overall the product is a success. Microsoft stock shoots up nearly $5 and holds there for the next two months. The stock doesn't return as much as the Queen had hoped, but earns a good profit anyway—or does it?

Unfortunately, the U.S. dollar was not holding up as well. Rumors in the interbank community that the U.S. Federal Reserve intended to lower interest rates weakened the greenback. The dollar plummeted in relation to the British pound sterling. The rate of USD to the GBP jumped 5% in the five months to 1.7120 USD/GBP, requiring more U.S. dollars to buy the same number of pounds.

The Queen tells her broker to take profits in the Microsoft stock and then convert the U.S. dollars to British pounds.

The Bahamian broker sells the stock at an average price of 104 ⁷/₈ and converts the USD to GBP at 1.7120 USD/GBP. The commissions for closing the transactions are another $170.

The results of the sell were:

Sold 81,320 shares @ 104 $^7/_8$ USD (104,875) = 8,528,435 USD
8,528,435 USD proceeds – 170 USD commissions = 8,528,265 USD
Sold 8,528,265 USD @ 1.7120 USD/GBP =   4,981,463 GBP
Initial 5,000,000 GBP – proceeds 4,981,463 GBP = -18,537 GBP

The final results show a loss on the transaction due to the currency risk exposure on a stock transaction in a foreign currency. The total loss on the transaction for the fair Queen is 18,537 GBP.

CHAPTER 4

Buyer Beware— Be Very Aware

One cannot discuss the risks, rules, or regulations of forex trading without first describing the unique regulatory environment of this investment venue. As an investor explores forex regulatory issues, it becomes abundantly clear that international forex trading does not have a uniform regulator.

Some argue that forex trading is totally unregulated, but that is a false assumption. For anyone to assume that a market could grow to the magnitude of the foreign exchange market without rules would be preposterous. The Bank of International Settlements has estimated that the global net daily turnover in the cash foreign currency exchange currently exceeds $950 billion per day. In a speech before the Financial Markets Conference of the Federal Reserve Bank of Atlanta, in February 1997, Federal Reserve Chairman Alan Greenspan said ". . . it is critically important to recognize that no market is ever truly unregulated. The self-interest of market participants generates private market regulation." The "self-interest" of the participants in international foreign exchange trading has created a body of conventions and contract law that "regulate" forex trading.

The most uniform contract created is the customer agreement drafted by the International Swap Dealers Association (ISDA), which stands as the boilerplate for many of the customer agreements of this marketplace. (The complete text of the ISDA agreement appears in Appendix A.)

With individual agreements playing such an important role in providing the body of rules under which investors and counterparties will interact, it becomes paramount for the investor to have detailed knowledge of the counterparty and to understand the risks assumed by the investor inherent in the customer agreement. If the investor finds the customer agreement to contain untenable provisions, then exchange-traded foreign currency markets would make more sense.

ATTEMPTS TO CREATE GOVERNMENT REGULATION

The history of attempts by U.S. regulators to regulate the forex market must begin with a discussion of a specific exemption from regulation and the ensuing attempts by a government regulator to carve out an area of regulatory turf within the forex market.

The Commodity Exchange Act (CEA) was enacted in 1974. Congress crafted this important legislature to charter the Commodity Futures Trading Commission with the responsibility of overseeing and regulating the commodities futures industry and related markets. The CFTC's mission to protect the public was reinforced by a broad jurisdiction and regulatory authority.

As the Senate Agriculture Committee pondered this legislation in 1974, the Department of the Treasury expressed its concern that the inclusion of off-exchange transactions in foreign currencies, government securities, and certain other financial instruments could inhibit these markets and reduce their efficiency. The Treasury noted that the foreign currency market in the United States consisted primarily of sophisticated participants such as banks and dealers, and many of these participants were already regulated. The Treasury further argued that it would be inappropriate to impose an additional layer of CFTC regulation on what was a highly complex and actively traded market.

The Treasury was able to convince Congress that protecting foreign currency and government security markets from unnecessary regulation was warranted and suggested a specific exemption from the CEA for off-exchange foreign currency, government securities, and other financial instruments.

The specific language of the so-called Treasury Amendment was written practically verbatim as proposed by the Treasury Department. The Treasury Amendment provides as follows:

> *Nothing in this act shall be deemed to govern or in any way be applicable to foreign currency, security warrants, security rights, resale of installment loan contracts, repurchase options, government securities or mortgages and mortgage purchase commitments unless such transactions involve the sale thereof for future delivery conducted on a board of trade.*

To better understand how the Treasury Amendment has impacted forex regulation (or at least has attempted to impact forex regulation), it is appropriate to discuss three precedent-setting federal cases.

Salomen FX versus Tauber

Salomen Forex, Ind. v. *Lazlo Tauber*, 8 F. 3d 966 (4th Cert. 1993) *cert. denied*, 114 S. Ct. 1540 (1994).

This case was heard in the Fourth Circuit of the U.S. Court of Appeals and involved Salomen FX pursuing a debit collection claim against its customer, Tauber. Tauber raised defenses in an attempt to defeat the claim.

Lazlo Tauber, a wealthy surgeon and non-U.S. citizen, lost $25 million dollars in foreign currency forwards and options transactions. Dr. Tauber claimed that his transactions with Salomen were illegal, off-exchange futures contracts and therefore sought to avoid this by claiming the contracts violated the Commodity Exchange Act of 1974 and were thus unenforceable.

In its decision, the Fourth Circuit pointed to the broad language of the Treasury Amendment to exclude those transactions from the CEA and that Dr. Tauber was a sophisticated investor and therefore was subject to the CEA exclusion provided by the Treasury Amendment.

Salomen FX, Inc. v. *Tauber* reinforced two important elements of FX trading: (1) the Treasury Amendment provided an exemption for sophisticated investors from regulation under the Commodities Exchange Act and therefore was not within the jurisdiction of the CFTC, and (2) the legality of the contract (the customer agreement) between the counterparty and the investor.

The Fourth Circuit Court cautioned against a narrow interpretation of the Treasury Amendment that could inhibit the smooth functioning of currency markets and jeopardize outstanding transactions. The Court appeared to agree with the Treasury Department that a broad interpretation of the Treasury Amendment is necessary to maintain an efficient, global, foreign exchange market for the sake of its institutional participants.

Although not implicit in the Court's decision, *Salomen FX* v. *Tauber* went a long way towards providing a legal benchmark to support the counterparty customer agreement contracts.

The Court held that "individually negotiated foreign currency options and futures transactions between sophisticated large-scale foreign currency traders" are within the Treasury Amendment exclusion. With this, the Court appeared to support one of the CFTC's contentions that the Treasury Amendment exemptions were limited to financially sophisticated and informed parties. The CFTC therefore found some comfort in the Fourth Circuit's decision and was not inhibited in seeking the prosecution of boiler room and other fraudulent activities performed in the foreign exchange market arena.

CFTC versus Frankwell

CFTC and Commissioner of Corporation of the State of California v. Frankwell Bullion Limited; Frankwell Investment Services, Inc.; Frankwell Investment Services (Texas), Inc., Frankwell Management Service (New York), Inc. [1994-1996 Transfer Binder] Comm. Fut. L. Rep. (CCH) Par. 26,484 (US Dist. Ct., Northern District of California, August 1995).

In June 1994, the CFTC and the California Commissioner of Corporations brought a complaint against the Frankwell Group of Companies for entering into illegal, off-exchange foreign currency and precious metal contracts with members of the general public.

Frankwell Bullion, Ltd. is a Hong Kong corporation, established in 1987, and a member of the Frankwell Group of Companies that conducts business through several American-based affiliates. Frankwell was characterized by the Court as a worldwide organization.

Frankwell marketed to the general public transactions involving foreign currencies in predetermined, specified lot sizes. Actually, Frankwell's foreign currency transactions were identical in size to futures contracts traded on the International Monetary Market of the Chicago Mercantile Exchange.

Frankwell's customers were not permitted to negotiate the purchase or sale or the quantity of the foreign currency. All transactions involved the standardized lot size marketed by Frankwell. Frankwell's customers could either open a long (buy) position or a short (sell) position in these markets at a price set by Frankwell. Frankwell claimed price quotes were obtained from the interbank spot market in Hong Kong. Frankwell's customer agreement provided that the customer was to pay initial margin for each lot of approximately $1,000 for a day trade, or $2,000 for an overnight trade. Additional margin would be required if the market price moved adversely to the customer's position.

At no time was the customer required to pay full purchase price for the foreign currency, unlike a true spot (cash) transaction. Instead, Frankwell allowed its customers to satisfy their contractual obligation either by entering into an offsetting position or by taking or making delivery of the underlying currency.

Frankwell calculated customer profits or losses based on the difference between the spot price at the time the position was established and the spot price when the position was offset.

Frankwell's customer agreement did make reference to taking and making delivery of the foreign currency, but there was little evidence presented in the case that there was an expectation for the customer to do so. Frankwell's sales agents told customers that physical delivery of the foreign currency was not required. Customers were assessed a carrying charge calculated by Frankwell for each day a position was left open.

In summary, the Frankwell foreign currency contracts appeared to be an illegitimate marriage of a futures market contract and a forex transaction.

Frankwell recruited customers and account executives by placing classified advertisements in newspapers of general circulation. Frankwell also purchased customer leads and instructed its sales agents in cold-calling techniques and provided them with scripts.

The Federal District Court initially granted the CFTC's temporary restraining order, but then denied its application for preliminary injunction. Frankwell argued that the CFTC lacked jurisdiction over foreign currency transactions at issue based on the Treasury Amendment and that such transactions were spot (cash market transactions) rather than futures contracts.

The District Court found in favor of Frankwell. The judge in his decision looked to the "plain meaning" of the Treasury Amendment, holding that the Treasury Amendment exempts all off-exchange transactions in foreign currency from CFTC jurisdiction regardless of whether such transactions are offered or sold to the general public. The court held that the language of the Treasury Amendment conclusively reveals Congress's intent that off-exchange transactions in foreign currency are exempt from the CEA, and rejected the CFTC's argument that the Treasury Amendment is a limited exclusion for sophisticated and informed institutions. The judge stated that the language of the Treasury Amendment makes no distinction based on the type of investor involved and looks instead solely to whether trading is off-exchange or on-exchange.

This Court surmised that had Congress intended to exempt only transactions involving banks and other sophisticated institutions, it would have used language specifying that intent rather than exempting all off-exchange trading.

The Court found that the broad interpretation of "board of trade" would render the Treasury Amendment meaningless, as every organization engaged in selling foreign currency futures could then fall outside its scope. At the same time, the Court stated that the distinction between sophisticated, large-scale investors and private, unsophisticated investors would be arbitrary and nearly impossible to apply. The Court found that a jurisdictional standard, based on an investor's level of sophistication, would be arbitrary and also impossible to apply.

This case marked the first time that a court had interpreted the Treasury Amendment as ousting the CFTC's jurisdiction over foreign currency contracts offered and sold to the general public.

The CFTC claimed that this decision was inconsistent with the Fourth Circuit's decision in *Solomon FX v. Tauber* and sought to appeal the District Court's decision. Regulated futures exchanges across the United States argued in support of the CFTC's motions to reverse the Frankwell decision.

The exchanges argued, given the broadness of the District Court's decision, that any entity, no matter how unscrupulous or undercapitalized, would be free to operate as a dealer in futures and options contracts (including exact replicas of those traded on the exchanges). Furthermore, those instruments could be offered to any customer (including those that now trade on the exchanges) without the entity complying with any of the regulatory dictates of the CEA. Nonexchange entities could replicate the futures exchanges' business while escaping CEA regulation of futures and options trading.

On appeal to the Ninth Circuit Court of Appeals, the CFTC prescribed a broad meaning of the "board of trade" and a narrow reading of the term *transactions in* foreign currencies. The CFTC contended that the term *board of trade* encompassed non-exchange entities making markets in futures contracts as well as futures exchanges. The CFTC pointed out that the CEA defines a *board of trade* to include and mean "any exchange or association either incorporated or unincorporated of persons who are engaged in the business of buying or selling any commodity or receiving the same for sale on consignment." They argued that under this definition, Frankwell is a board of trade and is hence ineligible for exclusion from regulation by virtue of the Treasury Amendment.

The CFTC claimed that legislative history surrounding the Treasury Amendment demonstrates that the Amendment was adopted to carve out types of transactions already effectively supervised by bank regulatory agencies. The Treasury Amendment was intended to exclude from the CEA only those futures transactions in foreign currencies that were between banks and other sophisticated institutions and already subject to regulation by banking regulatory authorities.

On October 29, 1996, the Ninth Circuit of the U.S. Court of Appeals affirmed the holding of the District Court. This ruling by the Ninth Circuit

Court focused additional attention on the *CFTC v. William C. Dunn, et al.* case to be heard before the Supreme Court in the following month.

CFTC versus William C. Dunn et al.

CFTC v. William C. Dunn and Delta Consultants, Inc. Delta Options, LTD., and Nopkine Co., LDT., 58 F. 3d 50, 53 (2d Circ. 1995), *cert. granted*, 116 S. Ct. 1846 (1996) Dunn et al. v. CFTC et al. 95-1181.

There are significant differences between *CFTC* v. *Dunn* and the *CFTC* v. *Frankwell,* not the least of which is the fact that the Dunn case alleges fraud. No count of fraud was alleged in the Frankwell case. Despite their differences, both cases point to the legitimacy of the CFTC's claim for jurisdiction.

The CFTC filed a civil injunctive action against Dunn et al., alleging fraud in connection with commodities options transactions. The CFTC asserted that Dunn disseminated false information concerning the risks and rewards of currency trading in general, and of investing with the defendants in particular. Investors were also deceived as to the success of the defendants, trading and the success of the investors' accounts. Phony statements were sent out, which showed impressive returns on investments, convincing investors to open and maintain accounts with Dunn.

By all appearances, the Dunn defendants were engaged in what is commonly known as a *Ponzi scheme.*

Dunn solicited investments from a number of individuals, partnerships, and companies. Customers were told that Dunn would execute sophisticated investment strategies involving the purchase and sale of call and put options in various foreign currency markets. These trades, using various combinations of sales and purchases of different forms of options, created relatively exotic positions in foreign currencies.

Weekly printouts sent to customers suggested large returns. convincing them to "roll over" their funds, and as long as these funds remained in the accounts and new investors were found, the Ponzi scheme persisted. In the second half of 1993, however, it began to unravel. Investors began to receive strange communications from the defendants, and promises to repay monies at certain dates were not honored. Apparently some of the money, totaling nearly $20,000,000, had been transferred to Switzerland.

The CFTC prevailed in the lower court, proving its fraud and other claims, but the defendant appealed the lower court's decision, asserting that the CFTC lacked jurisdiction because foreign currency options were "transactions" in foreign currency and therefore were excluded from the CEA by the Treasury Amendment.

The Second Circuit Court upheld the CFTC's jurisdiction in this case, but Dunn appealed to the Supreme Court and, to the surprise of many observers, the Supreme Court reversed the Appeals Court decision.

The Supreme Court said that transactions in foreign currency, such as those in the Dunn case, are explicitly exempt from the Commodity Exchange Act, and that no other interpretation of the statute makes sense. The justices said arguments about whether such transactions should be included in the CFTC jurisdiction ought to be addressed to Congress rather than the courts. In February 1997, Senators Lugar, Harkin, and Leahy introduced a bill to amend the Commodity Exchange Act. This bill, the Commodity Exchange Amendment Act of 1997, addresses and further clarifies the jurisdiction of the Commodity Futures Trading Commission. Time will tell if this bill provides adequate clarification to avert further controversy regarding forex regulation.

No one can deny the importance of the CFTC's focus on shutting down fraudulent foreign currency schemes, pursuing boiler-room operations that seek to lure vulnerable investors through high-pressure sales tactics and false promises, and protecting the public interest. But clearly the ultimate imperative is to protect the public without discouraging the global economic function of the foreign exchange markets.

REGULATION BY SELF-INTEREST OF MARKET PARTICIPANTS

As stated earlier, a basic customer agreement has been created by the ISDA for the purposes of delineating the responsibilities of the parties in a foreign exchange transaction. It is extremely important for customers in the foreign exchange markets to thoroughly read and understand the provisions of the agreements and contracts they have entered into with the counterparty.

From the onset, it is extremely important to understand that the ISDA agreement is primarily designed to protect the interests of the counterparty and that the provisions of the agreement are governed in accordance with contract law. There is no formal regulatory body to which the customer agreement must comply. The primary content of the agreement describes the obligations, responsibilities, and procedures of the customer. In addition to other issues, the following are some important commitments made by a customer who signs a customer agreement:

1. The customer has a limited amount of time to object to any details or terms of a customer confirmation, usually one day. A confirmation of transactions is delivered to the customer by the counterparty. The terms of this confirmation are deemed conclusively correct unless the customer objects within a designated period of time. This makes the customer's attentiveness to trade confirmations critically important.

2. In the event that the customer is an options buyer and fails to pay the premium before the premium payment day (the second business day immediately following the trade date), the options buyer is responsible to pay all loses, expenses, costs, and damages incurred in connection with the option premium. All calculations of option premiums, netted contracts, or other amounts required for payment by the customer are computed by the counterparty. Therefore, the customer must carefully examine these calculations for accuracy to ensure that the customer account is being properly credited or debited after a transaction.

3. The customer agreement prescribes important time deadlines after which the customer has little recourse. For instance, failure to provide a written notice by an option buyer of an exercise of an option may cause an exercise on the following business day in the case of American-style options, or in the case of a European option, to become null and void.

4. The customer must be a duly organized, valid, existing entity that is solvent and acting properly within its certification of corporation and/or by-laws. The individual signing the agreement must be authorized and acting properly as a principal in the contract.

5. The customer agrees to provide a properly secured pledge of collateral and provide to the counterparty all assurances required by the counterparty of its ability to meet the terms and conditions of the contract.

6. The customer must represent and warrant that it is a sophisticated institutional investor entering into the agreement and that the foreign exchange transactions are solely in connection with its business and investment purposes.

This is a short list of obligations prescribed by the basic foreign exchange customer agreement and is not intended to be comprehensive. There are numerous other covenants of the basic agreement that should be thoroughly understood by the customer before agreeing to the provisions.

It is important to notice the limited number of provisions that obligate the counterparty beyond executing and providing confirmations of transactions. The customer agreement saddles the counterparty with very few obligations. Actually, under the category of responsibilities of the counterparty, the agreement describes what the counterparty is *not.* The counterparty is not acting as a fiduciary and has no responsibility to comply with any law, rule, or regulation governing the conduct of fiduciaries, foundation managers, commodity pool operators, commodity trading advisors, or investment advisors. The counterparty also seeks to be indemnified for its advice so that the customer cannot seek to hold the counterparty responsible for any losses sustained by the customer as a result of any prediction, recommendation, or advice made or given by a representative of the counterparty.

Noticeably absent from the customer agreement are risk disclosures, disclosures of conflicts of interests, notices of the financial responsibility of the counterparty and its capitalization, assurances that customer funds will be segregated from the operating funds of the counterparty, or an acknowledgment of the forum for the resolution of disputes. These would all be common provisions in a customer agreement for transactions in a regulated market.

To reiterate: Since the typical foreign exchange customer agreement is so heavily weighted to the benefit of the counterparty, it behooves the customer to have a thorough understanding of the procedures and business practices of the counterparty before entering into any agreement. In short, if the customer is not a sophisticated investor, then foreign currency trading is not an appropriate venue.

BECOMING A SOPHISTICATED INVESTOR

In *CFTC v. Frankwell,* the Ninth Circuit Court of the U.S. Court of Appeals affirmed that a jurisdictional standard based on an investor's level of sophistication would be arbitrary and also impossible to apply. Yet considering the nuances of forex trading, it would only seem reasonable that some measure of sophistication is not only appropriate but necessary.

Historical precedents for determining "sophistication" exist. Generally, knowledge, experience, and/or capitalization are criteria applied in considering the sophistication of the investor. Knowledge and experience may be the most difficult to measure and quantify, but given the complex world of forex investing, these qualifications may be the most important.

Various regulatory agencies have attempted to define sophisticated investors. Part 4 of the Commodity Exchange Act describes a "qualified eligible participant" (QEP). Included in this definition are future commissions merchants, broker dealers, registered commodity pool operators with assets in excess of $5 million, Registered Commodity Trading Advisors providing trading advice to accounts totaling in excess of $5 million, individuals owning securities with an aggregate market value greater than $2 million, an investment company, a bank, an insurance company, an employee benefit plan, and a corporation with total assets in excess of $5 million. A natural person whose individual net worth is greater than $1 million or whose annual income exceeds $200,000 for the two most recent years may also be considered sophisticated.

The Securities and Exchange Commission similarly describes an accredited investor for Regulation D investment pools as an individual with a net worth greater than $1 million or $200,000 annual income for the past two years and an expectation for a $200,000 income in the current year. Until such specific measures are used to define the sophisticated investor, it will be left to the investor to decide if he or she possesses adequate knowledge, experience, and/or wherewithal to be a participant in this marketplace.

Eradicating Fraud, Manipulation, and the Unscrupulous

Since the CFTC was created in 1974, it has brought over 28 cases involving the illegal sale of foreign currency futures or options contracts to the general public—and over 19 since 1990. These 19 cases involved more than 3,200 customers investing over $250 million in fraudulent schemes. The CFTC prevailed in all but two of these cases.

The CFTC has been an effective force in fighting fraud and manipulation. Its diligence in combating white collar crime extends to the new technology of the Internet, where its federal enforcement effort is particularly effective because state authorities have neither the resources nor the broad-based jurisdiction to cope with the problem. Federal banking regulators and the Securities and Exchange Commission (SEC) have had marginal success in fighting forex fraud and manipulation, since neither federal banking laws nor federal securities laws currently provide the regulatory protections necessary for the sale of futures and options to the general public, as the CEA does.

CHAPTER **5**

Are You Qualified to Invest in Forex?

Given the regulatory environment (or the lack thereof) described in Chapter 4, the investor is left to decide for him/herself if forex is a suitable investment opportunity. While reading this book (and others on forex trading) provides a knowledge base that is important for the forex investor, that alone falls far short of the education taught by the marketplace. Individual investors and multinational corporations alike can find investment opportunities in forex trading, but it can also be their undoing.

The appropriate investor for any investment venue may be best defined in terms of preparedness rather than degree of sophistication. Many highly sophisticated multinational firms are reluctant to use the foreign exchange market to hedge their foreign exchange exposure even though they are aware of the financial damage caused by currency exchange rate fluctuations, primarily because the management team may not understand foreign exchange or may consider these markets to be speculative and risky. There is considerable evidence to show that a transaction error in the foreign exchange markets will cause greater damage than the benefit of performing the correct transaction.

RISK OF THE UNKNOWN

It is extremely important for the investor, large or small, to have a thorough understanding of the risks involved in any investment. Since the forex market is largely unregulated by traditional regulatory agencies, risk disclosure is not mandated. The investor is left to determine the risks involved.

The Forex Market Is Not the Futures Market

Investors who do not have the resources or inclination to thoroughly survey the operational and facility risks involved in forex trading should utilize a highly regulated market environment such as the futures market. Currency trading in the Chicago Mercantile Exchange (CME) IMM Division is regulated by the Commodity Futures Trading Commission, the National Futures Association, and the CME. These regulators provide assurances of a fair marketplace with financial safety controls to ensure the investor receives proper risk disclosure plus unparalleled protection against counterparty risk. For instance, the structure and regulation of the CME assure the investor that every transaction on the exchange is backed by the composite financial statement of every clearing member FCM of the exchange, in addition to the book value of the exchange itself. The unregulated environment of the forex market provides nothing close to this financial backing. Plus, trading on a regulated exchange assures that investors will receive detailed risk disclosure and equitable treatment in the marketplace.

The Quality of the Counterparty Is Your Only Protection

The forex investor's only protection lies in the procedures and operations of the financial institution that provides the investor access to the interbank market. The firms providing access to the forex market range from the most highly capitalized banks in the world down to boiler-room bucket shops. Unfortunately the average individual is much more likely to encounter a smooth-talking telephone salesperson than a multinational bank. Therefore, before investing, it is important to ask some simple questions.

Ask to see the firm's audited financial statement and a detailed description of operations and procedures. Since there are no minimum capital requirements for a forex firm, it is left to the investor to determine if the firm is adequately capitalized to handle the transactions the investor expects to perform. In addition, it is critical to determine if the firm segregates customer deposits from the firm's operating capital.

Customer segregated accounts are required by regulation in the futures industry, but the same is not true for forex. Segregation of forex customer funds is voluntary.

Many of the financial institutions offering forex are firms regulated by a government agency monitoring other facets of their business, such as banking and securities and futures brokerage, or are affiliated with financial institutions supervised in such a fashion.

To examine other procedures and operations, the investor should ask for a step-by-step description of the procedures the firm performs when a customer places an order. From this description, the investor should be able to determine if the firm is the actual counterparty for the transaction or a banking member of the interbank market, or if the firm places the order with another counterparty who is a banking member of the interbank market. In the latter case, the investor should request the name of the counterparty and the name of a contact. A follow-up call to the contact may reveal if the counterparty is adequately capitalized for the investor's needs.

Ask to see any documents, prospectuses, risk disclosure statements, or other written explanations of the firm's procedures and investment products. Firms peddling fraudulent investments seldom take the time to create detailed written documents. On the other hand, investors should be cautious if the documents contain more style than substance. Some of the worst Ponzi schemes uncovered by the CFTC, FBI, and the U.S. Postmaster General were perpetrated by firms that provided very flashy mailing pieces. A simple rule: If it's too good to be true, it probably is.

Ask for the names of the firm's principals and officers, and other financial institutions the firm deals with. Determine the background of these individuals and entities, how long they have been in business, their prior business activities, and how long they have been involved in their current business.

Read Documents in Detail

The futures industry has clear requirements for the documents that must be put into the hands of the investor prior to an account opening. The lack of such mandates for forex gives firms the latitude to write into the customer agreement provisions that may be wholly untenable for the customer. It is key for the investor to read and understand all agreements and contracts he or she signs.

Warning Signals

The investor should be very skeptical of any salesperson offering:

1. The expectation of a large profit
2. The assurance of low risk
3. An urgent or limited-time offer

CHAPTER 6

A Little Preparation Goes a Long Way

Hedgers and speculators in the forex market begin with a common challenge: to determine how to best benefit from the foreign exchange marketplace. The speculator must focus on opportunities to generate profits, while the hedger often concentrates on avoiding the evaporation of profits due to exchange rate fluctuation. In either circumstance, the forex trader is best served when operations in forex are treated as any other business challenge. The most common approaches to developing a business plan can be summarized with the following steps:

DETERMINE AN OBJECTIVE

This step may seem to fit the practices of the hedger better than the procedures of a speculator, but both entities benefit if they begin with a thorough understanding of what they intend to accomplish in the forex market.

Without a clearly thought-out objective, the speculator may believe that he or she is being overly swayed by the emotionalism of day-to-day exchange rate fluctuation.

RESEARCH AND RESOURCE

Accumulate historical information and facts both internal and external. External information may include historical exchange rate fluctuation (charts and tables), interest rate patterns, historical economic information, political considerations, and other factors that relate to the analysis of the forex market itself.

Internal information includes an assessment of the forex trader's makeup. For the hedger, this means an assessment of foreign exchange risk exposure, an evaluation of the impact of foreign exchange fluctuation on the hedger's ability to compete, accounting considerations, and other business factors. Since the hedger is likely to be a multinational firm, tax considerations must be evaluated along with the potential for regulatory and/or bylaw restrictions. For the foreign exchange hedger, exposure can be divided into two categories: accounting or translation exposure and economic exposure.

For the speculator, research may not be nearly as complex as that of the hedger, but it is no less important. In addition to gathering statistical and economic information (external information), the speculator must come to terms with the amount of risk capital he or she is willing to devote to the enterprise (internal information). Determination of risk capital will help the speculator avoid the exaggerated effect of emotions on trading decisions. Risk capital is best defined as the amount of money the speculator could lose without impacting lifestyle, standard of living, retirement, and emotional well-being. Risk capital is a wholly subjective consideration but is seldom greater than 15% of total net worth.

DEVELOP A PLAN

This is the "what, how, and who" step. What is the forex trader going to do? How is the trader going to do it? With whom is the trader going to implement the plan? The more specific the plan is, the better. Specific, but not inflexible: The exchange-rate landscape can change rapidly, sometimes redefining even basic principles. An inflexible plan can be a formula for disaster. "What-if" scenarios are important. The speculator must ask, "What should I do if my analysis is correct, and what should I do if my analysis is wrong?"

IMPLEMENT AND EXECUTE THE PLAN

For beginning hedgers and speculators, the key here is to start small. Even the best-designed plan will show flaws and a need for minor refinements when applied to the "real world." Starting with a smaller position will also reduce emotionalism and enable the forex trader to make a more detached evaluation.

MONITOR THE PLAN

The forex trader should monitor the plan to determine if it is being followed, and if it is meeting objectives, reaching benchmarks, or achieving other desired results. For the speculator, this is a good time to evaluate the emotional and financial impact of the investment on his or her well-being.

EVALUATE THE RESULTS

It will be important for the hedger to objectively evaluate the transaction(s) on the firm from both an exchange risk and an accounting perspective. An independent assessment by an outside accounting or consulting firm may be appropriate to assure objectivity. The speculator must determine if the results justify the headache.

Whether a person is a hedger or a speculator, the creation and implementation of the plan are likely to involve forecasting the future price movement of currency exchange rates. The two most common forecasting methods are fundamental analysis and technical analysis.

FUNDAMENTALLY FOREX

Fundamental analysis is the study of all underlying factors influencing the supply and demand equation to determine the future price direction of a market. For a physical commodity, supply and demand factors include current and expected inventory, production, and usage. This is not an easy task.

Gathering such supply and demand information is a colossal effort even for minor commodities. For the forex market, accumulating fundamental information may require a team of researchers. Obviously, when an analyst applies the supply and demand factors of inventory, production, and usage to currency markets, much more is involved than counting beans. A few currency analysis techniques are widely held as preliminary approaches. A sample list of approaches or theories includes purchasing power parity (PPP), unbiased foreign rate theory (UFR), balance of payments analysis (BOP), interest rate analysis or international Fisher effect (IFE), as well as economic and political factors.

Purchasing Power Parity (PPP)

Purchasing power parity (PPP) is one of the most popular and widely respected theories of exchange-rate pricing. PPP suggests that there should be parity among the world's currencies in regard to their ability to purchase goods. In theory, if it takes three deutschemarks to purchase a bag of apples and two U.S. dollars to purchase a bag of apples, then three deutschemarks will equal two dollars. In a perfect world, this may be true. But in the real world, trade barriers, tariffs, and currency market manipulation distort this natural balance.

Comparing the cost of a basket of goods such as the U.S. Consumer Price Index (CPI) with a similar inflation measure of a different country is problematic because all countries do not have the same items in their "basket." Problems of precise calculation reduce the effectiveness of the PPP theory for evaluating the short-term trading opportunities in foreign exchange markets.

The formula to compute purchasing power parity (PPP) exchange rates is:

$$\frac{\text{Index number of price in one country}}{\text{Index number of prices in another country}} \times \begin{array}{c}\text{Rate of exchange in}\\\text{base period between}\\\text{the two countries}\end{array}$$

$$= \quad \begin{array}{c}\text{Purchasing power}\\\text{parity rate}\end{array}$$

The PPP can be useful in identifying currencies that have become widely overvalued or undervalued and can also serve as one of a number of factors used to evaluate a foreign exchange market.

Unbiased Forward Rate Theory (UFR)

This theory relies on the efficient markets theory, which states that a broadly traded market, accessible to all participants, unmanipulated, and equally available to competitive forces, will produce a value that is truly the composite of all factors affecting its price. The UFR asserts that if a forward exchange rate is produced in an unbiased efficient market, then it should equal the expected future spot exchange rate.

The unbiased forward rate theory can be stated simply as:

The expected exchange rate = The forward exchange rate

In actual practice, the spot exchange rate has an equal probability of being above or below the forward rate at the delivery date of the foreign market. Therefore, the greatest value of UFR may be in determining the impact of unexpected exchange rate changes due to international events.

The UFR may not be particularly useful in determining the most important position to establish in the market, but it does teach us a very important lesson—an exchange rate determined in an efficient market will be the result of the composite opinion of all participants and thus a composite of all factors governing the market at that moment in time.

Balance of Payments Analysis (BOP)

BOP is the calculation of transactions made between the people of one country and the people of the rest of the world for a given time frame. BOP is broken down into three components of supply and demand: current, capital, and official settlements (see table below). Sources of demand (or inflows) represent sources of demand for a country currency. In order to buy goods from a country, the buyer must convert its currency to the currency of the seller. When the people of one country import goods from another country, they must sell their currency in exchange for the currency of the other county. In short, when a country exports goods, it accumulates another country's currency, thereby increasing its reserves of that currency. Importing has the opposite effect of reducing the reserves of a country's own currency.

The general structure of the balance of payments analysis is shown in the following table.

Sources of Demand (Inflows)	Sources of Supply (Outflows)
Current Account	
Physical trade: export of goods	Import of goods
Nonphysical trade: export of services	Import of services
Interest income from abroad	Debt service
Capital Account	
Short-term investments by foreigners	Short-term investments in foreign countries
Long-term investments by foreigners	Long-term investments in foreign countries
Official Settlements Account	
Increases in reserves	Declines in reserves

By definition, the balance of payments is always in balance. The sum of the current and capital accounts will be equal to increases or declines in reserves. If a country experiences a trade deficit, then that country's reserve will be reduced by the amount of the deficit. The decline in the reserve will finance the deficit.

Interest Rate Analysis, or International Fisher Effect (IFE)

The IFE suggests that if an investor in a low-interest-rate country, such as Japan, converts investment funds into the currency of a high-interest-rate country, such as the United States, the gain will be offset by the loss caused by foreign exchange rate changes. Countries with high interest rates will have currencies of lesser value than countries with lower interest rates. The expected change in the exchange rate should be equal to the interest rate differential. Therefore the expectation for higher interest rates should devalue the currency.

The international Fisher effect can be written as follows:

The expected rate of change of the exchange rate
= The interest rate differential

Deviations in the IFE can persist for considerable periods of time. Therefore, this analysis has reduced effectiveness in making short-term trading decisions.

Economic and Political Factors

A country's mismanagement of its fiscal policy can be devastating for the value of its currency. Therefore the analysis of a country's economic condition may be the single most important factor in determining the trend of a currency.

Expanding, healthy economies tend to have rising currency values. Countries experiencing recessions will experience a decline in the value of their currency. Exceptions to these rules are particularly remarkable. In the case of Japan, an expanding economy will boost imports, reducing its trade surplus, and have a negative impact on its currency.

If a country needs to tighten monetary policy to avoid the repercussions of inflation, it will force interest rates sharply higher, and a sharply decreased value for its currency is likely to result.

Regardless of a country's fiscal policies, political factors can widely distort the value of its currency. The opposite is certainly true. Even though the United States is a "debtor nation," its currency remains relatively strong due to the stable political condition of the country. The less stable a country's government, the more volatile its currency's exchange rate.

THE TECHNIQUES OF TECHNICAL ANALYSIS

Futures markets and forex markets are often described as efficient markets due to their worldwide participation, accessibility, and lack of manipulation. Both markets offer narrow differences between bid and offer prices, as these trade prices are widely known. Distortion in the differentials between bid and offer prices and between the prices of individual markets quickly evaporate as the wide universe of market participants quickly take action to realign prices.

Since these are "zero-sum markets" in that there must be a unit sold for every unit bought, price rises and declines occur in reaction to the aggressiveness of either the buyer or the seller. If buyers are more aggressive, prices will rise. If sellers are more aggressive, prices will decline.

The underlying reason for the aggressiveness of a buyer or seller may be a reaction to a publicly distributed news release such as a government report. On the other hand, the reason for the aggressiveness may not be discovered for days or weeks.

For the fundamental analyst, the impossibility of knowing all changes affecting supply and demand can seriously affect profit potential. Few will argue that a thorough knowledge of fundamental factors will provide an excellent forecast for exchange rate changes, but this fatal flaw of fundamental analysis has caused traders to look for other analysis techniques.

Technical analysis has become the preferred analysis tool for many forex traders. Technical analysts theorize that since prices are created in an efficient market, the price represents a value reflecting the impact of every single fundamental factor known by anyone, anywhere. The trader does not need to know the fundamental factor that has moved the price, only that the price has moved for a reason.

A price created in this tug of war between the world's buyers and sellers becomes an expression of their composite opinion. In short, price is the composite opinion of all the people who are willing to put their money where their mouth is. If prices are rising over a period of time, then it stands to reason that the factors observed by the buyers are inspiring greater aggressiveness then the factors observed by the sellers.

Moreover, prices created in an efficient market tend to be anticipatory. Not only do traders respond to what they know is true, but they also establish positions based on ramifications of what they know. This is particularly true of forward markets. Based on everything that is known today, what will tomorrow bring?

Bar Charts

Bar charts are the single most common tool of the technical analyst. The basic bar chart will show the opening, high, low, and close prices for a trading period, typically as a vertical line connecting the high and the low with a short, horizontal tick mark on the left representing the opening and another on the right indicating the close.

In the foreign exchange market, a daily price chart can show the opening price in the Pacific Rim and the closing price in the U.S. market, with the high and low established by any interbank price created between the Pacific Rim opening and the U.S. closing.

Bar charts can be created for nearly any time period, from a few seconds to weeks, months, and years. Weekly and monthly bar charts for many important forex markets appear in Appendix B.

The individual vertical bar of a bar chart should be viewed as the record of the tug of war. The strength of the buyer was able to pull the price to the high, while the strength of the seller was able to pull the price to the low. At the end of the day, the center of the rope was at the closing price. Through time, the pattern of bars will express a trend. The trend can be up, down, or sideways.

An uptrending market is typically delineated by a line connecting the lows; a downtrending market by a line connecting the highs. A sideways trending market is usually expressed by drawing a channel with one line connecting the highs and another line connecting the lows (see Figures 6-1 through 6-3).

Over time, price charts usually develop a sawtooth pattern. Prices rise for a few days, then decline for a few days, and so forth. This is often viewed by the technical analyst as a market cycling from being overbought to oversold. Traders may aggressively buy the market until the price reaches a short-term extreme high. At that moment, short-term traders may begin taking profits, sellers may see a selling opportunity, or a combination of both, causing the market to decline. As the aggressiveness of the seller dissipates, the market will reach a short-term extreme low and the buyers may see opportunities.

As long as successive lows are at or above an uptrend line, the uptrend remains intact, but a low below an uptrend line changes the trend by definition. For technical analysts, any time a trend is broken, there is reason for concern. This does not necessarily mean that a trend is reversing; it simply confirms that the trend has changed.

Trends can also change when the angle of the trendline becomes more steep. Successive increases in the angle of the trend will create fan trendlines, an indication that the market is becoming excitedly more bullish or bearish.

Changes in Trends Can Be Reversals of Trends

Technical analysts typically create rules for each market to differentiate changes in trends from indications of reversals. Some markets have a

FIGURE 6-1

Uptrend

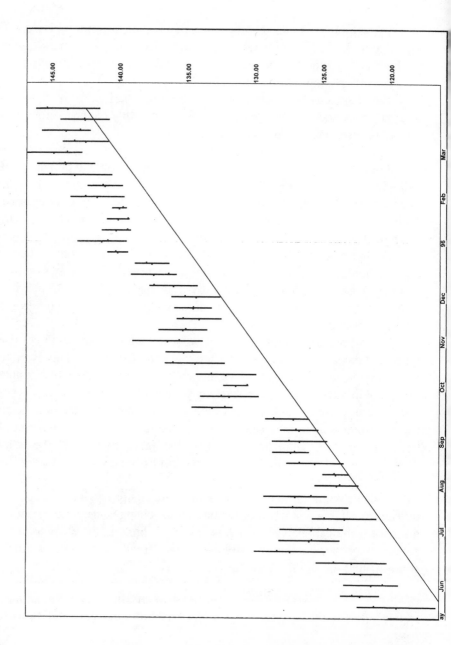

FIGURE 6-2

Downtrend

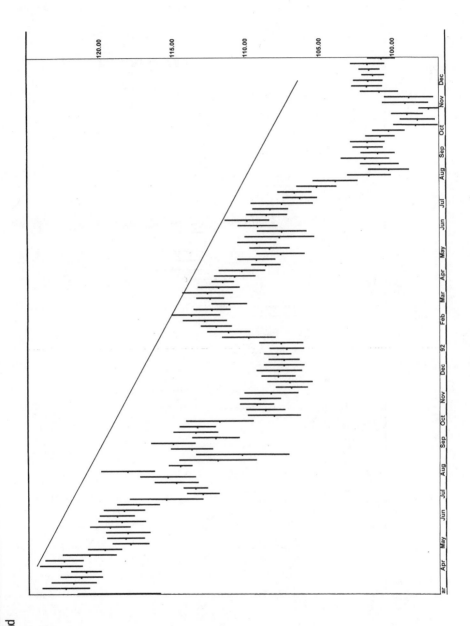

FIGURE 6-3

Sideways

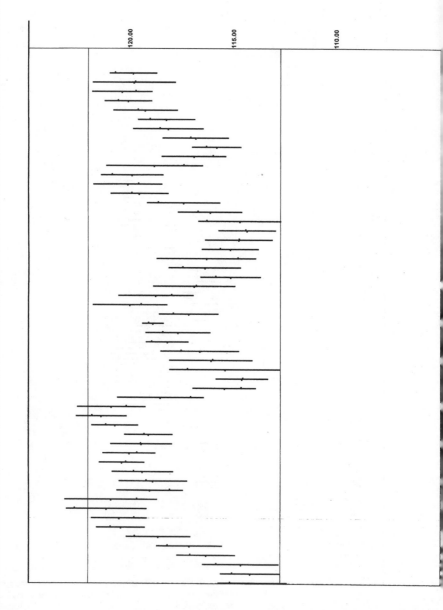

tendency to change trend often without reversing, while other markets maintain tidy trends that are not broken unless the market is reversing. The prices in some markets experience short-term volatility, which breaks trendlines without violating the long-term integrity of the trend. In these cases, confirmation or a trend reversal must be found. A confirmation rule may be that the closing price must close under the trendline, not just at the low under the trendline. Or, the market price must close in two successive trading periods below the trendline.

Breakouts often cause action and are seldom ignored even by the most stalwart fundamental analyst. Breakouts from sideways price channels can also be momentous (see Figure 6-4).

The market psychology that creates a sideways price pattern can be apathy, balanced supply and demand, and/or little news, providing limited cause of action for either buyers or sellers. The market simply moves from being modestly overbought to modestly oversold.

A trade above an upper channel line or a trade below a lower channel line of a sideways market tells the technical analyst that something important may be happening or about to happen. Certainly the channel of apathy has been broken.

Technical analysts often view upper channel lines to be an area of technical resistance and lower channel lines as technical support. As prices rise to the upper channel, buying weakens and sellers become stronger. The strength of the sellers resists a continued price rise. The opposite occurs as prices decline to areas of technical support with buyers supporting prices. Technical analysts also describe previous major highs and lows as resistance and support and will take particular notice if these levels are exceeded (see Figure 6-5).

If one day's low is higher than the previous day's high (or its high is lower than the previous day's low), a gap will occur on the chart. This is typically a very aggressive signal for the technical analyst. In the forex market, gaps are very unusual since the trading day is nearly 24 hours. To create a gap in a cash currency chart, an important event must have occurred, for example between the U.S. market close and the Pacific Rim market open.

Four Basic Gaps

A *common gap* occurs within a short-term trading pattern and is quickly closed with succeeding trading days. The common gap is closed when a future day of trading causes a price range to occur within the price gap area.

FIGURE 6-4

Breakout

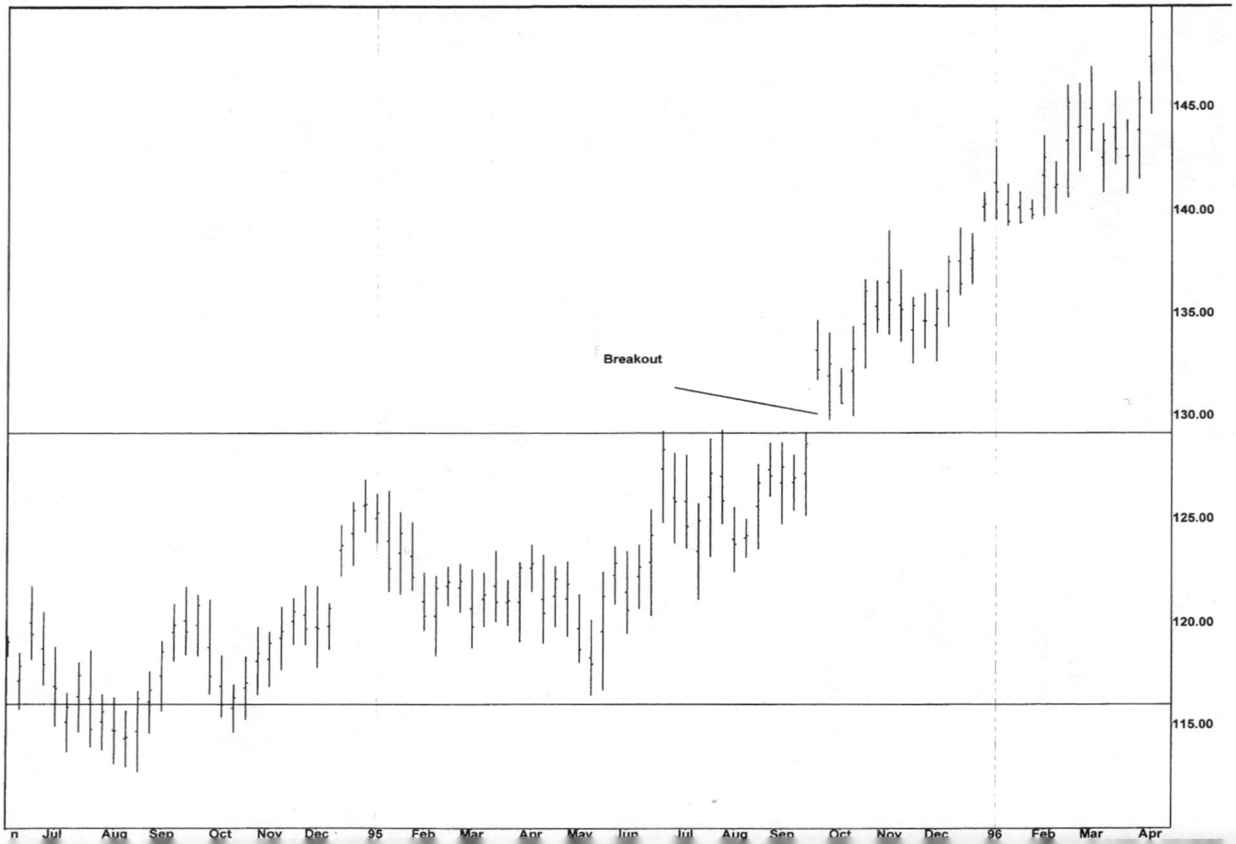

FIGURE 6-5

Support and Resistance

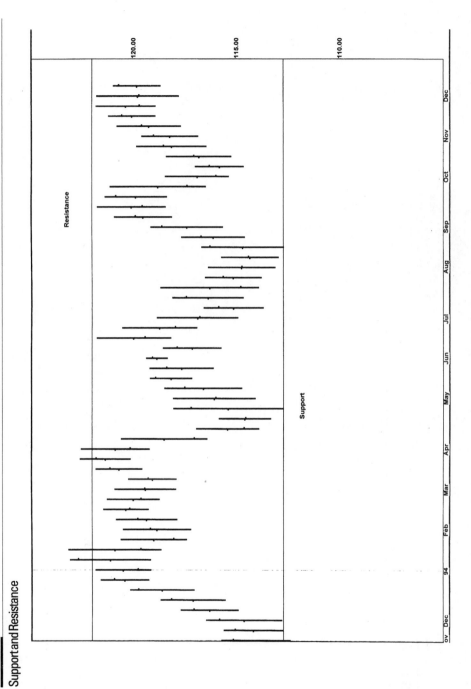

FIGURE 6-6

Gaps

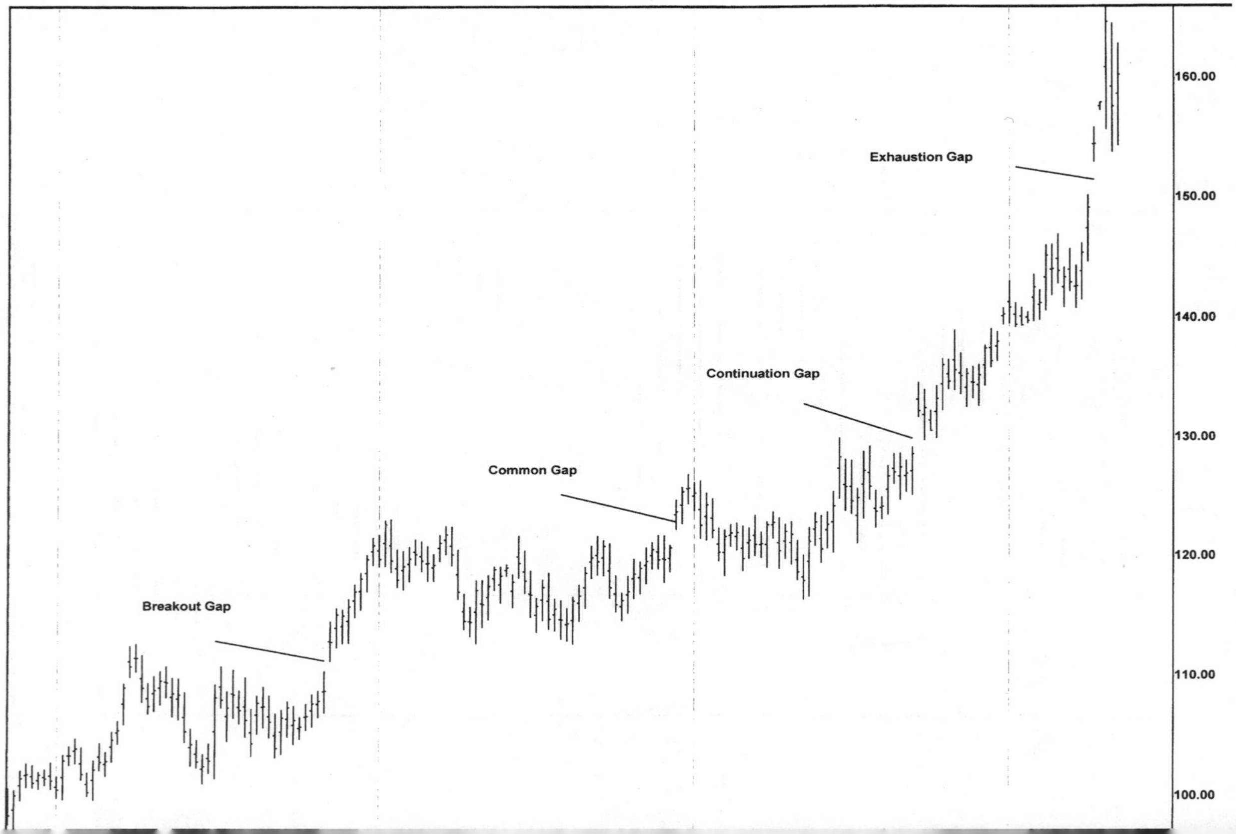

Exhaustion Gap
Continuation Gap
Common Gap
Breakout Gap
160.00
150.00
140.00
130.00
120.00
110.00
100.00

A *breakaway gap* occurs in combination with the breakout of a trend or channel. This gap is considered very meaningful by technical analysts and is often a significant indication that an important bullish or bearish move has begun.

Continuation gaps signal the technical analyst that a powerful trend is under way and accelerating.

An *exhaustion gap* is the last gasp of the market, occurring just before a major high or major low and often preceding a market spike (see Figure 6-6).

A spike in price is usually a wide range in price at either an extreme high or extreme low. If the spike is followed by a day of trading in the opposite direction, then a spike can provide strong evidence of a reversal. Forex markets often experience spike highs and spike lows since trend changes in currency are seldom subtle.

Technical analysts observe price patterns to provide justification for entering and exiting the market. They also attempt to find price patterns that have historically indicated that trends will continue. Continuation patterns are useful as confidence builders. Whether a market is trending higher or lower, there will be conflicting news reports that may shake the confidence of the trader. Continuation patterns are typically short-term periods of consolidation in price that form flags and pennants in the price chart. A flag formation occurs when parallel channel lines can be used to connect the highs and connect the lows. Pennant formations are actually the convergence of very short-term up and down trends. As the market price breaks out of a pennant or a flag in the direction of a trend, the technical analyst is convinced that the trend will continue (see Figure 6-7).

Technical analysts are in constant search of major top and bottom formations. Although it is seldom realistic for an analyst to pick a top and bottom, an understanding of these price formations is often useful in retrospect and can provide the technical analyst with some confidence that the new trend has long-term potential.

Double tops and bottoms (M or W formations) are actually indications of major resistance and support, respectively. The technical analyst should be aware, though, that two matching major highs do not make a double top. Confirmation of a double top occurs when prices drop below the lowest price between the two tops. Failure to wait for this confirmation may trap the trader in a period of consolidation—a sideways trend. Triple tops and bottoms have the identical confirmation rule of a double top or bottom.

FIGURE 6-7

Flags and Pennants

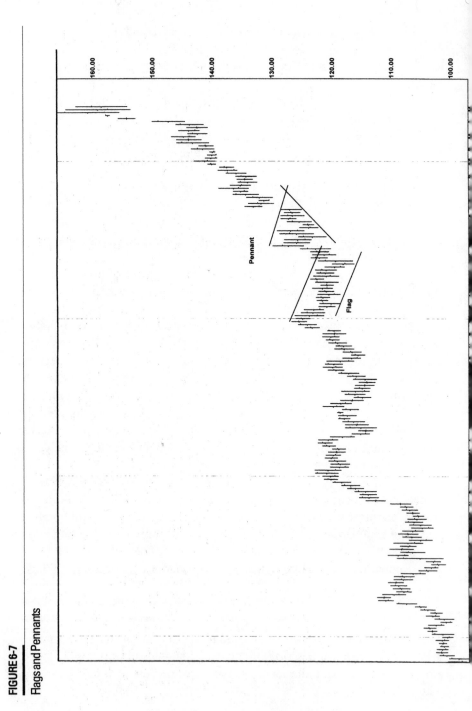

FIGURE 6-8

Head-and-Shoulders Formation

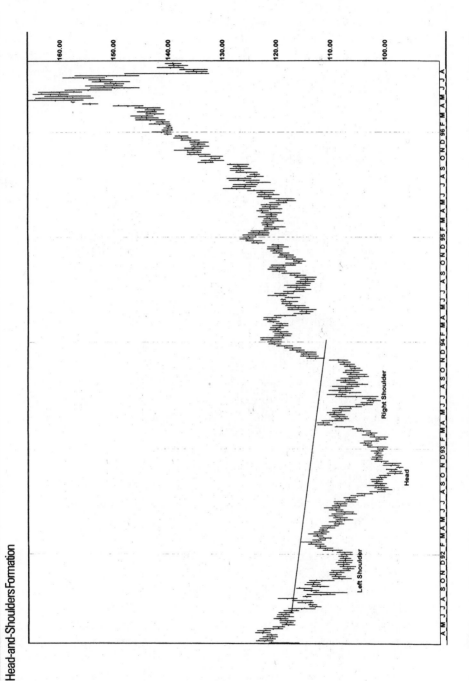

Historically, one of the most reliable reversal formations is the head-and-shoulders formation. Head-and-shoulders tops (or bottoms) are actually three successive prices. The first thrust is an important high (or low). The second thrust exceeds the previous rally (or decline), but the third rally fails to make a new high. When prices drop below the "neck line" created by the previous reaction low (or high), the head-and-shoulders is complete and the technical signal is confirmed (see Figure 6-8).

ANATOMY OF A BULL MARKET

Some major bull markets have characteristic anatomies that enable the technical analyst to understand how fundamental factors are displayed in prices. Early acknowledgment of the similar characteristics of a major bull market gives the technician the potential for major profits at relatively low risk. The foundations for a major bull market can be observed with fundamental analysis, as well as technical analysis, if the trader is willing to exercise the patience necessary to discover the illusive benchmarks.

Stage One: The Birth of the Bull

The origins of a bull market, surprisingly, are often found in surplus situations. It is agreed that the very high prices achieved in a bull market develop as shortages are realized, but surplus supplies actually set the stage for an explosive rally. Surpluses widen the arteries, fill the pipelines, and foster new sources of demand. An industry whose raw materials are in surplus is likely to have the confidence to expand and to contract long-term commitments. In terms of the forex market, a nation's currency that is in abundance (surplus) in the hands of its trading partners will be of diminished value. The relative strength of the opposing currencies will increase purchases of the nation's underpriced goods and services. For example, in theory, if the U.S. dollar is in surplus in Germany, and the Bundesbank has huge reserves of the greenback, then the dollar will be devalued relative to the deutschemark (DM). The greater value of the DM provides greater buying power for the Germans for U.S. goods and services.

Technically, a surplus market is observable as a rounded bottom, the early signs of which are progressively shallowing downtrends and narrower trading ranges. Many major bull markets begin as a rounded bottom technical formation. The absolute bottom of a rounded bottom often occurs when the fundamental information is the most bearish, while the commodity price meanders sideways in a narrow range. Passive market activity after bearish news is your first bull sign.

Stage Two: Shallow Uptrend

The next benchmark the technician will look for is modestly increasing prices. This is exhibited as the right side of the rounded bottom, a very shallow uptrend. Often, this is accompanied with wider price ranges. Fundamentally, there is little change in the supply. But a "what-if" scenario may be debated among fundamentalists—e.g., what if interest rates increase? Because of the intangible nature of the "what-if" scenario, stage two offers very little price improvement other than the gradual increase in price mainly due to carrying charges.

Stage Three: Breakout

The third stage of a major bull market often occurs with very little public fundamental information. It may be described in business publications as a "technical breakout," which is a newswriter's way of saying "The market has made a dramatic move, but we don't know why." Technically, the market is breaking out of the rounded bottom and often will have a modest rally for a few days, sometimes weeks. This rally often breaks down, as little fundamental news is forthcoming and the market develops what is technically termed a *platform*. A platform is sideways market activity at the area of the rounded bottom breakout. This is a period of confusing information. Often, fundamental and technical data during this time frame conflict, as various pieces of market information are contradictory.

Stage Four: The Rally Begins

The fourth stage develops as the major market information becomes more succinct. Often, rumored fundamental information comes into play. Also, some of the "what-if" scenarios begin to develop. This is a nervous, choppy rally, with labored price increases and sharp, quick dips. The rallies and subsequent dips are usually able to hold a solid trendline, and the technical trader may be confident, buying the dips back to the trendline.

Stage Five: The Explosive Newsmaker

Technically, gaps are left on the charts during this time period, and the bullish fundamental scenario enjoys wider acceptance. Buyers often scramble, while sellers are reluctant.

Stage Six: The Steep Rally

The sixth stage of the bull market is typically a steep rally with few minor retracements and wide trading ranges, fueled by very bullish fundamental information. Public attention is attracted to the market rally. Also during this stage, major U.S. news magazines provide extensive coverage, often in lead articles.

Stage Seven: The Shearing

This is when the most bullish information is very abundant and the public is being inspired into involvement. Technically, the market will gap higher sometimes for two or more days, and then "the sheep are shorn." It is after stage seven that the industry is plagued with outcries for greater regulation.

Neither fundamental analysis nor technical analysis is the golden grail, but they do provide important snapshots of the market and often serve as important starting points. Neither fundamental analysis nor technical analysis will be successful without the implementation of a serious, well-conceived plan.

CHAPTER 7

If You Can't Manage Your Investment, Who Can?

INTRODUCTION

Most investors new to currencies don't have any idea where to start. They have this nest egg of money in scattered investments that may never be affected by another currency. These investors have an appetite and a desire to get into FX trading, but no experience doing so.

Financial textbooks about currencies have been no help in the past because they were written for financial whizzes managing millions of dollars for banks or major international corporations. The investment public thinks that unless they have millions of dollars to invest they cannot buy and sell currencies for investment without going to their local bank to convert money at expensive, gigantic spreads. These investors typically shy away from the mysterious FX world, believing it to be untouchable.

The purpose of this chapter is to bridge the gap between investor and investment. Investors considering trading currencies for the first time should think seriously about hiring an investment manager. The limitless number of currency trading institutions have realized through expensive lessons that casual inspection of the market is not going to give them enough knowledge to produce a return by trading currencies. Trading institutions invest significant sums researching their traders and investments in the market. They know that the market is not going to lie down and let people pick its pockets.

Remember that for every loser there is a winner. The odds are always going to be on the side of the best prepared. This brings to mind the poker adage, "When you sit down at the table and look around, if you don't see the sucker, it is most likely you." The same is true for the big interbank market of currencies. When you look around and do not know who the sucker is, put your money back in your pocket.

WHO TRADES FOREX?

This chapter focuses on the currency investment managers who invest for speculators and hedgers. Typically an investment manager is considered to be independent and separate from the investor, but that is not always the case. Many major corporations build entire departments around their investment managers.

Fortunately for investors, in managed forex trading there is a whole army of highly qualified traders who left banks due to the shrinkage of bank forex departments from the high level of competition for customers and the decreases in profit margins as a consequence of the tighter spreads offered to these customers. Some of these same highly qualified traders who were making millions for banks are now starting up their own managed trading firms in order to give customers the opportunity to invest with an experienced bank trader. The only small caveat is that it is much different to trade for proprietary funds than for a bank's principal position.

The reason for the difference in trading proprietary funds as compared to bank funds is that a bank trader constantly receives the "edge" in the market from a customer coming to the bank to find a "market." The bank trader is then given a position better than the market. The dealer also doesn't enter the position due to market-trading decisions, which are susceptible to the enemies of sound trading, greed and fear. The dealer's only decision is how to exit as best as possible. Exiting may also be done for the dealer by another customer requesting a market in the opposite direction. The edge is then again in the dealer's favor. The combination of the two edges given by the customer makes even more money for the dealer. Therefore, the reliability of a trader's performance in the dealing environment versus the proprietary trading environment is shaky at best. The key is that traders have deep experience in the currencies and how they react in different scenarios.

Forex Money Managers

When trying to decide who can manage your money better than you, as an investor, you must look at the investment and decide whether or not there are any opportunities beyond those of what is considered the *random walk theory.* The random walk theory states that if there is a zero-sum gain on an investment, then for every winner or every positive return there is a loser or a loss in an investment. In the random walk theory, markets move in random directions if there is a zero-sum gain and information is publicly distributed equally. If this theory is true, then the markets move in a random direction and no one manager or investment decision by any one person is going to be better than any other.

According to the random walk theory, there are different levels of information available to the public. There are the fundamental analysis, technical analysis, and insider information. Those different levels of information make it possible for certain individuals to take better advantage of market moves. The theory states that traders with insider information are the only people who have an actual advantage over the market. Insider trading on foreign currencies would mean that central bankers taking advantage of currency flows would have an advantage over others using either fundamental analysis and/or technical analysis.

Fundamental analysis is the deepest form of analysis possible (short of insider trading, that is). The idea behind fundamental analysis is that somebody who studies the markets and the fundamental factors that affect the market—such as balance of payment, interest rates, and expected inflation—may find some important information. Those fundamental factors would be considered as having a good probability of producing successful returns.

The lowest level is technical analysis, which says that markets follow a certain pattern or trend, or signal changes in direction. These signals are almost a type of self-fulfilling prophesy, as investors who look for them invest according to what they believe the signal is indicating—thereby self-professing the direction of the market.

For example, say that significant technical analysis has been done in the market, and analysts see a head-and-shoulders top to the market, which may indicate to technical analysts that the market is going to go down. If enough analysts with money in their pocket think that the market will decline on account of the head-and-shoulders formations, they could *create* the market turndown by reacting to the information, selling the currency that just made the head-and-shoulders top.

In the currency business, insider traders don't necessarily have a chance of beating the rest of the market. In many cases central bankers have lost to speculators in the foreign currency markets, therefore proving that even insider trading may fail.

Currency Trading versus Other Asset Classes

Some characteristics of forex versus other asset classes make it a viable investment, even though it is considered to have a zero-sum gain of investment (meaning that every time an investor makes money buying Swiss francs and selling U.S. dollars, for instance, the opposite side of that transaction loses money). The difference between foreign exchange and many of the other asset classes is that foreign exchange has a wide base of participants.

Participants in Foreign Exchange

In foreign exchange there is a wide base of participants willing to offset their risks. Hedgers, governments, and central bankers constantly are transferring currency balances. They have to buy Swiss francs or U.S. dollars because they have a payment in those currencies. Their concern is making the payment and getting the currency, and they have to do it now.

Since this is the case, speculators who are willing to take the risk of following a different market direction for a period, and who believe that the market is going to move in a certain direction, will be more likely to have an opportunity to take advantage of the market. In other investment vehicles, the market is mostly controlled by speculators who are buying just as willingly as they are selling, and the hedgers make up a much smaller proportion of the market. Many institutions are willing to give up opportunity by hedging in the market today. This willingness to give up a "good position" provides opportunities to speculators who wish to take advantage of fluctuations in the currencies.

A cash flow manager for a major, multinational corporation may realize that he or she needs to make a payment of 10 million deutschemarks today, and does not care where the price of deutschemarks to the U.S. dollar is during the purchase. The manager has to buy 10 million deutschemarks and needs to sell the equivalent U.S. dollar amount. Speculators can take advantage of that opportunity.

Speculators can also take the opposite side of that transaction, selling the deutschemarks and buying U.S. dollars when the market is uptrending in the favor of U.S. dollars over deutschemarks. Speculators still have an opportunity to lose, and the opportunity may be just equal to the gain, but the hedger may be willing to give up that opportunity in order to make the payments. In short, there are many different opportunities available in the foreign currency market.

Opportunities in Currencies

There are basically three ways of profiting in the foreign currency market. One is by the method of arbitrage. In the following chapters, different methods of arbitrage will be analyzed. How different types of arbitrage can give investors opportunities in foreign currency trading will become apparent.

Also, many traders think that the currency markets trend on a long-term basis better than most other markets. Currencies trend better due to government economic cycles, inflationary trends, interest rates, and long-term policy decisions. Considerations such as these make investing in currencies a more viable method of investment for trend followers.

The third method of opportunity in foreign currency trading is based on the inefficiencies between the futures versus the spot market or the forward versus spot market. Since there are many different markets for trading currencies—futures markets, options markets, over-the-counter markets, over-the-counter forward markets, and spot markets—there may be many opportunities for investors to take advantage of price discrepancies between the spot and the forward markets or the option markets. If a trader feels confident about the volatility of the underlying option market or the interest-rate base difference between the spot and the futures or forward market, he or she can trade changes in these prices.

However, investing blindly in the currency market can be very dangerous for the novice investor as markets rise and fall. To add to the danger, trading in the currency markets is frequently done on a very highly leveraged basis, meaning that only 10% of an investment may be needed on deposit to take advantage of a 100% move in the market.

For example, at 10% leverage an investor with $100,000 is able to buy $1 million worth of a non-U.S. currency. He or she may decide to buy $1 million U.S. dollars and sell that equivalent in Swiss francs at the current market price. Buying dollars and selling Swiss francs at a price of 1.4520 Swiss francs to the U.S. dollar, and selling often, the market moves from 1.4520 to 1.4540, a 20-pip move in the market. A 20-pip move equates to approximately $1,375 U.S. dollars on $1 million with only $100,000 on deposit. This move could occur in less than one second. Leverage of 10 to 1 creates drastic swings in profits and losses. A 1% gain on $1 million is $10,000. That $10,000 is 10% of a $100,000 investment. So 10 to 1 leverage drastically increases the amount of profit or loss potential on any given position.

The leverage of this example is not even as close as some of the leverages available in the market today. Many major corporations are able to trade on a credit basis with zero margin on deposit. Many institutions that are not necessarily sophisticated trading institutions are able to trade at much lower levels of margin or higher leverage levels, such as 20 to 1 or 30 to 1. At 20 to 1, a person with $50,000 could trade a $1 million investment.

FOREX CURRENCY ADVISORS

Obviously, with the many different opportunities for investment that exist and the many possible pitfalls of investing in foreign currencies, it is wise to look for foreign currency investment managers. There are basically four viable options for foreign currency investment managers: bank proprietary investment departments, foreign exchange advisory firms, registered investment advisors, and commodity trading advisors.

Bank Proprietary Investment Departments

Bank proprietary investment departments are basically not available for outside investors on a direct basis but possibly indirectly. A stock investment in a bank that has many proprietary investments in the currency markets is an indirect way to take advantage of the possible opportunities that exist in foreign currency trading. Some banks offer funds that are traded by the bank's proprietary traders. Bank proprietary investment departments have been, in the past, a major form of profit for banking institutions around the world. Many banks which have shown losses in all major departments have been able to show profits overall to their investors or stockholders by producing very large profits in the foreign currency proprietary trading department. This is partly due to the vast amount of information that banks have in regard to currency and currency flows. Also, banks are able to make very large amounts of money on offering their currency trading facilities to large corporate clients at a cost. This cost is usually the spread that they offer to their corporate customers in their currency conversions. These bid/ offer spreads may be as wide as 10% of the current spot currency market. That would reflect a $10,000 cost on a $100,000 currency conversion. It may seem radical for banks to profit so much in currency conversions, but many times, as stated earlier, corporations are willing to buy or sell currencies without necessarily great regard to the conversion price. As efficiencies increase, the profitability of bid/offer spreads decreases, as the participants become more savvy about other trading vehicle opportunities.

Foreign Exchange Advisory Firms

The second type of currency manager is foreign exchange advisory firms, which offer publications, newsletters, hotlines, market commentary, and information on the direction of foreign currency trends. They often also offer the opportunity to invest through their trading operations and their advisory firm in the foreign currency market. They may utilize banks, limited partnership funds, pools, or trading houses for executing foreign currency transactions. Due to the amount and the value of the information in the foreign currency market, there are many good advisory firms that offer information on foreign currencies. This information is quite expensive: Institutional investors are willing to pay well for information that could produce better opportunities. These firms also will often point investors in the direction of fund managers or banking institutions in which they may invest. Some of those advisory firms are run by the next two types—registered investment advisors and commodity trading advisors.

Registered Investment Advisors

Registered investment advisors are registered under the Securities Exchange Commission. There are strict rules on what a registered investment advisor is able to do and not do. Those rules don't necessarily pertain to the activities of foreign currency trading, which remains an unregulated investment in the United States at the time of this book's publication. Yet registered investment advisors and commodity trading advisors do provide one very important characteristic that other advisors and money managers may not— a registered capacity. This means that they are responsible to a regulatory agency that reviews them regarding other activities and their background.

Commodity Trading Advisors

Commodity trading advisors are not allowed to be approved for registration if they have committed a felony, unless the NFA permits them to do so due to special circumstances. They are also statutorily disqualified from registration if they have forged records in the past or if they have violated the rules of another registered capacity to the point of suspension or expulsion. As in any situation there are exceptions, but with a registered capacity there are ways to review their background and overall compliance in the respective industries. Other investors who are not trading with registered commodity trading advisors or registered investment advisors may not have information available beyond that which is supplied to them by the advisor, whose background may not be reviewed, audited, or inspected from outside agencies. This gives investors one more level of protection when they put their funds with an advisor.

Reviewing Currency Managers

There are certain characteristics to look for in investment advisors if you are a foreign currency investor who would rather invest with an experienced investor instead of rolling the dice and investing money in the currency yourself. These include their trading style and whether they are position traders or arbitrage traders. Other characteristics are the required capitalization methods of the account, the traders' bias versus the trading benchmark, the minimum account size of the trader, the fee structure that the advisor is charging for trading an investor's account, past performance of the advisor, and risk relationship to profitability.

Investment Strategy

The first characteristic the investor should look for is whether the manager is a position trader, arbitrage trader, or combination of both.

Position Traders

Position traders have a tendency to establish a position and hold it for time periods greater than a day. They may buy currencies and hold on to them for a period from one day to 10 years, taking advantage of currency fluctuations, economic cycles, interest rate movement, and inflationary trends. Position traders normally fall into short-, medium-, or long-term traders. The *short-term trader* is anyone who trades in a direction less than a week. A *medium-term trader* is anyone who trades a position for one week to a month. A *long-term trader* is anyone who trades or holds a position for longer than a month. In currency trading, most position traders fall into the first and second categories rather than the third. Short- and medium-term traders in the foreign currency markets are willing to buy or sell into a position on the idea that the market is trending in a certain direction and they want to take advantage of that direction. They hold a certain risk perimeter to which they are willing to allow the market to go against them before offsetting the position and taking losses on it. They normally have a profit objective or a target point to which they believe the market is going to trend.

Arbitrage Traders

Arbitrage traders enter and exit a trade immediately and simultaneously, meaning that they will be buying in one market and selling in another, locking in a spread differential between the two markets. As the markets approach each other and the opportunity disappears, they will exit their positions in the markets, taking advantage of the markets' arriving at equilibrium. Complex arbitrage positions may take a longer time period to move into equilibrium and move against arbitrageurs while they are waiting for the market to approach equilibrium. A market that is not in equilibrium may force a manager to take a loss due to the lack of capitalization needed to hold the position until equilibrium occurs. This results from volatility in the market or wide fluctuations in interest rates. Also, an arbitrageur usually has the ability to invest in many different markets. Arbitrageurs are usually required to possess a very large amount of capitalization in order to access and fund positions in many different markets. The customer or investor who wants to invest with an arbitrageur must usually put up a large amount of capitalization. In contrast, long-term position traders normally will put on a position knowing that they are going to be able to withstand a movement against their position and will not leverage themselves as dramatically as an arbitrageur. Therefore they have the capitalization to withstand movements against their position, allowing the long-term trend or the opportunity to become available to them.

Methods of Capitalization   The second characteristic the investor should be aware of is the different methods of capitalization advisors require. Methods of capitalization such as a letter of credit or a banking relationship may allow an investor to invest with no additional capitalization requirement.

- *Credit lines.* An investor may have millions of dollars at a certain bank in the form of CDs, treasury bills, or bonds that the bank is holding as custody, as well as cash deposits. These deposits in themselves may not be put up as margin in currency transactions. There may be no additional margining of currency transactions required because the customer of the bank has so many funds on deposit with that bank. Not having to put up funds with a trading institution reduces the amount of opportunity costs on interest flows and other investment opportunities that may be available to the investor.

- *Marginal lines.* Investors who don't have banking relationships equivalent to millions of dollars may set up with certain advisors the ability to invest on margined accounts. Margined accounts allow leverage as low as 50 to 1 or 2% of margin on the transaction that they are executing. Some leveraged transactions can give investors the opportunity to invest much smaller amounts than normal yet receive the same advantages. This is considered *notional funding.*

    Notional funding allows advisors to permit customers to invest with them on a greater leverage basis than what is considered to be their normal minimum standards. An investor may put up $50,000 with an advisor, telling the advisor that they may trade those funds as if the customer invested $100,000. Thus, a 2% return on a transaction would actually be reflected as a 4% return on the amount of funds on deposit. Likewise a 2% loss on the $100,000 notional funds would actually be a 4% loss on the $50,000 invested. Notional funding is used in circumstances where investors may have many funds with many different advisors while maintaining only a marginal amount with any one manager.

Correlation to Benchmarks   The third characteristic an investor should look for in an investment advisor is the trader's bias versus trading benchmarks. A trading benchmark is a similar investment that is used to measure an advisor's performance. The trader who has a bias of buying dollars and selling foreign currencies may perform better in bull market situations for the U.S. dollar than in times of depreciating U.S. dollars versus foreign currencies. An investor looking for an advisor who takes opportunities in bull markets for the U.S. dollar will look for advisors who perform well during bull markets. An investor should compare or correlate that investor's past performance with the movement of different currency indexes which are important to the investor. In certain cases, an advisor may not perform as well as a direct investment into the currency market itself due to getting in and out of the market at unfavorable levels, buying when the market has peaked rather than when the market has bottomed in an attempt to take advantage of a trend in the market. Even though benchmarks are important, an advisor who is bullish on U.S. dollars or any other currency may still lose while the market is moving in a bullish direction.

Account Minimum   The minimum account size is the fourth characteristic the investor should investigate. The minimum account size requirement of many advisors makes them inaccessible to customers or investors, even though they would like to invest with that advisor. Advisors usually increase their minimum account size as they begin to perform better. Since fees are typically a percentage of the investment, the larger the investment size the larger the fee payment to the advisor and the smaller amount of management costs per customer due to a smaller number of large accounts.

Fee Structure   Foreign currency trading advisors have fees and compensation that are disclosed to the investor, but that may also have deals or methods of compensation that the customer or investor is not necessarily aware of, bringing us to our fifth characteristic. In the unregulated industry of foreign currency trading, an advisor may be compensated not only by normal fees such as incentive fees and management fees but also by commission rebates and rebates on pips of the price in which they executed trades for the customer.

The management fees are usually a percentage of the amount of funds under management deducted on a quarterly or annual basis. These fees could range anywhere from zero to 8% on an annual basis. The management fee is the cost of the advisor monitoring and keeping statements for the customer while managing the customer's positions relative to the investment size.

The *incentive fee* is a fee that an advisor charges an investor on the profits produced in the account. A common example may be a 20% incentive fee for profits. If an advisor produces a 20% return on a $100,000 investment ($20,000), the advisor (assuming a 20% incentive fee) would receive $4,000 of that profit, the investor $16,000. Some incentive fees have been set up so that an advisor has to reach above a certain percentage return on a monthly basis before he or she receives an incentive fee for trading. This is called a *hurdle rate*. An example is an incentive fee of 20% for profits only greater than 15%: The advisor has to produce a return above 15% to receive a 20% incentive fee—a great incentive for producing higher returns.

Some of the hidden fees that may be charged by advisors due to the amount of power that they wield in the investment environment are commission rebates on commissions charged to investors trading in the currency markets and rebates on commissions on a per transaction basis. Investment advisors are sometimes compensated by what is termed *pip rebates*, available to them per pip of a transaction. A pip rebate applies when an investment advisor places trades with a banking counterparty and the banking counterparty pays a one-pip rebate as an incentive for the advisor to trade through them. In order to stay competitive, many banks have compensated advisors by this method. These methods of compensation may or may not be disclosed to the investor. The investor should take the opportunity to check the background or request from the advisor information regarding the total fees hidden or not hidden being charged to the customer.

Past Performance   The sixth characteristic that should be considered when looking for an investment advisor is past performance. It is obviously important to consider that the performance of an advisor does not guarantee that he or she will produce results. Past performance is not necessarily indicative of future events. A currency trader or currency advisor may have been extremely successful over the past five years with buying U.S. dollars due to a temporary bull market in U.S. dollars, but that advisor may have much different performance in trading proprietary funds or funds for an investor versus trading funds on a market-making basis for a banking institution—the difference being that while making markets for a banking institution the advisor is able to buy and sell at the better bid/ask price due to the customer entering the trade with the banking institution. *Trading on the edge*, as it is termed, gives the advisor the ability to buy at better levels and therefore hold a position better than an investor who must go into a trading institution and lose the edge entering the trade at a loss. This edge can produce a great difference in the advisor's profitability.

When considering the past performance of investment advisors, it is important to look at their ability to trade funds on a notional basis versus a fully capitalized basis, the difference being that some investment advisors are able to trade better at different levels of capitalization. An investment advisor trading million-dollar quantities may not be the same as an investment advisor trading 100-million-dollar quantities due to the amount of profits and losses occurring in each transaction. It is important to consider the advisors' past performance in relation to the investment you are about to make with them.

Risk to Reward   The seventh characteristic is one of the most important and should be considered when choosing an advisor. It is the advisor's risk relationship to profitability. There are different measures of risk relationships to profitability: (1) volatility against losses, (2) standard deviation as a measure of risk, (3) the standard deviation of profit versus deviation of losses, (4) maximum loss in any one position versus the maximum return, (5) negative performance versus other similar traders or managers as a level of risk consideration, and (6) correlation to similar portfolios or investments.

Qualitative Factors   Finally, certain qualitative factors can point out which advisor suits an investor's needs, such as the trader's accessibility and information about what the trader is doing at any current time in the market.

The level of information available about the advisor through past experiences, registrations, and background checks is abundantly important in choosing an advisor, as the following section explains.

Commodity Trading Advisors

Commodity trading advisors (CTAs) and registered investment advisors are good choices for investors who wish to enter into foreign currency trading. The foreign currency environment is an environment in which the basis for protection of customer funds and investments is unregulated. Any unregulated environment is prone to fraud, misrepresentation, manipulation, and other abuse. Many times the unregulated industries of the financial world are considered safe harbors for criminals prohibited from the registered investment environment. Yet paradoxically, in the foreign currency industry, the environment is actually a very viable one, free the costs of regulation. Forex investing offers many opportunities for many different types of investors, but like any investment it can be misused and manipulated in ways that take advantage of the customer.

Registered investment advisors or CTAs give customers additional protection in trading foreign currencies. Even though the foreign currency trading aspect of CTAs or registered investment advisors is unregulated, they may hold and pool funds without the need of a clearinghouse, bank, or counterparty to hold the funds. And there is one more level of protection that a CTA or registered investment advisor offers that is unavailable from an advisor who is not regulated or registered by a governmental agency: CTAs have registration status with the National Futures Association (NFA), a self-regulatory agency of the futures industry which registers members under the Commodity Futures Trading Commission (CFTC). The CFTC is the regulatory agency set up for futures trading. In futures trading a CTA is very heavily regulated. An investor can achieve additional protection and comfort by trading in currency futures through a CTA rather than through the interbank market through a CTA. This basically creates three tiers of security for investors. They can invest through an advisor who is not registered or regulated by any investment agency. They can put their funds with a CTA who is trading in the interbank market and whose trading activities aren't necessarily monitored by a regulatory agency. Or they can invest with a CTA who is trading in futures and has a trading disclosure document and track record that is audited and heavily regulated. In each one of these situations there are pros and cons. Having a CTA trading futures means that the markets might not be as flexible and liquid and therefore as efficient for the investment advisor as trading directly through the interbank market. Without a wealth of liquidity, flexibility, and multi-marketplaces from which to take opportunities, the investment advisor may not produce as great an amount of returns.

An advisor registered by the NFA has a background that has been reviewed and a registration which tells the customer that the advisor has had no statutory disqualifications. A *statutory disqualification* is a disqualification from registration due to fraudulent activities or misrepresentations, as in name or forgery. An applicant for registration would be statutorily disqualified from registration if he or she were disqualified from registration in another governmental agency. There are obvious exceptions to statutory disqualification, but in general they are disclosed in registrations with government agencies. Also, a registered commodity trading advisor has his or her address, name, and background information disclosed to a regulatory agency. Therefore, it is easy to do reliable background checks on a CTA. Registered CTAs have an agency that is supervising at least their background activities if not their foreign exchange trading activities.

A forum exists for settling certain disputes involving a registered CTA. Disputes that involve foreign currency trading might not be resolved through the arbitration format or the complaint format of the NFA or SEC; however, other aspects regarding representation and misrepresentation may be available for settlements through an arbitration forum in front of the National Futures Association or the Securities and Exchange Commission.

CTAs who invest in foreign currencies through the futures market also provide one extremely valuable aspect and additional level of comfort to the customer by having an audited track record of past activities. A track record is simply a history of the CTA's trading performance. A track record of a CTA who has been trading over time would show the trader's past performance on a monthly basis, in terms of the amount of assets on deposits, the amount of funds withdrawn and added each month, the ending balance, profit or loss, and any commissions or fees that were charged. Since this information is available and reviewed by regulated agencies, it is considered to be highly reliable—much more reliable than that of someone who is not subject to such scrutiny.

An investor must always remember that even in an environment that is highly scrutinized, such as the futures market, there is always the possibility of abuse. There have been examples of commodity trading advisors who had pooled funds for trading in foreign currencies only to take those funds and disappear out of the country, leaving almost no mechanism for the customers to get their funds back.

CHAPTER **8**

Multinational Corporation Derivative Hedging and Other Complex Topics Made Easy

Before we dive right in, take a moment . . . .

The amazing thing about mysterious, in-depth concepts such as Eurodollars, swaps, arbitrage, and multinational business is that they would not be extremely difficult and complex if someone would just explain them in simple English instead of trying to sound academic by using complex jargon. The concepts are very basic and fairly simple to put to use.

Before jumping into the mix of high finance there are some important points to remember. One, don't get too caught up in the big words and, two, remain skeptical of the mathematical formulas. The formulas are accurate in theoretical terms, but some of their assumptions may not be obtainable.

For example, financial arbitrage is at the core of financial formulas. Financial arbitrage will be discussed over and over in this chapter, but for now just consider financial arbitrage as the taking advantage of price discrepancies. Restated, financial arbitrage is when a trading institution takes advantage of price discrepancies between the market value of an item and the "real" value of an item. Due to this thing called *financial arbitrage*, market prices generally adhere to their "real" or theoretical value.

In the study of FX, financial arbitrage in theory "guarantees" the price and interest rate of a currency. The key word is *theory*. Theories assume that there is no human element and unlimited deep pockets protecting the arbitrage. The easiest way to think about theories and probabilities is to think of casinos.

Casinos are founded on probabilities and risk/reward balances. A casino considers the risk and reward of every bet and allows gamblers to bet with the odds in the favor of the casino. In investment terminology consider "bet" equal to investment, "gamblers" equal to investors, and "casino" equal to market. Remember, though, that the market is not exactly equal to a casino because you the investor can determine if you want to be the gambler or the casino, whereas in gambling the gamblers never get to be the casino.

A casino always has the edge in a transaction. Since the casino always has the edge it should always be successful over time. The edge means that the odds are in favor of the casino. The odds are always 50% or greater for the casino, meaning that at least 50% of the time the casino will win. The "at least" part of the phrase "guarantees" the casino will make money over time. The problem with this theory, and any pricing theory, is that it doesn't include the human element and the fact that nobody has an unlimited deep pocket in the financial world.

Why are these two factors so important? Consider the gambling example again. A new casino opens up and starts allowing gamblers to frequent their tables. The casino has a roulette wheel where there is a bet that the ball will fall either on a red or a black spot. The roulette wheel has the same number of black spots as red spots; also, there are the two green spots, 0 and 00. The two green spots on the wheel make the odds slightly less than 50/50 for the gambler. In the study of probabilities, the casino over time should win slightly greater than 50% of the time if the casino pays out 1 for 1 on the bet (i.e., a gambler who risks one dollar receives one dollar if he or she wins).

By all studies of theories, the casino should be more successful the more investors gamble. The problem occurs when the casino only has $1 million dollars in capitalization to pay the gamblers' winnings and a gambler comes to the table with $2 million dollars to bet on the roulette table. The casino knows that in theory the amount of money should not matter because the odds are in its favor, but the casino also realizes that it cannot afford to lose on the bet. This points out the problems that are associated with a casino not having unlimited deep pockets. In arbitrage the same problem exists.

Let us consider a financial example. A importer/exporter knows that they are going to need to buy deutschemarks with U.S. dollars three months from now. The importer/exporter looks at the market and realizes that if they locked in the forward price at the forward price's current rate, they would lock in a profit on the goods they will be importing in three months in exchange for deutschemarks. The importer knows that if they buy deutschemarks at the forward price, they will be able to convert the U.S. dollars they will receive from the proceeds of the sale. The importer/exporter executes a forward buy of deutschemarks on credit with their counterparty and then waits to count their money in three months. The problems start to occur as the forward price starts to loss money in relation to the U.S. dollar and their counterparty requests funds to meet the variation loss in the position. The importer/exporter might not yet have the U.S. dollars from the sale of the goods they are going to be selling once the importer/exporter receives them from Germany. The importer/exporter is stuck closing the position because they can't make the variation request from the counterparty at a loss and they can't receive the profits from a favorable move in the underlying cash market because the three months have not yet passed. The theoretical hedge that should have locked in a guaranteed profit instead put the importer/exporter out of business because they could not meet the variation margin.

Furthermore, theoretical equations do not account for a complete loss of liquidity. If there are no buyers for it, there is no value to the instrument or asset. An asset is only as valuable as what someone else is willing to pay for it. An apple in the United States doesn't necessarily cost 1 dollar because in Japan that same apple costs 124 Japanese yen and the rate of Japanese yen to U.S. dollar is 124 JPY/USD. If no one in the United States likes apples, you can't sell them to complete the final leg of the arbitrage.

Remember to be skeptical at all times when these complex formulas are discussed because of human factors and lack of unlimited funds. Let us now proceed with making the complex look easy.

COMPLEX STRATEGIES MADE SIMPLE

Multinational corporation derivative hedging is an example of an intimidating phrase used to describe some fairly basic concepts. Like any language, the language of foreign exchange and finance as a whole can be broken down into smaller parts that make simple sense.

For example, the concept of multinational corporation derivative hedging is broken down into three elements: multinational corporations, derivatives, and hedging.

Simply stated, a multinational corporation is one that not only buys and sells goods and services but also produces goods and services internationally. There is even a term to describe a corporation which has offices for production, financing, taxation, and sales in multiple countries for different parts of the corporation—a *transnational corporation*. Interestingly enough these terms are just more detailed descriptions of the different levels of international corporations.

Derivative is simply a word to describe a financial instrument whose value is derived from or highly correlated to another financial asset. For example, stock options are derivatives whose underlying asset is the stock. The underlying asset of a gold futures contract—another derivative—is actual gold bars. Currency futures and forwards are derivatives of their underlying currencies. Returning to *multinational corporation derivative hedging*, a multinational corporation in standard business practice receives and pays cash flows in many different currencies. Since there are many inflows and outflows of different currencies at known dates in the future, the use of currency futures or forwards may be used to "hedge" their upcoming currency value.

Hedge describes the reduction of risk by the use of a derivative product. Something is considered hedged if the value of one asset increases while the asset it is protecting decreases, and vice versa. For example, a mutual fund manager may be concerned about an upcoming crash in the stock market. The fund manager is concerned that if the stock market crashes the assets of the fund will decrease in value. Instead of selling the stocks in the fund, the fund manager could sell stock index futures, such as the S&P 500 futures on the Chicago Mercantile Exchange. The value of the S&P 500 futures would increase in value as the value of the stocks in the fund as a whole decreased. As the value of the fund increased, the value of the sell position in S&P 500 futures would decrease in value. The overall position of the fund manager does not change much in value while a hedge is maintained; therefore risk is reduced but so are returns. In other words, hedging is an investment strategy where risk and return are reduced. Hedging is used every day when a consumer buys insurance. Car owners who buy collision insurance are paying money to reduce the cost (or loss) from a collision. If an accident occurs, their risk of loss is reduced by the value of the insurance. If an accident never occurs, their risk of loss is the cost of the insurance over time without receiving any compensation from the insurance company.

Finally, by combining all these definitions, we discover that multinational corporation derivative hedging is simply the process whereby an international corporation uses currency futures to protect against decreases in value of its currency cash flows from sales, exports, and production costs of its factories in foreign countries.

The term *multinational corporation derivative hedging* should now seem like a very simple concept. It is definitely not a concept that requires a Ph.D. in international finance to comprehend.

Now that the curtain has been pulled back to reveal how mundane the mysterious Oz is, let us look at all the other concepts that seem deep, dark, and impenetrable.

Derivatives

In further discussions of derivatives, the focus will remain on derivatives in the FX business. As the FX market is the largest market in the world, FX derivatives are the largest derivative market in the world. Actually, any transaction valued for a future delivery date (or value date or settlement date) is considered to be a derivative. Normally "spot" transactions have a value date two days from execution. (An exception to the rule is the Canadian dollar which has a value date of one day.) Therefore all transactions are derivative prices based on the underlying asset of the currency itself. A currency transaction with a value date within seven days of the execution date (trade date) is commonly considered to be a spot transaction and not a forward transaction for practical terms.

Forwards

Forward contracts are very much like spot contracts, except forward contracts extend further out in time. There are organized markets on forward contracts for major currencies such as the German mark. Figure 8-1 indicates that there is an organized market for the 30-day, 90-day, and 180-day forward for the mark. The difference between the spot—the first line, which indicates a price range of 1.6876 to 1.6785—and the 30-day forward, which is 1.6848 and 1.6757, is the interest rate that is applied between the U.S. dollar and the deutschemark. Examples of that will be shown later in the section.

Currency futures look like a forward contract except that they are standardized contracts traded on a regulated board of exchange or board of trade. Futures contracts cannot be traded in just any size. There are standard sizes for different futures contracts. For example, on the Chicago Mercantile Exchange the Swiss franc is traded in 125,000 Swiss francs per contract, the German mark is 125,000 marks per contract, the British pound is 62,500 pounds per contract, and the Japanese yen is 12,500,000 yens per contract. The different contract sizes are standardized per number of contracts. When trades are executed in the futures markets, the person placing

FIGURE 8-1

Wall Street Journal, "Foreign Exchange Rates," February 12, 1997 (Reprinted by permission of *The Wall Street Journal,* © 1997 Dow Jones & Company, Inc. All Rights Reserved Worldwide.)

Germany (Mark)	.5926	.5958	1.6876	1.6785
30-Day Forward	.5935	.5968	1.6848	1.6757
90-Day Forward	.5959	.5991	1.6781	1.6692
180-Day Forward	.5996	.6029	1.6677	1.6586

the trade specifies the number of contracts he or she wishes to buy or sell. Two contracts of Swiss francs would indicate that the person wanted to trade 250,000 Swiss francs.

Another interesting characteristic about the futures market is that futures are quoted on the direct basis for the United States—the opposite of the way that the interbank quotes, which is on an indirect basis. Therefore, a futures quote would be quoted in the amount of U.S. dollars to one deutschemark or the amount of U.S. dollars to equal one Swiss franc. The futures market looks much the same way as the British pound does in the interbank market: The British pound sterling is quoted on a direct basis in U.S. terms, as is the futures contract.

Another interesting factor about currency futures is that they have a specified delivery date or settlement date. The delivery date of a currency futures contract is the third Wednesday of the contract's maturity month or delivery month. Therefore, the March Swiss franc contract would deliver on the third Wednesday in the month of March. The futures contract is traded for a specified location. For example, the Chicago Mercantile Exchange is a specified location and delivery location.

Another important characteristic of the futures markets is that the counterparty risk is the counterparty risk of the exchange rather than a bank or institution. An exchange has the backing of all of its members, which are possibly banks and large trading institutions. In addition, there is a standardized clearing system for clearing every transaction on a daily basis, and a standardized margin system. At this time, currency futures are not a large segment of the overall interbank market, representing approximately 1% of the foreign exchange market. A new facet of currency futures is the new emerging country currency interest rates and stock index futures. New currencies such as the Mexican peso and the Brazilian real, which do not necessarily have a fairly liquid interbank market, have a fairly liquid futures market.

Options

An option is another type of derivative. Currency options allow but do not require an investor to buy or sell a specified amount of foreign currency at a specified price at any time up to a specified date.

Call and Put Options

The buyer of a call option is given the right to buy a foreign currency at a specified price, the strike price.

A buyer of a put option has the right to sell a foreign currency at a specified strike price. For acquiring the right to buy at a specified price on a call option, the buyer has to pay premium to the seller of that option. The same holds for a put option: The buyer of a put option pays a premium to the seller to acquire the right to sell at a specified strike price.

These options are traded on organized exchanges worldwide as well as in the interbank market. There are markets for options on futures, forwards, and spot contracts. Options on futures are traded on the Chicago Mercantile Exchange, and options on the spot contracts are traded on the Philadelphia Exchange. One is considered a futures contract, the other a security. Options account for approximately 5% of the total foreign exchange market activity. Derivatives such as foreign market currency futures and options enable financial institutions to protect themselves by hedging or reducing their risk (and their return) on their underlying currency positions.

Arbitrage

Arbitrage is one of the single most important aspects of currency trading. Arbitrage is simply the risk-free buying of a currency in one market for immediate or simultaneous resale in a second market in order to profit from the price discrepancy. Arbitrage is the driving force in maintaining prices within a certain band and maintaining consistency of currency prices with their theoretical value. There is arbitrage, and then there is forward market arbitrage. An example of arbitrage is simply the arbitrage of spot prices. Two different locations might be offering two different prices.

Purchasing Power Parity—the Law of One Price

One of the most common forms of arbitrage in theoretical terms is the arbitrage of goods for currency, which is the concept behind purchasing power parity. Commodities or similar products, even though bought and sold in different currencies, should maintain the same price. For example, if the amount of deutschemarks to U.S. dollars is 1.67 deutschemarks to one U.S. dollar, then a $1 candy bar in the United States should be equal to 1.67 deutschemarks in Germany. If there is a discrepancy between the price of a candy bar in the United States versus a candy bar in Germany and the exchange rate, then theoretically someone could buy the candy bar in the cheaper location and sell it in the more expensive location, making it a risk-free, automatic process. This does not include certain factors such as transportation cost, transaction cost, taxes, and the time factor of going from one country to another. But all those factors aside, theoretically, the product should cost the same in one country as in another country. If the two objects aren't the same in price—meaning that the $1 candy bar is not equal to 1.67 deutschemarks in Germany, the law of one price says that arbitrage will continue until the two prices coincide.

The price of tradable goods when expressed in the common currencies will tend to equalize across countries as a result of exchange rate changes. The theory behind purchasing power parity doesn't necessarily focus on the products but rather on the flow of currencies. For example, in the case of the candy bar, if it is cheaper to buy the candy bar in Germany in marks than it is in the United States in U.S. dollars, the flows of money will move to the United States. People will then sell U.S. dollars and buy deutschemarks. The buying of deutschemarks will increase their value against the U.S. dollar until the two prices reach a level of parity. Obviously, this theory is not intended for just one item, such as a candy bar, but rather is considered as a way to look at goods as a whole.

Big Mac Example   Probably one of the best examples of purchasing power parity is the Big Mac example. Economists periodically publish the prices of McDonald's Big Mac around the world. The value of the Big Mac around the world differs depending on the country in which the restaurant is located. Obviously, in certain locations the Big Mac has a higher or lower value depending on factors such as supply and demand.

One of the reasons why people look at the Big Mac example, or the examples of purchasing power parity, is that it gives a quick view of the value or the possible misalignment of exchange prices between one country and another. It may signal a new coming change in exchange rates. The Big Mac example or the candy bar example might not show the exact differences, or an upcoming and pending dip in the deutschemark. However, looking at goods and services as a whole by comparing the standards of living from one country to another becomes very relevant.

When using purchasing power parity, it is interesting to look at the standard of living in Germany versus the standard of living in the United States. The value of a house in Germany versus the value of a house in the United States on average increases and decreases. This may show a shift in inflation and a shift in the exchange rates. Therefore, many international economists follow purchasing power parity in arbitrage of goods as an important factor for valuing the spot rates of different currencies. But probably the most important factor for valuing currencies is the arbitrage of money.

Arbitrage of Money

Arbitrage of money is the single largest factor in evaluating individual currencies. Traders in every major banking institution and trading institution around the world are constantly monitoring the price discrepancies in currencies, trying to take advantage of them. As long as foreign exchange prices in the market are not in equilibrium, traders will profit through arbitraging money—buying the cheap currency and selling the expensive currency.

Geographic Arbitrage (Two-Point Arbitrage)

Arbitrage of money leads us to two-point, or geographic, arbitrage. Geographic arbitrage is done by finding price differences between two locations, such as New York and London. London, the largest geographic location for interbank trading, might have the dollar versus the pound trading at 1.65 dollars per pound. In the same instant, New York might be trading the dollar versus the pound at 1.66 dollars per pound. Unusual as it may seem, a difference could exist even at the exact same time. Arbitrage opportunities are quick, fleeting moments in the highly technical world of interbank trading. Arbitrageurs constantly focus on the different prices in different locations while buying and selling as quickly as the differences appear and vanish.

On the previous example, if dollars versus pounds were trading at 1.65 dollars to the pound in London and 1.66 dollars to the pound in New York, someone could easily buy the dollar in London at 1.65 and sell the dollar to the pound at 1.66 in New York, instantly gaining 100 pips on that transaction. Obviously, in today's interbank trading the actual differences between one geographic location and another are usually much smaller than 100 pips. There might be only half-pip or 1-pip discrepancies between the exchange rate of one currency and another. As people start buying the pound in London and selling the pound in New York, the prices in New York start decreasing 1.66 closer to the price in London of 1.65.

Once the prices reach equilibrium, arbitrage no longer exists; the two prices have again reached parity. One of the important factors of arbitrage is the cost involved. Currency arbitrage is different from goods arbitrage in that it does not usually involve many different transaction costs. The transaction costs for the major currencies in interbank trading are very low. Since the currency is exactly the same from one location to another, there may be no transportation or shipping costs. The value of buying deutschemarks in Germany and the value of buying deutschemarks in New York are the same. Even the phone cost can be decreased as the use of Internet trading facilities have been used.

Goods arbitrage involves the costs of shipping the goods and the transaction itself. There might be some sales tax and barriers in transporting the goods from one location to another. The bid/ask spread between what the goods are bought and sold at might be too dramatic for a profit to be made. The time required to move the goods from one location to another is a cost that might decrease the value of the arbitrage. In goods, arbitrage is not necessarily "perfect," "pure," or "risk-free."

In the arbitrage of money, when somebody buys dollars and sells pounds in New York and sells dollars and buys pounds in London at two different exchange rates and locks in a profit, that profit does not generally have any great cost besides the cost of trading lines and maintaining funds at different locations. Use of credit lines eliminates even the cost of maintaining funds.

The next level of arbitrage is called *three-point arbitrage*.

Three-Point Arbitrage with Cross Rates

Three-point arbitrage involves a cross rate and the indirect and direct rate of two different currencies. For example, the dollar Swiss rate, the Swiss mark rate, and then the dollar mark rate might move out of parity. These rates are constantly watched and have even become more of a factor than the direct rate as traders are constantly looking for arbitrage opportunities that do not exist in the direct currencies because of constant monitoring by traders worldwide. The Swiss mark rate becomes a very important consideration for arbitrage opportunities.

Looking at the cross rates from the *Wall Street Journal* tells us that the dollar mark rate (amount of marks to one U.S. dollar) was 1.6876. The amount of Swiss francs to the one dollar was 1.4520. At these two rates, the amount of Swiss francs to the mark would be an implied rate of .86039:

$$CHF/USD = 1.4520$$
$$DEM/USD = 1.6876$$
$$CHF/DEM = 1.4520$$
$$1.6876 = .86039$$
$$\text{Arbitrage at } CHF/DEM = .8650$$

The Swiss mark rate can be quoted directly in itself. One of the interbanks or one of the geographic locations may be quoting Swiss mark at .8650 at the same time that the dollar mark is being quoted at 1.6876, while still the dollar Swiss is being quoted at 1.4520. If that is the case, then arbitrageurs can take advantage of these price discrepancies by buying Swiss to the dollar at 1.4520 and selling at the same time marks to the U.S. dollar at 1.6876, then selling the Swiss mark of .8650 at that geographic location, and constantly doing so until the rates coincide.

Taking advantage of this arbitrage opportunity, the parity of cross rates is brought in line with the value of currencies that are quoted on indirect and direct basis. The three-point arbitrage is becoming more and more common as the cross rates of currencies not using the U.S. dollar and not involved with the U.S. dollar are transacted. For example, there are cross rates for the yen to the deutschemark, the Swiss franc to the mark, the pound to the mark, or the pound to the yen. Each one of these cross rates generates more and more arbitrage opportunities.

The large world of interbank trading intricately weaves all the different currency links together to form a tapestry of exchange rates. A large move in the U.S. dollar to the mark, even though directly affecting the U.S. dollar and the mark, will also affect other currencies—the mark/Swiss franc, mark/yen, dollar/yen, dollar/Swiss franc, and so on. That's why the activities of Federal Reserve leaders such as Alan Greenspan have become such monumental factors in the international finance of today.

The next form of arbitrage is actually an arbitrage on interest rates rather than on the underlying currencies.

Covered Interest Arbitrage

Interest rates and the value of the currencies are dramatically interlinked to create the exchange rates between one country and another country. It may seem confusing, but once we go through the example of covered interest arbitrage, it will become very easy to understand that the short-term interest rates in Germany must coincide with the short-term interest rate in the U.S. dollar, and the difference between the two is a factor of the exchange rate. If they are not, then the opportunity called *covered interest arbitrage* exists. Even though it is not as widely taken advantage of as two- and three-point arbitrage, it is one of the most important forms of arbitrage. Governments, multinational corporations, and treasury departments are constantly looking for the highest return for the lowest risk on their short-term, excess currency deposits. They are constantly looking for the interest rate that will give them the best return. They must also consider where that currency return is located. In order to take advantage of the interest rates of a given country, institutions must protect themselves or cover themselves from the exchange rate risk of that country.

For example, suppose the annual interest rate for a 90-day deposit is 5% in New York and 3% in Munich. Munich investors would be eager to earn the higher returns available in New York. To do so, they must convert their marks to dollars in order to invest in New York. However, the Munich investors ultimately want marks, not dollars, so they must reconvert the dollars back to marks at the end of the 90 days. Also, they must consider what the mark rate is today in relationship to what it may be in 90 days. If the decrease in that rate from today until the following 90 days does not make up the difference in the amount of interest that they gain from holding funds in New York versus holding funds in Munich, then taking advantage of the 5% interest rates in New York would not be a major factor.

By using covered interest rate arbitrage, the Munich investor can capture the higher New York interest rates by investing in the markets to lock in a 90-day forward exposure.

Let's put a dollar amount on this example. Suppose Munich investors have 1 million marks to invest, the spot mark rate is selling at 1.68 marks to U.S. dollars, and the 90-day forward mark rate is selling for 1.67 marks to the dollar. They have two choices. One, they can invest the money in Munich at 3% interest. Two, they can convert their marks to dollars today, invest in New York at 6% interest, and in 90 days liquidate their New York investment and convert it back to marks. If the Munich investors choose the first option and invest their funds in the Munich money market for 90 days at 3% annual interest or 75% for 90 days (the 75% is calculated by taking 90 out of 360, which is one quarter of a year; 75% is one-quarter of 3%), at the end of 90 days their mark investment in Germany at 3% interest would return 7,000 marks.

Likewise, they can invest their money in New York for 90 days. To do so they must first convert their marks into dollars at the prevailing rate of 1.68 marks to the dollar, which equals $595,238.10 dollars (1,000,000 divided by 1.68 DEM/USD), then invest the dollars at the 6% annual interest rate available in New York, or 1.5% for 90 days (dividing 6% by 4). Their investment will grow in 90 days to the sum of $595,238.10 times 1.015, or $604,166.67. If they want to avoid the exposure of the exchange rate fluctuations, they can sell the $604,166.67 today in the 90-day forward market at the current 90-day forward rate of 1.67 marks to the dollar, thereby yielding at the end of the 90 days $604,166.67 x 1.67 marks to the dollar, or 1,008,958.33. The Munich investors thereby have made 8,958.33 marks by investing their marks in the U.S. interest rates rather than the deutschemark interest rates, a risk-free profit due to the arbitrage opportunities of interest rates and the spot and forward rates.

As time goes on, investment money will move to the location granting the higher return, thereby moving the short-term interest rate in New York closer to the short-term interest rate in Munich, and the spot rate of the mark will coincide more closely with the forward rate of the mark. In the spot market, the demands on the dollar will increase, thereby rising the spot price of the dollar. In the 90-day forward market the supply of dollars increases, thereby lowering the forward price of the pound. Loanable funds will continue to flow from Munich to New York until the return of the investment is the same in New York as it is in Munich. Only then will the arbitrage opportunity be completely eliminated.

In practice, the short-term interest rates between one country and another are the forward points and discount points. In this example, the buying of the spots against the forward rate is actually considered a swap.

Swaps

A *swap* is simply the buying and selling of the same currency at the exact same time with delivery at two different points in time.

Spot against Forward Swap

The most common form of swap is the spot against the forward swap. Another common swap is the swap from one two-day spot period to the next two-day spot period, usually referred to as a *roll*. In the interbank market, swaps account for approximately 39% of overall foreign exchange transactions. Interest rates create the value of the forward price due to the differentials in the two currencies that are involved. In terms of covered interest arbitrage, the short-term interest rates are in direct correlation to the exchange rates of one country's currency for another's. If they are not, then arbitrage opportunities exist until the two currencies and interest rates reach parity.

Forward Discount/Forward Premium

If forward prices are less than the spot price, the currency is considered to be offered at a forward discount. If the forward price is higher than the spot price, then the currency is selling at a forward premium. In turning back to our deutschemark example (Figure 8-1), you'll notice that in the third and fourth column, the spot rate is quoted at 1.6876 for the spot price and the 90-day forward is quoted at 1.6781. Therefore, the forward prices are at a discount to the spot price. The interest rate differential implied by this 90-day forward can be found by subtracting the spot price from the forward price and dividing it by the spot price.

If you multiply that times the period in the year (for example, 90 is one-quarter of a year, so you would multiply it by 4), you will find the implied discount factor. In our example, forward price equals 1.6781, spot price equals 1.6876, and the number of periods in a year is four. The annualized forward discount is equal to negative .02252, or a annualized discount of 2.25%. In terms of interest arbitrage, this forward discount is a factor of the short-term interest rate of the United States versus the short-term interest rate of Germany. Therefore, a short-term interest rate differential other than 2.25% is an opportunity.

Hedging Cost

The cost of hedging is directly calculated by the forward discount or premium of a currency exchange rate from one to the other.

For example, if a firm needs to buy forward 1 million deutschemarks against the U.S. dollar for the purchase of a tractor, it should use the outright forward rate, which is the appropriate rate for its business in the future.

In other cases, it may be more appropriate to use the spot rate. If you are considering an investment, you will probably want to express the hedging cost or profit as a percentage of the original investment and therefore probably use the spot rate. Compared to the previous example of deutschemarks, a forward discount in the spot of 2.25% is the cost of hedging 1 million deutschemarks by selling in the 90-day forward market. There is a cost of 2.25% on an annual basis, as opposed to going directly into the spot market and buying deutschemarks versus the U.S. dollar not knowing which way the deutschemarks are going to go until the 90 days passes and you must pay in deutschemarks. Therefore, you can either pay 2.25% today for locking in a hedge or wait and possibly lose the opportunity.

The Euro Market

Most concepts that involve an interest rate are considered complex. The Euro market is the money market for foreign exchange prices. The Euro market consists of the Euro dollar, the Euro mark, the Euro Swiss, and the Euro yen. These are simply dollar deposits that are traded outside the United States. Euro dollars are the main interest rate used in FX.

Let's say, for example, that there is a bank in London which places U.S. dollar deposits with another bank in London. The interest rate on those U.S. dollar deposits located outside the United States is the Euro dollar deposit rate. The major difference between the Euro dollar rate and the short-term T-bill rate in the United States is that the Euro dollar rate does not reflect the costs of the Federal Reserve requirements. Therefore, a non-U.S. foreign bank holding U.S. dollar deposits in London could undercut its U.S. domestic competitor because the non-U.S. bank does not have strict U.S. Reserve requirements that cost loss of interest. The Euro dollar is much more efficient than the short-term interest rates in T-bills. The Euro dollar deposit market has grown to a multitrillion dollar market today.

The Euro currency market originated in the early 1950s when the Soviet Union controlled the governments of central and eastern Europe and needed dollars to finance the international trade, but feared the U.S. government would confiscate or block their holdings of dollars in the United States for political reasons. The Communist government solved this problem by using European banks to maintain the dollar. Thus were created Euro dollar and U.S. dollar deposits in European bank accounts.

As other currencies became stronger, the Euro currency market broadened to include Euro yen, Euro mark, Euro Swiss, and other currencies. Some $6 trillion worth of Euro currencies are in deposits in banks worldwide. Of that, roughly two-thirds of these deposits are in the form of Euro dollars. The Euro dollar interest rate is used to calculate the forward rate on different currencies. The interest rates on the Euro dollars compared to the

Euro mark rate create the differential called *forward premium* or *forward discount.*

The Euro market plays two key roles. It provides a link between the spot rate and the forward rate of foreign exchange markets. The foreign exchange rates in covered interest rate arbitrage are determined by the relative interest rate differentials between Euro currency deposits of one currency and another. It also provides a mechanism for taking and placing deposits free of domestic central bank restrictions. Therefore, due to less regulation and fewer government restrictions, the international banking system is able to offer more diverse and innovative types of loans. The end value of the Euro dollar deposit is that any person in the United States will accept U.S. dollars held outside the United States (Euro dollars) for full payment of goods and services from the United States.

The quotation of rates in (Figure 8-2) shows the diverse levels of interest rate products and their interest differentials.

The Euro currencies in Figure 8-3 (Euro dollar, Euro yen, and Euro mark) are actively traded in the futures markets, where hedgers and speculators predict future short-term interest rates.

FIGURE 8-2

The Wall Street Journal, "Money Rates," Wednesday, February 12, 1997 (Reprinted by permission of *The Wall Street Journal,* © 1997 Dow Jones & Company, Inc. All Rights Reserved Worldwide.)

MONEY RATES

Wednesday, February 12, 1997
The key U.S. and foreign annual interest rates below are a guide to general levels but don't always represent actual transactions.

PRIME RATE: 8.25% (effective 2/01/96). The base rate on corporate loans posted by at least 75% of the nation's 30 largest banks.

DISCOUNT RATE: 5%. The charge on loans to depository institutions by the Federal Reserve Banks.

FEDERAL FUNDS: 5 3/8% high, 2% low, 3% near closing bid, 5 % offered (Rates reflect settlement activity). Reserves traded among commercial banks for overnight use in amounts of $1 million or more. Source: Prebon Yamane (U.S.A.) Inc.

CALL MONEY: 7%. The charge on loans to brokers on stock exchange collateral. Source: Dow Jones Telerate Inc.

COMMERCIAL PAPER placed directly by General Electric Capital Corp.: 5.26% 30 to 44 days; 5.27% 45 to 89 days; 5.28% 90 to 179 days; 5.29% 180 to 270 days.

COMMERCIAL PAPER: High-grade unsecured notes sold through dealers by major corporations: 5.38% 30 days; 5.39% 60 days; 5.40% 90 days.

CERTIFICATES OF DEPOSIT: 4.98% one month; 5.00% two months; 5.08% three months; 5.33% six months; 5.47% one year. Average of top rates paid by major New York banks on primary new issues of negotiable C.D.s, usually on amounts of $1 million and more. The minimum unit is $100,000. Typical rates in the secondary market: 5.32% one month; 5.37% three months; 5.48% six months.

BANKERS ACCEPTANCES: 5.23% 30 days; 5.23% 60 days; 5.23% 90 days; 5.24% 120 days; 5.24% 150 days; 5.24% 180 days. Offered rates of negotiable, bank-backed business credit instruments typically financing an import order.

LONDON LATE EURODOLLARS: 5 3/8% - 5 1/4% one month; 5 7/16% - 5 5/16% two months; 5 1/2% - 5 3/8% three months; 5 17/32% - 5 13/32% four months; 5 9/16% - 5 7/16% five months; 5 19/32% - 5 15/32% six months.

LONDON INTERBANK OFFERED RATES (LIBOR): 5 7/16% one month; 5 17/32% three months; 5 5/8% six months; 5 13/16% one year. The average of interbank offered rates for dollar deposits in the London market based on quotations at five major banks. Effective rate for contracts entered into two days from date appearing at top of this column.

FOREIGN PRIME RATES: Canada 4.75%; Germany 3.15%; Japan 1.625%; Switzerland 3.75%; Britain 6.00%. These rate indications aren't directly comparable; lending practices vary widely by location.

TREASURY BILLS: Results of the Monday, February 10, 1997, auction of short-term U.S. government bills, sold at a discount from face value in units of $10,000 to $1 million: 5.02% 13 weeks; 5.07% 26 weeks.

OVERNIGHT REPURCHASE RATE: 5.29%. Dealer financing rate for overnight sale and repurchase of Treasury securities. Source: Dow Jones Telerate Inc.

FEDERAL HOME LOAN MORTGAGE CORP. (Freddie Mac): Posted yields on 30-year mortgage commitments. Delivery within 30 days 7.82%, 60 days 7.87%, standard conventional fixed-rate mortgages; 5.625%, 2% rate capped one-year adjustable rate mortgages. Source: Dow Jones Telerate Inc.

FEDERAL NATIONAL MORTGAGE ASSOCIATION (Fannie Mae): Posted yields on 30 year mortgage commitments (priced at par) for delivery within 30 days 7.78%, 60 days 7.85%, standard conventional fixed rate-mortgages; 6.55%, 6/2 rate capped one-year adjustable rate mortgages. Source: Dow Jones Telerate Inc.

MERRILL LYNCH READY ASSETS TRUST: 4.89%. Annualized average rate of return after expenses for the past 30 days; not a forecast of future returns.

FIGURE 8-3

The Wall Street Journal, "Eurocurrency Futures," Wednesday, February 12, 1997 (Reprinted by permission of *The Wall Street Journal,* © 1997 Dow Jones & Company, Inc. All Rights Reserved Worldwide.)

EURODOLLAR (CME)-$1 million; pts of 100%

	Open	High	Low	Settle	Chg	Yield Settle	Chg	Open Interest
Feb	94.50	94.50	94.49	94.50	....	5.50	....	20,072
Mar	94.48	94.48	94.46	94.48	+ .01	5.52	- .01	395,427
June	94.36	94.36	94.33	94.35	....	5.65	....	378,768
Sept	94.22	94.23	94.19	94.21	- .01	5.79	+ .01	290,148
Dec	94.03	94.05	94.00	94.03	- .01	5.97	+ .01	209,944
Mr98	93.94	93.94	93.91	93.92	- .02	6.08	+ .02	180,105
June	93.82	93.84	93.80	93.82	- .01	6.18	+ .01	139,888
Sept	93.74	93.76	93.72	93.74	- .01	6.26	+ .01	104,514
Dec	93.63	93.64	93.60	93.62	- .02	6.38	+ .02	81,829
Mr99	93.60	93.62	93.58	93.60	- .01	6.40	+ .01	65,442
June	93.54	93.56	93.53	93.54	- .01	6.46	+ .01	68,146
Sept	93.49	93.51	93.48	93.49	- .01	6.51	+ .01	54,902
Dec	93.40	93.42	93.39	93.40	- .01	6.60	+ .01	46,045
Mr00	93.40	93.42	93.38	93.39	- .01	6.61	+ .01	41,151
June	93.35	93.37	93.33	93.34	- .01	6.66	+ .01	35,087
Sept	93.29	93.32	93.28	93.29	- .01	6.71	+ .01	31,851
Dec	93.21	93.24	93.20	93.21	- .01	6.79	+ .01	25,272
Mr01	93.21	93.23	93.21	93.21	- .01	6.79	+ .01	25,623
June	93.16	93.18	93.16	93.16	- .01	6.84	+ .01	20,559
Sept	93.12	93.14	93.12	93.12	- .01	6.88	+ .01	12,537
Dec	93.04	93.06	93.04	93.04	- .01	6.96	+ .01	10,334
Mr02	93.05	93.06	93.03	93.04	- .01	6.96	+ .01	5,759
June	93.00	93.01	92.98	92.99	- .01	7.01	+ .01	5,148
Sept	92.96	92.97	92.94	92.95	- .01	7.05	+ .01	5,278
Dec	92.88	92.89	92.86	92.87	- .01	7.13	+ .01	5,715
Mr03	92.89	92.89	92.86	92.87	- .01	7.13	+ .01	4,835
June	92.84	92.84	92.81	92.82	- .01	7.18	+ .01	3,636
Sept	92.80	92.80	92.77	92.78	- .01	7.22	+ .01	4,781
Dec	92.71	92.72	92.69	92.70	- .01	7.30	+ .01	3,937
Mr04	....	....	....	92.70	- .01	7.30	+ .01	2,044
June	....	....	....	92.65	- .01	7.35	+ .01	3,738
Sept	....	....	....	92.61	- .01	7.39	+ .01	3,054
Dec	....	....	....	92.53	- .01	7.47	+ .01	3,678
Mr05	....	....	....	92.53	- .01	7.47	+ .01	1,929
June	....	....	....	92.48	- .01	7.52	+ .01	2,256
Sept	....	....	....	92.44	- .01	7.56	+ .01	1,608
Dec	....	....	....	92.36	- .01	7.64	+ .01	1,107
Mr06	....	....	....	92.36	- .01	7.64	+ .01	2,187
June	....	....	....	92.31	- .01	7.69	+ .01	796
Sept	....	....	....	92.27	- .01	7.73	+ .01	571
Dec	....	....	....	92.19	- .01	7.81	+ .01	253

Est vol 193,766; vol Tue 183,989; open int 2,306,880, -3,822.

EUROYEN (CME) -Yen 100,000,000; pts. of 100%

	Open	High	Low	Settle	Change	Lifetime High	Low	Open Interest
Mar	99.46	99.46	99.45	99.46	- .01	99.50	98.09	5,085
June	99.43	99.44	99.43	99.43	- .01	99.50	97.80	5,385
Sept	99.38	99.38	99.37	99.37	....	99.39	97.50	5,244
Dec	99.26	99.26	99.25	99.25	- .01	99.27	97.30	3,814
Mr98	99.11	99.11	99.09	99.09	- .01	99.12	97.04	1,719
June	98.93	98.93	98.91	98.92	....	98.94	96.81	2,149
Sept	....	....		98.73	....	98.74	96.62	1,081
Dec	98.52	98.52	98.51	98.51	- .02	98.55	96.39	437
Mr99	....	....		98.30	- .02	98.33	96.67	221

Est vol 2,979; vol Tue 760; open int 25,197, +214.

STERLING (LIFFE)-£500,000; pts of 100%

	Open	High	Low	Settle	Change	Lifetime High	Low	Open Interest
Mar	93.72	93.72	93.69	93.72	+ .01	94.13	90.20	103,133
June	93.48	93.50	93.42	93.49	+ .02	93.81	90.05	115,675
Sept	93.28	93.31	93.22	93.30	+ .02	93.54	89.92	79,647
Dec	93.14	93.17	93.09	93.16	+ .02	93.33	90.10	54,015
Mr98	93.07	93.07	93.00	93.06	+ .02	93.16	90.58	37,733
June	93.00	93.00	92.93	92.98	+ .01	93.04	90.89	35,278
Sept	92.93	92.93	92.89	92.93	+ .02	92.95	91.30	21,968
Dec	92.83	92.88	92.83	92.87	+ 0	92.88	91.27	18,537
Mr99	92.83	92.83	92.79	92.82	+ 0	92.83	91.45	8,699
June	92.75	92.75	92.74	92.79	+ .02	92.78	91.53	7,021
Sept	92.70	92.73	92.69	92.74	+ .02	92.73	91.92	7,014
Dec	92.68	92.68	92.65	92.70	+ .02	92.68	91.94	5,209

Est vol 93,234; vol Tue 65,831; open int 493,929, +4,697.

LONG GILT (LIFFE)-£50,000; 32nds of 100%

	Open	High	Low	Settle	Change	Lifetime High	Low	Open Interest
Mar	113-15	113-24	112-29	113-16	+ 0-06	113-24	105-22	193,562
June	112-30	112-30	112-15	113-01	+ 0-06	112-3	107-27	6,064

Est vol 89,539; vol Tue 64,741; open int 199,626, -1,444.

EUROMARK (LIFFE)-DM 1,000,000; pts of 100%

	Open	High	Low	Settle	Change	Lifetime High	Low	Open Interest
Feb	96.86	96.87	96.85	96.86	- .01	96.93	96.85	3,249
Mar	96.89	96.90	96.88	96.89	- .01	96.94	96.26	200,946
Apr	96.90	96.90	96.89	96.89	- .01	96.95	96.86	3,961
June	96.92	96.92	96.88	96.90	+ 0	96.96	96.20	171,981
Sept	96.85	96.86	96.81	96.83	- .01	96.87	92.06	150,942
Dec	96.70	96.71	96.65	96.68	- .01	96.72	91.94	164,787
Mr98	96.54	96.56	96.49	96.52	- .01	96.56	92.00	118,288
June	96.37	96.37	96.30	96.33	+ 0	96.37	92.59	105,602
Sept	96.13	96.13	96.07	96.11	+ .01	96.13	93.38	78,078
Dec	95.86	95.89	95.81	95.86	+ .01	95.89	93.40	67,360
Mr99	95.62	95.64	95.58	95.62	+ .02	95.64	93.24	46,860
June	95.38	95.38	95.33	95.37	+ .02	95.38	93.29	24,997
Sept	95.11	95.12	95.07	95.11	+ .02	95.12	93.80	20,413
Dec	94.86	94.87	94.82	94.86	+ .02	94.87	94.19	17,907
Mr00	94.63	94.63	94.61	94.64	+ .03	94.63	94.26	1,780
June	....	....		94.42	+ .03	94.40	93.97	464
Sept	94.22	94.22	94.22	94.24	+ .03	94.22	93.92	350
Dec	....	....		94.06	+ .03	93.98	93.70	735

Est vol 140,780; vol Tue 116,074; open int 1,178,700, +6,344.

EUROSWISS (LIFFE)-SFr 1,000,000; pts of 100%

	Open	High	Low	Settle	Change	Lifetime High	Low	Open Interest
Mar	98.33	98.35	98.28	98.34	+ .03	98.43	96.72	30,216
June	98.33	98.36	98.29	98.35	+ .03	98.36	96.47	30,180
Sept	98.24	98.27	98.19	98.24	+ .01	98.27	96.28	11,972
Dec	98.05	98.07	97.98	98.05	+ .02	98.06	96.02	7,890
Mr98	97.82	97.86	97.80	97.85	+ .02	97.86	96.90	4,398
June	97.62	97.62	97.62	97.65	+ .02	97.62	97.25	1,023

Est vol 16,995; vol Tue 16,539; open int 85,679, +730.

3-MONTH EURO LIRA (LIFFE)
ITL 1,000,000,000; pts of 100%

	Open	High	Low	Settle	Change	Lifetime High	Low	Open Interest
Mar	93.02	93.05	92.94	92.97	- .03	93.72	89.41	94,979
June	93.58	93.62	93.48	93.52	- .05	94.17	90.30	78,142
Sept	93.95	93.98	93.85	93.87	- .05	94.42	90.49	45,985
Dec	94.15	94.16	94.05	94.07	- .04	94.56	91.72	35,149
Mr98	94.19	94.20	94.13	94.15	- .01	94.53	92.26	16,235
June	94.19	94.20	94.14	94.15	+ 0	94.50	93.92	10,496

Est vol 55,511; vol Tue 46,409; open int 280,986, +1,691.

GERMAN GOVT. BOND (LIFFE)
250,000 marks; pts of 100%

	Open	High	Low	Settle	Change	Lifetime High	Low	Open Interest
Mar	103.07	103.25	102.76	103.10	+ .19	103.25	95.15	240,674
June	102.20	102.29	101.93	102.24	+ .22	102.29	98.56	16,660

Est vol 217,007; vol Tue 173,990; open int 257,334, +9,130.

ITALIAN GOVT. BOND (LIFFE)
ITL 200,000,000; pts of 100%

	Open	High	Low	Settle	Change	Lifetime High	Low	Open Interest
Mar	131.10	131.38	130.85	131.02	+ .20	132.38	116.30	108,249
June	130.61	130.69	130.40	130.52	+ .20	131.80	126.66	14,305
Sept	....	....		130.50	+ .20	131.73	129.22	600

Est vol 60,621; vol Tue 65,396; open int 123,154, +3,472.

In the next chapter we consider the various kinds of risk and how they affect foreign currency trading.

CHAPTER 9

The Sensitive Question
of Risk, Risk, Risk...

The greatest risk is the risk that is not conceived possible. Many risks are known, evaluated, and monitored, yet the most dangerous are those not identified by companies and shareholders. "What-if" scenarios analyzed by the Monte Carlo computer simulations looked at thousands of possibilities, yet they still couldn't conceive of the 1929 stock market crash, the United States S&L failures, the Mexican government's default on debt obligations, and so on.

An inconceivable U.S. Treasury coupon payment default would be a wild card that would crash the perceived security of U.S. Treasuries and make U.S. dollar-based interest rates skyrocket. This book is not forecasting such doom, but rather illustrating the damage of such unknowns. Even though the objective of this chapter is not to speculate on inconceivable unknowns, it is important to point out that much risk is left unmeasured.

Risk exposure is generally broken down into the three "C"s: currency risk, counterparty risk, and country risk. *Currency risk* is the actual risk associated with a currency position and the valuation of those positions in spot and forward terms. *Counterparty risk* is the possibility that a customer or counterparty will default on their contracts. *Country risk* is the geographical risk of countries and their regulations regarding currency trading.

A later section in this chapter explains how these risks are monitored and by whom. Some advanced systems have evolved along with innovations in computer technology and the bank transfer systems that take some of the uncertainty out of foreign exchange currency trading.

CURRENCY RISK

Market Risk

Currency risk is the market risk of a specified portfolio. Counterparties, customers, and investors that enter into the foreign exchange business and industry are confronted with certain market risks, from an open position, a hedge position, or an option position. These risks are broken down into four different sections: the exchange rate risk, or the risk of the movement of the different exchange rates; the basis risk, which includes both interest rate risk and the relative yield curve risk; volatility risk; and liquidity exposure. With liquidity exposure, there is also additional risk that needs to be considered, which is called *forced sale risk*. In a currency portfolio there might be positions that are long U.S. dollar, short Japanese yen, long deutschemark, or short Swiss franc, both outright spot positions and cross positions in a bank's or a counterparty's portfolio.

These positions have some inherent risk due to market volatility and market movement. For example, when a bank receives positions from a customer, the bank is making a market by offering a price the customer may buy and bidding a price the customer may sell. The bank has a number of ways in which to offset the risk from making that position.

If a customer says he or she wants to buy dollars and sell Swiss francs, the counterparty then has a short dollar position and a long Swiss franc position. The counterparty can either hedge that risk or lay that risk off. By laying that risk off, it would be going to another counterparty and buying the U.S. dollar and selling the Swiss franc, leaving the counterparty with no open position. This goes on and on until every bank and counterparty have their respective positions that they desire to maintain open—meaning that if a customer has a long dollar bias in the market and desires to take advantage of that long dollar bias, he or she would hold open a long dollar position. A hedging of that position could be done either in the forward market, the futures market, or the options market. The market risk would be any movement in the exchange rates from the time that the customer opened the position until the time the customer closed the position. That market risk may change due to volatility, fundamental factors, or technical factors that may affect the market.

Exchange Risk

Exchange rate risk is the most obvious risk that customers encounter when opening a position. It is a known risk, one that is very obvious to the investor, the counterparty, or any banking institution. Those risks become a little more vague once you look at balance sheets, income statements, and currency of the assets or liabilities of different corporations. Evaluating the currency risk is simply a matter of looking at what the price is for that certain forward, spot, or option on the currency, in each specific market. Fortunately, the interbank market is liquid and capable of reporting a price on basically any major currency 24 hours a day. Therefore, different prices for currency risk are easily known, and the risk of a position is well understood.

Market risk becomes more difficult to understand when you look at coverage for a specific position. For example, when a counterparty is holding long dollars and short Swiss francs, it can hedge that position by going into the futures market and buying Swiss francs and selling U.S. dollars, thereby leaving their exposure flat. Now, if this position is a hedge against a spot position and not a hedge against a forward position, there is a basis risk that exists between the spot and the futures, or forward, position.

Basis Risk

Interest Rate Risk

Basis risk is susceptible to changes in the relative interest rate of each currency. If you go back and look at covered interest arbitrage, you will notice that the relative interest rate of the different currencies account for the forward price versus the spot price. If the interest rates were to change dramatically, the futures price versus the spot price would do the same.

Yield Curve Risk

Depending on the actual portfolio of a bank, counterparty, or customer there may be yield curve risk or basis risk on multiple levels of maturity, meaning that a 60-day forward versus a 1-year forward may not change in the same amount. For example, the interest rates may change a half a percent for the one-year interest rate but may only change a quarter of a percent on the 60-day interest rate. If there is a one-year currency forward contract and a 60-day forward currency contract, they would change by a different amount in basis to the spot rate. Therefore, if there is a spot coverage against a 60-day forward versus a one-year forward, the interest rate change would create a higher price change for the 1-year than for the 60-day forward. For forward and options trading, the basis trading or the basis risk could be quite dramatic. A forward position is held for longer time periods than a spot position which is rolled into the next spot time period. A forward position that is held longer would be affected more by the basis change. As each day goes by, the amount of change in the basis between the spot and the forward price becomes more dramatic. Each day the forward discount decreases as the forward price approaches the spot price.

For example, assume a 20-point discount. If the interest rate differential between two currencies, say, U.S. dollar and Swiss franc, were to increase by a half of a percent, it may change that forward discount from 20 to 22. A 20-point discount would mean that a Swiss franc that was trading at 1.4570 the spot rate would have a forward price of 1.4550. If it changed by two points, the forward price would be 1.4548. Two pips might not seem like a dramatic change, but on a $10 million position, a two-pip change can be a dramatic move in a market and the underlying position. A bank with million-dollar positions in different currencies is very interested in monitoring the basis risk and the relative interest rate.

Volatility Risk

Volatility risk can be viewed in two different aspects, options on currencies and risk parameters on market risk.

Volatility risk in regards to options on currencies is extremely important. Options on currencies are valued according to volatility and the underlying changes in the currency price. Volatility is the mysterious, unknown factor. It is such an unknown factor that different valuation techniques of volatility create dramatic differences in the underlying prices. If a bank, customer, or counterparty has a large option on currency portfolio positions, the change in volatility could dramatically change the value of the underlying position. In reviewing the risk of a portfolio of options, the investor does need to look not only at the underlying price change, but at the volatility of those price changes as well. If the volatility were to increase from 10 to 20%, which is a 100% increase in the volatility, the underlying option value would increase dramatically as well.

Volatility has a dramatic effect on market risk, not only for options but also for the valuation of underlying positions. A bank, customer, or counterparty must look at volatility and determine different risk perimeters for different customers accordingly. A customer who trades on credit, for example, may be asked to put down a percentage of margin for the positions he or she is holding. If the volatility starts to increase dramatically, the credit evaluation on each customer and counterparty needs to be reviewed. A customer who under normal volatility conditions would be considered a low-risk customer or counterparty may suddenly become a counterparty risk or a credit risk. For example, assume a customer has a $10 million credit limit with a bank. The $10 million position may change in value on a daily basis under normal market conditions, perhaps $40,000 U.S. If volatility increases, that $40,000 change in value per day may increase to $200,000, both positively and negatively for the customer. Obviously the main concern is any loss that may be incurred by the customer that the customer might not be able to afford. If the customer is unable to afford a risk, it becomes a risk of the counterparty, as if it were holding the position itself.

Liquidity Risk

In the interbank market, liquidity risk is not considered much of a problem, due to the high amount of liquidity in daily interbank operations on the major currencies. Yet there are different currencies which may not have as much liquidity, such as those currencies that aren't as actively traded. Even the actively traded currencies may lose liquidity during certain market conditions. If, for example, the U.S. Federal Reserve were to increase rates, for a short time liquidity might drop out of the U.S. dollar versus major currencies. If the liquidity drops out, then knowledge or price discovery may become difficult. Customers may not know the risk of their underlying portfolio because they do not know the price to evaluate their portfolio. If they are unable to know the price to evaluate the portfolio, the risk becomes too dramatic for them to hold. A customer trying to protect or exit a position in times of low liquidity may lose much more on exiting the position than expected.

For example, when customers call into a major bank, they may get a five to ten pip spread on a normal basis for entering and exiting a position. That would mean that a dollar mark position would be trading at, for example, 1.7085, 1.7090. If the market was trading at 1.7085 to 1.7090 during normal market conditions and the liquidity dropped out, that same market in the dollar mark might be trading at 1.7050 to 1.71. Obviously, if customers are trying to exit a position with normal valuations on their portfolio at five pips and the market suddenly is now evaluating at 50 pips, the risk of those underlying positions increase almost 10 times what they are used to. Another important aspect of liquidity risk is that many times customers will have a limit of how much movement in the market their position is allowed to maintain. For example, a customer who is holding a million dollar position versus a mark position at a price of 1.7050 marks to the dollar may be allowed to maintain a position as long as the position does not lose more than $11,000. An $11,000 loss on a dollar/mark position would only be 200 pips. If the market liquidity were to drop out and the price movement made it so that the spread of the dollar mark increased to 50 pip spreads, the customer would have moved from a 200 pip risk level to a 150 pip risk level and might be forced to liquidate his or her position.

Forced Sale Risk

A forced liquidation may force the customer out of a position and put at risk an opposite open position that was being hedged by that currency position. Using the previous example, the dollar/mark position might be a position that is hedging an option on a currency portfolio which had an open exposure of $1 million. The obvious risk would be that the customer would be forced to liquidate and the market would turn back around, so that the customer not only would lose on the underlying currency hedge, but may also lose on the option position, all due to a decrease in liquidity in the position and an increase in volatility in the market. (The Bank of England evaluates the London institutions on a risk measurement called the *forced sale liquidation*, which actually is forward positions that might not have a mechanism for offset.)

An example would be a complex derivative position that involves options and different swaps on forward settlement. On such positions there may be only one or two counterparties that the bank may go to in order to offset the risk. The bank may have a high risk on those positions because of a lack of counterparties able to offset that position. (Due to what is called a *forced sale risk*, the Bank of England would give a different evaluation on that bank or the institution's credit standing.)

Overall market risk can be evaluated per currency or for the entire portfolio. Many times a portfolio has a risk perimeter set on the net position. A customer that has a portfolio of long U.S. dollars and short 1,450,000 Swiss francs at the equivalent rate of 1.45 Swiss francs to U.S. dollars, and a position of short 2 million U.S. dollars and long 1,697,500 deutschemarks at the equivalent rate of 1.6975 deutschemarks to the U.S. dollar, and also has a position in its portfolio of long 1 million British pound sterling and short 1,636,500 U.S. dollars at the equivalent rate of 1.6365 U.S. dollars to the pound sterling, would have a net portfolio risk of 2,636,500 U.S. dollars:

(+1,000,000 USD - 1,450,000 CHF @ 1.4500 CHF/USD
(-2,000,000 USD + 1,697,500 DEM @ 1.6975 DEM/USD
(+1,000,000 GBP - 1,636,500 USD @ 1.6365 USD/GBP
net USD risk is 2,636,500 USD

The risk for the entire portfolio is almost equivalent to the risk of just one of those positions in the portfolio. The net risk of the entire portfolio is decreased due to its long and short U.S. dollar positions in the portfolio.

COUNTERPARTY RISK

Counterparty risk is an extremely elusive risk in the foreign currency market; losses occur due to counterparties that have high credit levels as well as counterparties that have low credit levels. Counterparty risk is constantly adjusted due to market volatility. Therefore, counterparty risk is as much based on name recognition and length of time dealing with a counterparty as it is on credit rating. Obviously, a counterparty with a high level of capitalization and low market risk is the ideal customer. Yet it is prudent to look at every customer and counterparty as a risk.

Counterparty risk can be evaluated on many different levels.

Name Reputation

As noted, counterparty risk is evaluated on name recognition or reputation—the trading activities of a counterparty, evaluations of the different risks or exposures that are involved in back office operations, the credit evaluation of outside or independent agencies, and the control risks that the counterparty takes in regards to its own systems. When most institutions evaluate their counterparties, they find that the most notable and interesting reason why customers will deal with a counterparty is not necessarily a credit evaluation or back office procedures, but the customers' relationships with their banks. Banking relationships have been found to be the number one reason why customers deal with that bank.

Ethical Standards

A bank said to have had problems with regulators, solvency, and ethical conduct will be less desirable as a counterparty regardless of credit standing, credit level, and risk perimeters. In all actuality, customers often choose a counterparty due to a referral from another institution with which the customers deal. Also, a customer may deal with a bank due to other activities done with that bank rather than basing the decision on the prices and execution level of that bank. If a customer's bank is doing all the loans and banking functions, such as wire transfers and checking, that customer is more likely to deal with the bank on other activities such as foreign currency trading. Usually, if these customers desire to execute a transaction in foreign currency trading, they will most likely look to the same banking relationship regardless of counterparty risk.

In evaluating counterparty risk, one must be aware of name reputation. Unfortunately, name reputation in the interbank industry might be completely unrecognized by the investment public. Therefore, it is important to evaluate and interview other counterparties in regards to their investment activities and operation standards. An obvious point in dealing with a counterparty is its ethical standards in dealing on day-to-day business. A counterparty or customer who is willing to cut corners may also be willing to take risks that it is not able to withstand.

Overexposure

In evaluating counterparty risk, one must know the level of trading activity and exposure. If a counterparty begins trading more actively and taking larger exposure, customers may decrease the amount of activity that it is putting at risk with that counterparty and place other transactions through another counterparty. The counterparty for a banking institution may also reduce the amount of credit they are willing to give to a customer or counterparty that is giving or doing larger activity. Therefore, the risk that is evaluated on a customer might be based not only on the net position that the customer is holding, but also on the depth of the positions that the customer is holding in different currencies, as well as the level of experience that the customer has in dealing with the currencies or the products that are being traded.

Dealing Room Procedures

The next factor in evaluating counterparty risk is dealing procedures. If a counterparty does not separate their dealing activities from their back office operations, the activities may be a dangerous risk to a customer or counterparty. It is extremely important for an investor, institution, or counterparty to separate back office operations from dealing operations, because dealing operations—and the profitability of those dealing operations—are easily manipulated by changes in back office reporting and risk evaluation. A counterparty may have internal risk controls which may be violated, putting the institution at risk unknowingly due to manipulations and hidden losses from the dealing operation. Rogue traders in the dealing operation have caused severe losses and scandals such as those at Barings Bank and Sumitomo. Those rogue traders had the ability to manipulate the back office reporting and risk evaluations of the positions of their institution. Any counterparty which does not separate dealing from back office activity is at risk in very much the same way.

Also, there is a risk in the way counterparties or customers evaluate their dealers. If a dealer is simply evaluated by the amount of return that he or she produces, regardless of the risk taken, the dealing operation is destined to be a great risk. Such a dealer might double up or hold losses too long instead of cutting the losses short and holding the profits long. A dealer who does not cut losses as part of a mandated rule of the institution puts the institution, counterparties, and customers at risk. The evaluations of a dealer should be based on risk adjusted returns. The risk-adjusted returns consider the amount of risk that was taken in order to make the returns that they have made. A customer that risked $10,000 to make $2,000 has a risk-adjusted return of 20%. A customer who returns $10,000 while risking $2,000 has a risk-adjusted return of 500%. Also, dealing operations of counterparties and customers should have set dealing limits and perimeters that any dealer may be able to take at any one time.

CREDIT RISK

The most obvious consideration in evaluating a counterparty is the credit risk of that counterparty. There are independent agencies that evaluate the credit risk of a counterparty; for example, the amount of limit put on a counterparty is normally fixed by the creditworthiness or perceived creditworthiness of the counterparty. The creditworthiness of a counterparty is difficult to evaluate due to the many intricate positions, products, and risks taken by that counterparty.

BIS Two-Tier System

An independent credit agency called the *Bank for International Settlement* (BIS) is perhaps one of the leading independent agencies for evaluating the risk of foreign exchange trading institutions on a global basis. BIS has put together procedures for evaluating the credit risk of counterparties by a two-tiered capital standard measured against risk-weighted assets. Tier one is defined as fully paid into shareholders' equity and returned earnings. Tier two includes subordinated debts, loan loss reserves, preferred stock, and certain high-bred instruments.

These capital standards look at a trading institution's entire list of assets and position risk and weights each risk of that institution by a certain percentage based on whether it is a tier-one or tier-two operation. The risk evaluations make it so that different counterparties are given different levels of creditworthiness due to the level of risk that is being held in different products. Assets and liabilities that have a low risk to outside customers or counterparties are given lower capital requirements than products or assets of high risk, such as options on illiquid currencies or complex derivative transactions with a low number of counterparties.

It is important again to remind customers and institutions that even though independent agencies have rated the creditworthiness of institutions, that does not mean they are infallible or cannot collapse.

Settlement Risks

Credit risk in reality is broken down into the risk on open positions of the counterparty and the risk of defaulting settlements from other customers for the counterparty. A counterparty may have low risk requirements and low credit standards for a whole list of customers with whom it is dealing. In taking on more customers and accepting customers with low credit standards, counterparties put themselves and other customers at risk of default on positions that they allow to trade on credit. Also, a counterparty that gives customers credit rather than making them put up a percentage of margin places their other customers at risk of those customers on credit defaulting, versus having a certain level of margin to withstand movements in open positions.

It is important to note that a trading institution that allows customers to trade on credit also allows them to do so according to set limits and perimeters. These limits and perimeters are an important consideration to the credit risk of that counterparty. Counterparties that do not offer credit lines are more creditworthy than those that give credit to customers. Much better than credit lines are margin lines. Margin levels give protection from marginal movements in open positions of customers.

Control Risks

The control risks that a counterparty takes also need to be evaluated.

Systems and Evaluation Risk

The systems and evaluation mechanisms that a counterparty uses in evaluating its own internal system should be reviewed by customers before they choose counterparties. A counterparty that uses sophisticated systems in evaluating its own risk perimeters and evaluates its back office operations and dealing operations separately would be considered a lower control risk than a counterparty that has unsophisticated evaluation systems and little separation in back and front office operations.

Back Office Risk

The most important aspect of control risk is the back office risk or back office exposure.

Inexperienced Staff   Trading institutions and operations often go through a high level of turnover of staff in back office operations. Inexperienced staff (due to turnover) may not recognize certain risks or problems inherent in the trading operation.

Corruption   Inexperienced back offices may also be more susceptible to corruption and hidden losses by traders and dealers who are compensated based on the profitability of their trading.

Closing Valuation Pricing   The back office evaluation system may also have different methods for evaluating the closing prices of an institution. How these systems evaluate the closing prices of different trading products is important, as different trading products correlate and protect (or cover) other positions that are established by the trading institution. A trading institution that evaluates futures, forwards, and spot positions based upon the same closing time frame will have a better evaluation of its overall risk than will an institution that evaluates its future positions, forward positions, and spot positions at separate closing times. For example, if a bank evaluates its spot positions based on its London closing, its futures positions on Chicago closing, and forwards on New York closing, it will have a wide discrepancy in the underlying risk of those positions due to the changes in exchange rates from each one of those closing time frames. Also, option volatility and the prices of the options must be evaluated by an independent back office representative rather than the dealer. Dealers might change their volatility figures in order to show a higher profit on a position than is actually realized.

Credit Risk—Conclusion

One mechanism by which counterparties can protect their customers and decrease the amount of risk of their trading operation is the futures industry in the United States, which is highly regulated. The futures regulators require clearinghouses and futures commission merchants to maintain customer funds segregated and separate from the operating income of the institution. This means that a trading institution is not allowed to use customer deposits for proprietary trading or operating expenses. In the interbank industry, it is uncommon for banking institutions and trading institutions to hold customer funds separate and segregated from the operating funds of the trading institution. Due to the commingling of customer funds with the funds of the trading institutions, certain losses may be hidden for large periods of time in a kind of Ponzi scheme. (A *Ponzi scheme* is when the losses of the investment firm are hidden by the deposits of new customers until all customer funds are lost and the customers are not able to withdraw their funds.)

Banking institutions generally receive deposits for the purpose of loans to other institutions. The risk that they take on those deposits are monitored by central banks and government regulators. However, bank deposits that are used to cover trading losses may put customers and counterparties at risk as the losses in banks are not separated from those of the customers' deposits, and therefore a loss due to the default of one customer may put the rest of the customers at risk unknowingly.

COUNTRY RISK

This is a macro risk which involves the risks of particular nations in which trading occurs as well as the global risk of the foreign exchange trading industry. Country risk can be broken down into political risk, regulation exposure, and legal exposure, all of which may have adverse effects on a customer or counterparty.

Political Risk

Political risk is the risk that multinational firms have within host countries and the political relationships between host countries and home countries. Usually when considering political risk, what comes to mind most readily is the risk of a country expropriating the funds of a corporation or trading institution for its own benefit. For example, after the Second World War, many corporations and institutions found their capital and assets seized by Eastern European countries, China, and Cuba. Obviously, in the present day and age such political risks are highly unlikely; still, traders today must, for example, evaluate the political risk of Hong Kong's being governed by Communist-controlled China.

In evaluating trading institutions, one must look at where their transactions originate, where they are completed, and any political risk might that might be associated with those institutions. For instance, is it possible for the institution to default due to government activities that are outside of the control of the trading institution?

Another political risk is possible changes in the trading environment that may occur because of how the government or the public of that government perceive the activity of trading institutions. It may seem odd that institutions trading in foreign currency could be considered wrongdoers by the public, yet in times of financial disaster, institutions that speculate or hedge in foreign currency trading can easily be made scapegoats. The crash of the stock market in 1987, for example, was blamed on the activities of systematized trading operations. Ironically, those same arbitrage systems kept the market spreads tighter and maintained market valuation. Any possible government intervention with a counterparty, customer, or banking institution is considered a form of political risk that must be evaluated on a macro- and micro-basis in regard to the activity of the counterparty.

Regulation Risk

In the same vein, *regulation risk* is the risk of a government regulating and putting constraints on an institution which stop the trading of an institution. This risk must be considered when choosing counterparties or customers. In the United States the nonregulation of foreign currency trading increases the legal costs of interpreting case law in preparing for future possibilities of regulation. In the short term, nonregulation decreases the costs, and therefore the risk, of intervention and decreases the risk of a customer or counterparty defaulting due to government intervention.

Legal Risk

Another aspect of country risk is the legal risk of contract jurisdiction. The default of a foreign currency transaction may fall into the jurisdiction of a country that has unfavorable contract laws regarding such transactions, making them either illegal or invalid. When investigating customers and counterparties, one must consider the jurisdiction of the contract being executed.

There is also a risk in dealing with counterparties and customers from different countries in that banking laws and holiday markets vary among nations.

Country Holiday Risk

Religious holidays, political holidays, and government holidays all may shut down a country's financial systems. These holidays pose problems in the transfer of funds because banks from certain countries are closed during certain holiday markets; thus, it may be impossible for funds to be transferred in time to meet margin or capital requirements to maintain a position. A risk may be established that forces a trading institution to liquidate a position due to delays in transfers of funds from one country to another. Such potential forced liquidations should be evaluated in regard to potential customer and counterparty relationships.

Obviously, there are many risks, known and unknown, in transacting foreign currency. Due to the amount of risk involved, the size of transactions, and the importance of foreign currency trading, many risk monitors have been created.

RISK MONITORS

This section goes into depth about the risk monitors that exist in foreign currency trading, either on a global or on a national basis. Many risk monitors are national rather than global because different countries have established different procedures for netting positions or capital requirements for clearing foreign currency transactions. Foreign currency transactions in spot currencies and forward currencies are considered over-the-counter (OTC) transactions. OTC transactions are not executed on a regulated exchange. The different monitoring and evaluating techniques of nonregulated trading are normally scattered and inconsistent. Today, given the technological advances in the foreign currency industry, multinational business systems and techniques must be even more careful to measure the risks of trading in a self-supervised market.

Regulators, Authorities, and Central Banks

It is generally acknowledged that the regulatory authorities of the foreign currency trading industry are the world's central banks, which monitor the flows of currency between countries and the balance of payments between governments and banking institutions.

As noted in Chapters 4 and 5, the regulatory environment in the United States has been inconsistent in the past as regards government regulation of unsophisticated institutions. Generally, transactions between sophisticated institutions are monitored and regulated by the Treasury Department and the Federal Reserve banks. In many other countries, the same regulation of banking institutions has a long history, yet in nonbanking institutions this is not always the case. Many times in the case of nonbanking institutions, the sole regulation is caveat emptor—buyer beware. In this environment, trading relationships are mutually established and monitored by the counterparties instead of relying on a government regulator. If a counterparty defaults on its transactions, then that counterparty will not be able to transact in the future, or at least not as effectively. Here again, name recognition of counterparties comes into play.

Capital Requirements

As referred to earlier, the Bank for International Settlement has created risk-weighted evaluation and capital requirements for institutions that trade in foreign currency transaction and money market transactions. Capital requirements are an important aspect of controlling risk and customer funds segregation.

Clearing Systems

Some of the common clearing systems for the transfer of funds in currencies are the Chips and the S.W.I.F.T. systems (Appendix C of this book contains the S.W.I.F.T. codes for different currencies). The proper transfer of funds is an important aspect of protection against default in a wire transfer. The transfer system can guarantee that the funds will arrive correctly and according to disclosed instructions. Due to such clearing systems, it is easy to identify the creditworthiness of transactions and counterparties in certain spot and forward transactions.

Netting Systems

In the foreign currency industry, netting systems have become an important aspect of the overall evaluation of customer creditworthiness. Netting systems net the total long and short positions of different currencies against the current market price between counterparties. Different trading institutions and banks use netting systems to ensure that positions have netted according to the preset instructions of the transaction. For example, a transaction that buys 1 million U.S. dollars and sells deutschemarks at a set price would be marked to the market and netted against the books of the offsetting counterparty in that netting system. The netting system would show a buy of 1 million U.S. dollars and a sell of deutschemarks for one counterparty. The opposite side would show a sell of 1 million U.S. dollars and a buy of deutschemarks from the other counterparty of the transaction, netting the profit and loss with a closing price.

The futures industry is highly regulated by government regulators and exchanges. Futures transactions are cleared and marked to the market on an hourly and even minute-by-minute basis. The efficiency of futures clearinghouses is an example for the global foreign currency industry as a whole. The risks of transactions decrease dramatically when a clearing system automatically debits and credits the accounts and books and monitors the risk level of corporations on a mark-to-market basis.

Exchange Book/Ladder

Trading institutions are normally netted on what is considered an exchange book and exchange ladder. In the exchange books, all currency positions are netted to one established currency, for example, the U.S. dollar. This system reduces the net exposure of all currency transactions to one set currency. The exchange ladder is a netting system whereby the exposure is viewed by maturity rather than by currency.

By now it should be clear that the risks and the systems and monitoring mechanisms of foreign currency trading have many tiers of effectiveness and customization.

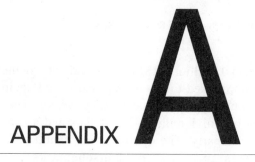

Standard Foreign Exchange Agreement

(Drafted by the International Swap Dealers Association)

FOREIGN EXCHANGE TRADING FACILITY

This letter agreement dated this _____ day of _____, 19____, is to confirm an agreement between _____ ("Customer") and _____ _____. The Foreign Exchange Trading Dealer ("FETD"), (individually or collectively referred to a "Party" or "Parties") pursuant to which FETD may effect spot ("Spot"), forward "(Forward")" and option ("Option") contracts (collectively, "Contracts" and each a "Contract") with the undersigned customer ("Customer") for the purchase or sale by Customer of foreign exchange ("FX"). The Parties agree that each Contract will be governed by the terms and conditions set forth in this document and Annex I attached hereto and the documents exchanged between the Parties confirming such Contract (each a "Confirmation"). This document and all the Confirmations constitute a single master agreement between the Parties (collectively, this "Agreement").

1.   Definitions

For the purposes of this Agreement:

a)   "Act of Insolvency" means, with respect to Customer, the commencement by such person as debtor of any case or proceeding under any bankruptcy, insolvency, reorganization, liquidation, dissolution, or similar law, or such person seeking the appointment of a receiver, liquidator, trustee, custodian, or similar official for such person or any substantial part of its property; the commencement of any such case or proceeding against such person, or the seeking of such an appointment by another which (i) is consented to or not timely contested by such person, (ii) results in the entry of an order for relief, such as appointment, the issuance of such a protective decree or the entry of an order having a similar effect, or (iii) is not dismissed within 30 days; the making by such person of a general assignment for the benefit of creditors, or the admission in writing by such person of such person's inability to pay such person's debts as they become due.

b)   "Aggregate Collateral Value" at any relevant time means (i) the value of any collateral in the "Pledge Account" (as defined in Section 9 hereof) less (ii) the Aggregate Unrealized Contract Loss (if any), as determined by FETD at such time (which determination shall be conclusive in the absence of manifest error).

c)   "Aggregate Unrealized Contract Loss" at any relevant time means the absolute value of the aggregate net unrealized loss to Customer (if any) after application of any unrealized gains to Customer under all of Customer's outstanding Contracts, as determined by FETD at such time (which determination shall be conclusive in the absence of manifest error).

d)   "American Option" means an Option which is exercisable on any Business Day from and including its Effective Date to and including its Expiration Date.

e)   "Business Day" means a day other than a Saturday or Sunday on which (i) banks in New York City, and (ii) solely for the purpose of settlement, banks in the financial center of the country of issuance to the Currency to be settled, are open for business.

f)   "Call" means an Option by which the Seller grants the Buyer the right to buy the Delivery Currency.

g)   "Collateral" refers exclusively to cash in U.S. dollars and/or U.S. Treasury bills.

h)   "Credit Event" means any (i) default by the Customer or any affiliate of the Customer in respect of any other agreement with FETD or any affiliate of FETD, or (ii) material adverse change in the Customer's creditworthiness or financial results.

i)   "Currency" means the lawful currency of any country or any "composite currency" such as the European Composite Currency.

j)   "Delivery Collateral" means Collateral with a value equal to the full amount of the Payment Currency which the Customer is obligated to pay to FETD in respect of any and all Contracts sharing a particular Value Date.

k)   "Delivery Currency" means the Currency stipulated at the time of quotation, which is to be exchanged for the Payment Currency stipulated at the same time.

l)   "Effective Date" means, with respect to any Option, the date specified as such in the related Confirmation.

m) "European Option" means an Option that is exercisable only on its Expiration Date.

n)   "Expiration Date" means, with respect to any Option, the date specified as such in the related Confirmation, provided that if such date is not a Business Day, the Expiration Date shall be the next succeeding Business Day.

o)   "Minimum Amount" at any relevant time, means an amount of Collateral which FETD in its sole and absolute discretion determines will cover the maximum one-day loss that the Aggregate Contract Value may incur. For normal trading conditions, FETD may use up to 5% or more of Net Aggregate Contract Value but will not be bound by such system recommendation of Minimum Amount if price volatility or general trading conditions are judged by FETD to require a greater amount for the protection of FETD and/or Customer.

p)   "Net Aggregate Contract Value" has the meaning set forth in Section 4.

q)   "Obligations" means all amounts payable at any time by Customer to FETD (including, without limitation, indemnification, and expense reimbursements obligations) and all other liabilities, covenants, agreements, and obligations of Customer to FETD under, or in connection with, transactions effected pursuant to this Agreement, or under, or in connection with, transactions effected pursuant to any other agreement between FETD and Customer (whether oral or written).

r)   "Option" means the right but not the obligation of the Buyer to purchase or sell, as the case may be, a predetermined amount of a Delivery Currency, at its Strike Price for a predetermined amount of a Payment Currency.

s)   "Option Amount" means, with respect to any Option, the amount of Delivery Currency to be delivered.

t)   "Option Buyer" means, with respect to any Option, the owner of such Option.

u)   "Option Seller" means, with respect to any Option, the party that grants the Option.

v)   "Option Settlement Amount" means, with respect to any Option, the amount of Payment Currency for which the Option Amount could be exchanged using the Strike Price as the applicable rate of exchange.

w)   "Payment Currency" means the currency stipulated at the time of quotation to be exchanged for the Delivery Currency, which is stipulated at the same time.

x)   "Premium" means, with respect to any Option, the purchase price of such Option.

y)   "Premium Payment Date" means the date on which the related Premium is due and payable.

z)   "Put" means an Option by which the Seller grants the Buyer the right to sell the Payment Currency.

aa)   "Strike Price" means, with respect to any Option, the rate agreed to at the time the Option is granted at which the Delivery Currency will be exchanged for the Payment Currency.

bb)   "Trade Date" means, with respect to any Option, the date specified as such in the related Confirmation.

cc)   "US Dollars" means the lawful currency of the United States of America.

dd)   "Value Date" means the date on which settlement is to be made under a Contract.

2.   Procedures

The Parties agree that Contracts will be entered into through binding oral agreements concluded over the telephone by their authorized representatives.

a)   Each Spot and Forward shall be described in a Confirmation substantially in the form of Annex 1 hereto. FETD shall promptly deliver to Customer a Confirmation evidencing a Spot or Forward which shall incorporate the terms and conditions of this Agreement. Customer shall acknowledge such Confirmation to FETD within one Business Day of receipt. Unless Customer objects in writing to the terms contained in any Confirmation within such one-day period, the terms of such Confirmation shall be conclusively deemed correct. Failure by FETD to issue, or Customer to execute, a Confirmation will not alter the rights and obligations of either Party under the Spot or Forward Contract. In the event of any conflict between the terms of a Confirmation and this Agreement, such Confirmation shall prevail.

b)   Each Option shall be described in a Confirmation substantially in the form of Annex 2 hereto. FETD shall promptly deliver to Customer a Confirmation evidencing an Option which shall incorporate the terms and conditions of this Agreement. Customer shall acknowledge such Confirmation to FETD within one Business Day of receipt. Unless Customer objects in writing to the terms contained in any Confirmation within such one-day period, the terms of such Confirmation shall be conclusively deemed correct. Failure by FETD to issue, or Customer to execute, a Confirmation will not alter the rights and obligations of either Party under the Option. In the event of any conflict between the terms of a Confirmation and this Agreement, such Conformation shall prevail.

3.   Payments

a)   Subject to the provisions of this Section 3, each Party will make each payment specified in each Contract as being payable by it.

b)   In consideration for granting of Options by the Option Seller, the Option Buyer agrees to pay the applicable Premium on the Premium Payment Date. Unless otherwise agreed to in writing by the Parties hereto, the Premium Payment Date for an Option shall be the second Business Day immediately following the Trade Date. If any Premium is not received on its Premium Payment Date, the Option Seller may cancel the related Option or accept a late payment of such Premium. In either case, the Option Buyer shall pay all losses, expenses, costs, and damages incurred in connection with any unpaid or late Premium or canceled Option, including, without limitation, interest in the same Currency on such Premium at a then prevailing market rate. If a Premium has not been received, the related Option may not be exercised.

c)   Notwithstanding subsection (a) if (i) a Contract is entered into by the Parties in which one or both of the currencies are the same and with the same Value Date as one or more Contracts previously entered into or outstanding, all such Contracts shall automatically and without further action be regarded as a single contract ("Netted Contract") which shall be substituted for a constitute notation of the Contracts so Netted, and the sole performance required by each Party with respect to all Contracts combined into a Netted Contract shall be to pay to the other on the Value Date the amount, if any, of each relevant Currency produced by netting amounts of such Currency to be paid and received by each Party under all Contracts so combined, or (ii) if the Premium Payment Dates for two or more Contracts shall fall on the same day, and FETD and Customer each is required to pay an amount in the same Currency under such Contracts, then the amounts payable by each Party shall be netted and the Party obligated to pay the larger aggregate amount will be obligated to pay on such Premium Payment Date to the other Party the excess of the larger aggregate amount over the smaller aggregate amount.

d) Payments under this Agreement will be made no later than the due date specified in the relevant Contract or pursuant to this Agreement.

e) All calculations required by this Section 3 shall be computed by FETD. FETD shall give prompt written notice to Customer of all such calculations. Any net amounts actually payable (i) by FETD to Customer shall be credited in accordance with Customer's instructions to an account or accounts acceptable to FETD, or (ii) by Customer to FETD shall be credited in accordance with FETD instructions, in each case under (i) and (ii) on the applicable Value Dates.

f) FETD and Customer may agree in writing that any Contract be settled in a different manner from that provided in Subsection 3(a) immediately above. Customer must notify FETD of such desire prior to 8:30 a.m., New York City time, on the Business Day prior to the applicable Value Date.

g) Payment by Customer to FETD as a result of notification by FETD to Customer to maintain the Minimum Amount required shall be received by FETD not later than one Business Day after such notification has been made.

h) Unless otherwise agreed to by FETD in writing, each Contract shall have a Value Date of not more than one hundred and eighty (180) days following the Trade Date.

4. Contract Limits

a) The net aggregate value of long Contract positions and short Contract positions for all currencies and Value Dates determined by FETD (The "Net Aggregate Contract Value"), expressed in U.S. dollars (and calculated in accordance with Section 12(g) hereof), shall not at any time exceed (_____) U.S. dollars ($_____) (the "Net Aggregate Contract Value Limit").

b)   The Net Aggregate Contract Value Limit may be decreased or increased at any time by FETD, upon written notification to Customer.

5.   Premiums, Exercise, and Settlement

a)   Written notice by the Option Buyer to the Option Seller of exercise of any American Option may be given on any Business Day from and including its Effective Date to and including its Expiration Date prior to 5:00 p.m., New York City time. Any such notice received by the Option Seller after 5:00 p.m., New York City time, on any Business Day shall, subject to Subsection 5(a)(ii) below, cause an exercise on the following Business Day. Notice by the Option Buyer to the Option Seller of exercise of any European Option may be given prior to 5:00 p.m., New York City time, on its Expiration Date only. (ii) Any Option for which notice of exercise is not received by the Option Seller prior to 5:00 p.m., New York City time on the Expiration Date shall expire and shall become void and of no effect. (iii) An exercised Option shall automatically become a Spot transaction on the terms set forth in the related Confirmation.

b)   In the case of an exercised Call, the Option Seller shall deliver to the Option Buyer the Option Amount on the second Business Day (or, in the case of an Option in Canadian dollars, on the first Business Day) after the date an Option is exercised, and the Option Buyer shall on the corresponding Business Day pay the Option Seller the Option Settlement Amount. In the case of an exercised Put, the Option Seller shall pay to the Option Buyer the Option Settlement Amount on the Second Business Day (or, in the case of an Option in Canadian dollars, on the first Business Day) after the date an Option is exercised, and the Option Buyer shall on the corresponding Business Day deliver the Option Amount to the Option Seller.

6.   Representations and Warranties of Customer
     Customer hereby represents and warrants to, and covenants and agrees with, FETD, as of the date of this Agreement and, for purposes of each Contract, as of the date of such Contract as follows:

a)   It is duly organized and validly existing under the laws of the jurisdiction of its incorporation.

b) Each provision of this Agreement, each Contract, and each confirmation has been duly authorized, executed, and delivered and is a valid and legally binding obligation enforceable in accordance with its terms, subject, as to enforcement, to bankruptcy, insolvency, reorganization, and other laws of general applicability relating to or affecting creditors' rights and to general equity principles.

c) In its execution and delivery of this Agreement and each Confirmation performance of this Agreement, such Contract and each Confirmation does not and will not contravene or constitute a default under any provision of its Certificate of Incorporation or Bylaws (or equivalent constituent documents) or any law, regulation, rule, decree, order, judgment, or contractual restriction binding on it or any of its assets and all authorizations, consents, approvals, and notifications necessary for such execution, delivery, and performance have been obtained and remain in full force and effect, and all conditions thereof have been complied with, and no other action by or in respect of, or filing with, any governmental body, agency, or official is required in connection with such execution, delivery, and performance.

d) The resolutions of the board of directors of Customer authorizing this transaction are reflected in the minutes of such board of directors, have been rescinded, amended, or otherwise modified, are in full force and effect, and are the only resolutions so adopted relating to this Agreement.

e) It is not, on the date of execution of this Agreement or any Confirmation, required to deduct or withhold any taxes with respect to any payment which is or could be required to be made by it pursuant to this Agreement or any Contract.

f) It is acting as principal in connection with all Contracts hereunder.

7. Credit Event
   If a Credit Event shall have occurred and be continuing, FETD may require Customer to deposit with FETD Delivery Collateral at least one Business Day prior to the Value Date of each Contract.

8. Default

a)   Any of the following shall be an Event of Default for purposes of this Agreement: (i) Customer fails to make any payment owed pursuant to Section 3 or 9 hereof on the date such payment is owed. (ii) Any representation or warranty of Customer made in connection with this Agreement or in connection with any Contract shall prove to have been incorrect in any material respect when made or would be incorrect if repeated at any time after the date of this Agreement or such Contract if repeated in the context of the circumstances then existing. (iii) An Act of Insolvency shall have occurred with respect to Customer. (iv) Customer fails to deposit with FETD Delivery Collateral on the date such is due.

b)   If an Event of Default shall have occurred and be continuing, FETD ("Non-Defaulting Party") may designate an early termination date ("Early Termination Date") upon two Business Days' notice to Customer (the "Defaulting Party"). However, an Early Termination Date will be deemed to have occurred in respect of all Contracts immediately upon the occurrence of an Event of Default specified in Sections 8(a)(iii) or 8(a)(iv). Upon the Early Termination Date, the Parties' obligations under this Agreement shall terminate, except for the obligation contained in subsection (c) below.

c)   Upon the Early Termination Date, the Non-Defaulting Party shall calculate (i) the sum of (X) the aggregate amount, if any, owed by the Defaulting Party to the Non-Defaulting Party under Section 3 as to all Contracts through the Early Termination Date and (Y) the Aggregate Unrealized Contract Loss which is owed by the Defaulting Party under Section 3 as to all Contracts through the Early Termination Date. If the Event of Default giving rise to the Early Termination Date is one or more of the events specified in Section 8(a)(i), (a)(ii), or (a)(iv), then the Defaulting Party shall pay to the Non-Defaulting Party within two Business Days of the Early Termination Date the amount, if any, by which (i) above exceeds (ii) above. If the Event of Default giving rise to the Early Termination Date is specified in Section 8(a)(iii), then the Party owing the higher amount under (i) and (ii) above shall pay to the other Party within two Business Days of the Early Termination Date the excess of the larger amount over the smaller amount. The Non-Defaulting Party shall deliver to the Defaulting Party a certificate containing in reasonable detail a computation of the amount owing pursuant to this Section 8(c), which certificate shall be conclusive evidence of such determination absent manifest error.

d)   If an Event of Default shall occur and be continuing, or if FETD shall, in its sole and absolute discretion, consider it necessary for its protection, FETD shall have the right, in addition to any other remedy available to FETD at law or in equity and in addition to any other action FETD may deem appropriate in the circumstances, immediately and without prior notice, to terminate this Agreement and to liquidate all or any outstanding Contracts in accordance with Section 8(b) hereof and to apply any of the Collateral or Other Collateral (as defined in Section 9) or any proceeds thereof to the Obligations. In this connection, FETD may borrow or buy any currencies, options, securities, contracts, commodities, or other property for customer's account and sell any Collateral or Other Collateral. In the event FETD's position would not be jeopardized thereby, FETD will make reasonable efforts under the circumstances to notify Customer prior to taking any such action. Any such liquidation, sale, purchase, or borrowing shall be made at the discretion of FETD privately or otherwise. Customer acknowledges and agrees that a prior demand for collateral of any kind from FETD or prior notice from FETD shall not be considered a waiver of FETD's right to take any action without notice or demand. In the event FETD exercises any remedies available to it, Customer shall compensate FETD for any and all costs, losses, penalties, fines, taxes, and damages which FETD may incur including reasonable attorney's fees incurred in connection with the exercise of its remedies and the recovery of any such costs, losses, penalties, fines, taxes, and damages.

Customer shall pay to FETD the costs and expenses of collection of any debit balance and any unpaid deficiency resulting from the foregoing, including, but not limited to, legal charges and expenses. Failure by FETD to exercise any of its rights or remedies under this Agreement or any Contract shall not constitute a consent or waiver by FETD, either generally or specifically in any case, or preclude FETD from exercising its rights and remedies to the fullest extent permitted or contemplated by this Agreement, any Contract, or otherwise.

9.   Grant of Security; Collateral

The obligations of Customer shall be secured by the pledge of Collateral in an amount and on the terms and conditions hereafter set forth. This Agreement constitutes, to the extent relevant with respect to any Collateral, a security agreement under Article 9 of the Uniform Commercial Code of the State of New York ("UCC").

a)   On or prior to the date hereof, Customer shall have established a pledge account with FETD (the "Pledge Account") for the purpose of holding custody of Collateral in accordance with the provisions of this Agreement.

b)   Customer shall at all times maintain Collateral in the Pledge Account having a value such that the Aggregate Collateral Value shall not be less than the then applicable Minimum Amount. In the event that the Aggregate Collateral Value shall be less than the Minimum Amount required (the difference between such Aggregate Collateral Value and such Minimum Amount being the "Shortfall") Customer will deposit with FETD, immediately upon FETD's request, Collateral in an amount at least equal to such Shortfall.

c)   As security for the prompt and complete payment when due and the performance by Customer of all Obligations, Customer hereby pledges, assigns, conveys, and transfers to FETD, and hereby grants to FETD, a first and prior security interest in and to, and a general first lien upon and right of set-off against, all of Customer's right, title, and interest in and to all Collateral paid or delivered to FETD. Customer agrees and acknowledges that all Collateral will at all times be, and the same are hereby subject to, a first lien and charge as continuing security for the due and punctual payment and satisfaction of all the Obligations. Any other property of Customer, including but not limited to any Delivery Collateral, at any time held in FETD or any affiliate of FETD, including but not limited to, property held in any accounts of Customer with FETD or any affiliate or agent of FETD, irrespective or whether or not FETD has made advances in connection with such property ("Other Collateral"), shall constitute additional and further security for the due and punctual payment and satisfaction of all the Obligations. It is expressly agreed that the rights of FETD with respect to any Collateral or Other Collateral so paid or delivered shall include the right to sell, pledge, repledge, hypothecate, set-off, or further assign such collateral or Other Collateral on any terms, privately or otherwise, and that, without prejudice to the generality of the fore-going, FETD may in its sole discretion use any Collateral or Other Collateral in the ordinary course of its business, without notice to Customer or any obligation to Customer for any benefit that may be derived by FETD therefrom. FETD shall pay interest to Customer of any cash Collateral at such rates as shall be agreed upon by FETD and Customer from time to time.

d)   Substitution of Collateral by Customer and any other administration of Collateral may occur on such conditions as FETD may in its sole discretion consider to be acceptable.

e)   Customer represents and warrants to FETD that Customer is and will at all times be the sole beneficial owner of all property which Customer has paid or delivered and will hereafter pay or deliver to the Pledge Account, and that, except as contemplated by the Agreement, all such property is and will at all times continue to be free from any mortgage, charge, lien, or any other form of encumbrance or security or any equity whatsoever.

f)   Customer covenants and agrees that it will, at its expense and in such manner and form as FETD may require, execute, sign, seal, deliver, file, record, do, complete, procure, and otherwise obtain all transfers, powers of attorney, further assurances or other approvals, consents, UCC financial statements, specific assignments, acts, deeds, and docu-ments which FETD may require (i) to realize the Collateral and Other Collateral, (ii) to vest the same in FETD or its nominee or a purchaser or transferee or (iii) to create, validate, perfect, protect, or preserve FETD's rights and interests in or pursuant to this Agreement or any Contract, and hereby irrevocably and by way of security appoint FETD and any person nominated in writing by FETD as the attorney of Cus-tomer in its name and on its behalf to execute, sign, seal, deliver, file, record, do, complete, procure, and otherwise obtain all transfers, pow-ers of attorney, further assurances, or other approvals, consents, UCC financial statements, specific assignments, acts, deeds, and documents which FETD deems necessary or desirable for the above-mentioned rights, interests, and purposes.

10.   Responsibilities of FETD

a)   FETD's responsibility. FETD is not acting as a fiduciary, foundation manager, commodity pool operator, commodity trading advisor, or investment advisor in respect of Customers, and FETD shall have no responsibility hereunder for compliance with any law, rule, or regulation governing the conduct of fiduciaries, foundation managers, commodity pool operators, commodity trading advisors, or investment advisors.

b)   Advice. Any advice to Customer with respect to Contracts transmitted by FETD is incidental to the conduct of FETD's business and such advice will not serve as the primary basis for any decision by or on behalf of Customer. FETD shall have no discretionary authority, power, or control over any decisions made by or on behalf of Customer, whether or not any advice of FETD is utilized in any such decision. Any such advice, although based upon information from sources FETD believes to be reliable, may be incomplete, may not be verified, and may be changed without notice to Customer. FETD makes no representation as to the accuracy, completeness, reliability, or prudence of any such advice or information. Customer shall not seek to hold FETD responsible for any losses sustained by Customer as a result of any prediction, recommendation, or advice made or given by a representative of FETD whether made or given at the request of Customer.

11.   Currency Indemnity
      If, under any applicable law and whether pursuant to a judgment against Customer or the liquidation, bankruptcy, or analogous process of Customer or for any other reason, any payment under or in connection with a Contract is made in a Currency (the "Other Currency") other than that in which it is due pursuant to this Agreement (the "Contractual Currency"), then to the extent that the payment (when converted into the Contractual Currency at the exchange rate computed pursuant to Paragraph 12(g) hereof on the first day after the date of payment on which it is practicable for FETD to effect the conversion or, in the case of a liquidation bankruptcy or analogous process, prevailing on the latest due date for determination of liabilities permitted by applicable process) actually received by FETD falls short of the amount due under the terms of the relevant Contract, Customer shall, as a separate and independent obligation, indemnify FETD and hold FETD harmless against the amount of such shortfall.

12.   Miscellaneous

a)   Amendment. This Agreement may be modified or amended only in writing signed by each of the Parties hereto.

b)   Successors and Assigns. This Agreement shall be binding on and inure to the benefit of the Parties hereto and their successors and the assigns of FETD. Neither Customer nor FETD may sell, transfer, or assign this Agreement or any of its rights or obligations hereunder without the prior written consent of the other Party hereto; provided, however, that FETD may, without notice to Customer, assign in whole or in part its rights and obligations under this Agreement and under any Contract to any affiliate of FETD, and such affiliates may reassign such rights and obligations to FETD or any other affiliates of FETD. No person other than the Parties hereto and their respective successors and the permitted assigns of FETD shall acquire or have any right under or by virtue of this Agreement.

c)   Termination. Either FETD or Customer may terminate this Agreement at any time upon 24-hour written notice to the other and following such termination, the rights and obligations of the Parties hereunder shall terminate, except with respect to Contracts entered into and to such rights or obligations arising at or prior to such termination.

d)   Notices. Any communication, demand, or notice to be given hereunder will be duly given when delivered in writing or received by telex or telecopy or given by the telephone to a Party at its address as indicated below, or to such other address as may from time to time be notified in writing by such Party to the other Party.

e)   A communication, demand or notice given pursuant to this paragraph shall be addressed:

If to Customer at: If to FETD at:

_____   _____

_____   _____

_____   _____

_____   _____

Attn.:   Attn.:

_____   _____

Telex/Answerback: Telex/Answerback:

_____   _____

Phone: Phone:

_____   _____

Fax: Fax:

_____   _____

f) Right to Refuse Orders. FETD reserves the absolute right, exercis-
    able at any time in its sole discretion, to refuse acceptance of any
    order to establish new Contract positions of Customer.

g) Currency Conversions. The U.S. dollar equivalent of any other Cur-
    rency will be determined on the basis of the relevant exchange rate
    for the purchase of U.S. dollars with such Currency prevailing at any
    relevant time or times as determined by FETD, which determination
    shall be conclusive in the absence of manifest error.

h) Agent for Service. Customer shall at all times maintain an agent for
    service of process in the City of New York, Borough of Manhattan.
    Such agent shall be _____ of
    _____ and any summons, complaint,
    writ, judgment, or other legal process shall be sufficiently served on
    Customer if delivered to such agent at such address. Customer under-
    takes not to revoke the authority of the above agent and if, for any
    reason, such agent no longer serves as agent of Customer to receive
    service of process, Customer shall promptly appoint another such agent
    and advise FETD thereof.

i) Contract to Applicable Law. To the extent that this Agreement is found
    to be contrary to or inconsistent with applicable law, this Agreement
    shall continue to be enforceable to the maximum extent permissible.

j) Rights and Remedies Cumulative. All rights and remedies arising under
    this Agreement as amended and modified from time to time are cu-
    mulative and not exclusive of any other rights or remedies which may
    be available at law or otherwise.

k)   No Waiver. No failure on the part of FETD to exercise, and no delay in exercising, any contractual right will operate as a waiver thereof, nor will any single or partial exercise by FETD of any right preclude any other or future exercise thereof or the exercise of any other partial right.

l)   Governing Law. This Agreement and the rules, obligations, and remedies of the Parties shall be governed by and construed in accordance with the laws of the State of New York applicable to contracts made and to be performed entirely therein.

m)   Consent to Jurisdiction. Customer submits to the jurisdiction of the courts of New York and of the Federal courts in the Southern District of New York with respect to any litigation with FETD relating to this Agreement, and consents to the service of process 9(i) by the mailing to Customer of copies thereof by certified mail to the address of Customer set forth herein, such service to be effective ten days after mailing, or (ii) by the delivery to Customer's agent pursuant to Section 12(h), such service to be effective upon delivery. Customer hereby waives irrevocably any immunity to which it might otherwise be entitled in any arbitration, action at law, suit in equity, or any other proceeding arising out of or based on this Agreement or any transaction in connection herewith.

n)   Status of Customer. Customer represents and warrants to FETD that it is a sophisticated institutional investor able to evaluate and assume the risks associated with transactions in currencies as contemplated by this Agreement; and that it is entering into this Agreement and all Contracts solely in connection with its business and for investment purposes.

o)   Payments in Agreed Currency. It is the essence of this Agreement that the respective Parties make the payments thereunder in the Currency provided for in such Contract.

p)   New York Time. All times referred to in this Agreement shall be deemed references to New York time.

q)   Headings. The headings used in this Agreement are for convenience of reference only and are not to affect the construction of or to be taken into consideration in interpreting this Agreement.

r)   Entire Agreement. This Agreement contains the entire agreement between the Parties relating to the subject matter hereof and supersedes
all oral statement and prior writings with respect thereto.

s)   Counterparts. This Agreement may be executed in counterparts, each
of which when so executed and delivered shall be deemed for purposes an original, but all such counterparts shall constitute but one
and the same instrument.

t)   Tape Recording. Customer is hereby informed that telephone conver-
sations with FETD may be taped. Customer hereby waives further
notice of such taping.

13.   Disclosure

a)   Customer   has   been   introduced   to   FETD   by
_____. FETD confirms that it has
opened a foreign exchange trading account in the name of Customer,
subject to the terms and conditions of this foreign Exchange Trading
Facility Agreement. FETD will provide execution and clearing services for each transaction presented to it by Customer.

b)   Customer understands that _____ is an
independent company and is not part of the _____.
Further, Customer acknowledges that FETD will deal as principal with
respect to transactions executed for Customer's account. Customer
understands that each transaction will normally generate revenue for
FETD and the FETD may pay a portion of the revenue generated by
each   foreign   exchange   trade   made   to   FETD   to
_____. The amount of revenue paid to
_____ in accordance with this paragraph will be
furnished to you upon your written request. Customer expressly accepts that FETD and _____ shall not be liable for
any advice given or views expressed to Customer by FETD or
_____, whether or not such advice or views
were solicited or unsolicited by Customer. Any telephone conversa-
tion between Customer, FETD, or _____ may
be electronically recorded for the parties' mutual protection.

If the terms and conditions set forth and incorporated herein reflect your understanding of the terms and conditions of our arrangement, please forward to us an executed counterpart of this letter, whereupon this letter shall become a binding agreement between us.

Very truly yours,
By: _____
Name: _____
Title: _____

Accepted and agreed to as of the date first above written:
_____[Customer]
By: _____
Name: _____
Title: _____

APPENDIX **B**

Cash Currency Charts

Deutschemark Monthly

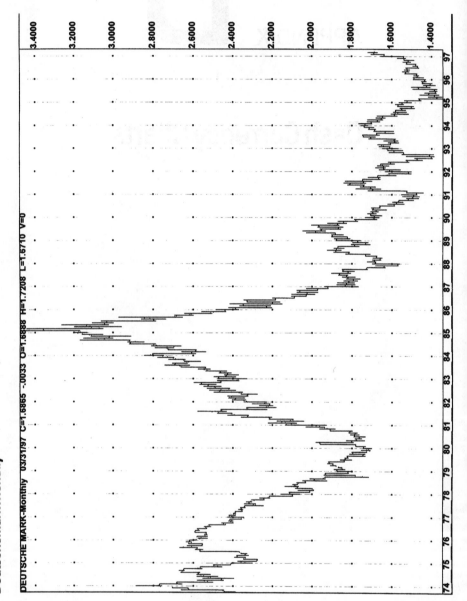

DEUTSCHE MARK-Monthly 03/31/97 C=1.6865 -.0033 O=1.6888 H=1.7208 L=1.6710 V=0

Deutschemark Weekly

DEUTSCHE MARK-Weekly 03/21/97 C=1.6865 -.0083 O=1.6941 H=1.6967 L=1.6710 V=0

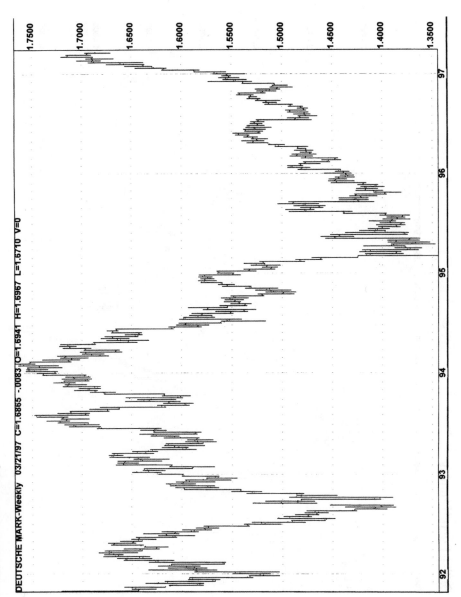

149

British Pound Monthly

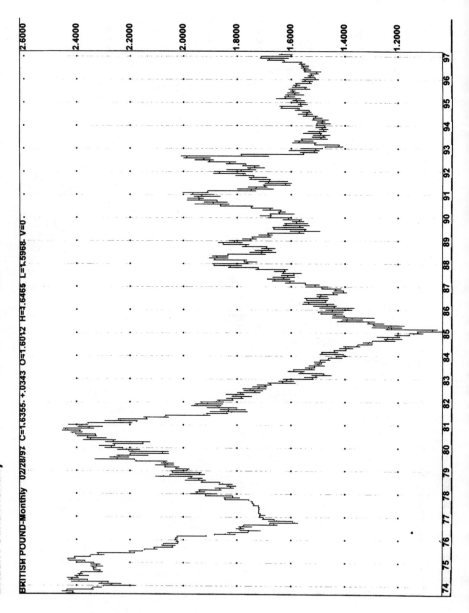

BRITISH POUND-Monthly 02/28/97 C=1.6355 +.0343 O=1.6012 H=1.6465 L=1.5968 V=0

British Pound Weekly

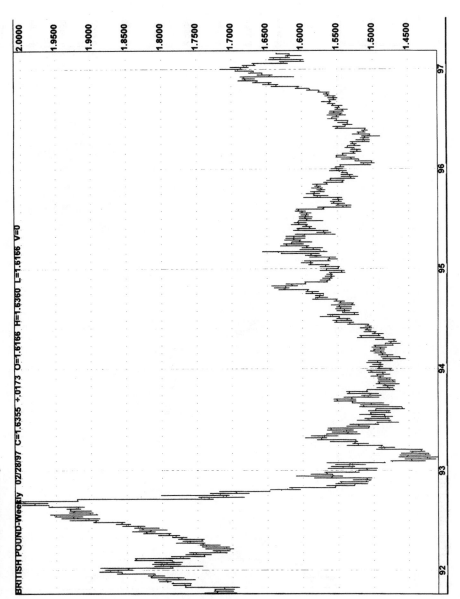

BRITISH POUND-Weekly 02/28/97 C=1.6355 +.0173 O=1.6166 H=1.6360 L=1.6166 V=0

Swiss Franc Monthly

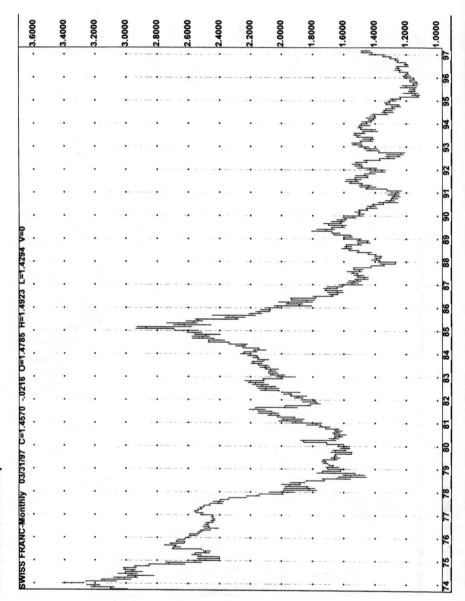

SWISS FRANC-Monthly 03/31/97 C=1.4570 -.0216 O=1.4785 H=1.4923 L=1.4294 V=0

Swiss Franc Weekly

SWISS FRANC-Weekly 03/21/97 C=1.4570 +.0012 O=1.4572 H=1.4625 L=1.4294 V=0

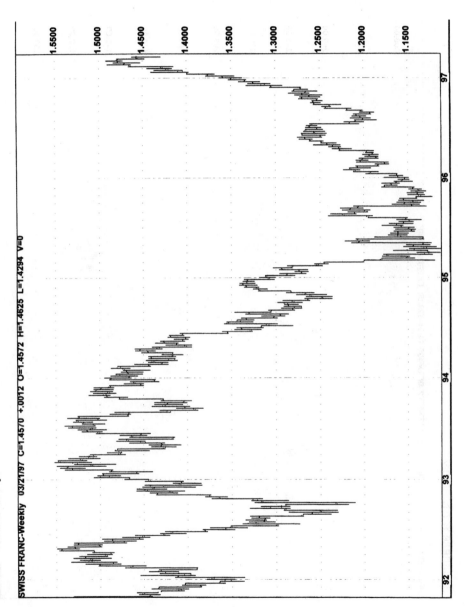

Japanese Yen Monthly

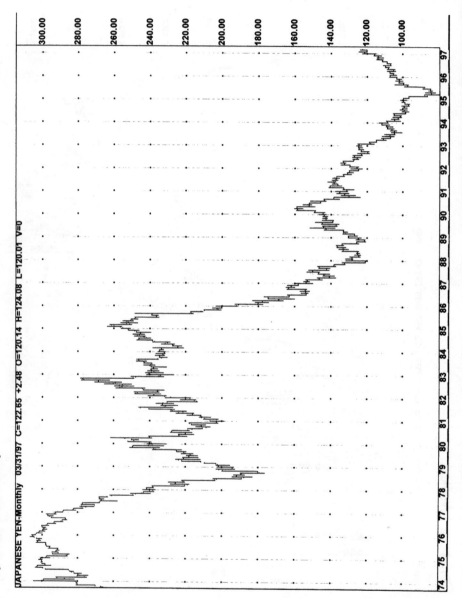

JAPANESE YEN-Monthly 03/31/97 C=122.65 +2.48 O=120.14 H=124.08 L=120.01 V=0

154

Japanese Yen Weekly

JAPANESE YEN-Weekly 03/21/97 C=122.65 -.80 O=123.36 H=123.98 L=122.11 V=0

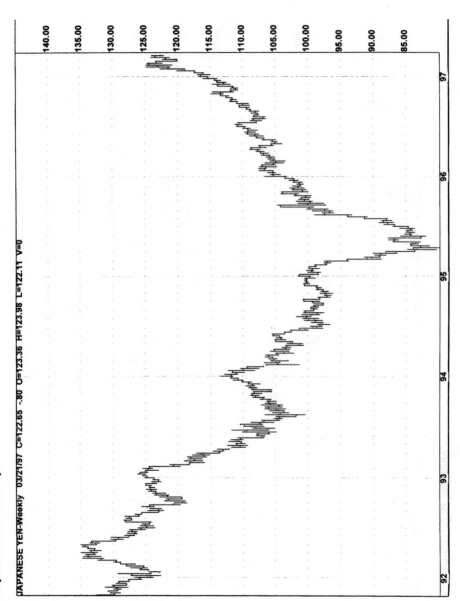

Canadian Dollar Monthly

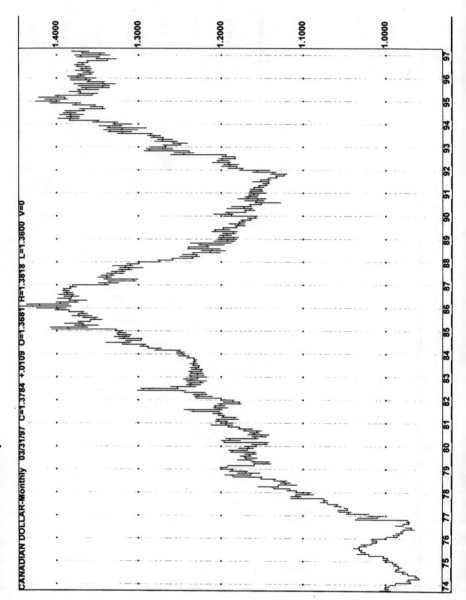

CANADIAN DOLLAR-Monthly 03/31/97 C=1.3784 +.0109 O=1.3689 H=1.3818 L=1.3600 V=0

Canadian Dollar Weekly

CANADIAN DOLLAR-Weekly 03/21/97 C=1.3784 +.0133 O=1.3648 H=1.3818 L=1.3638 V=0

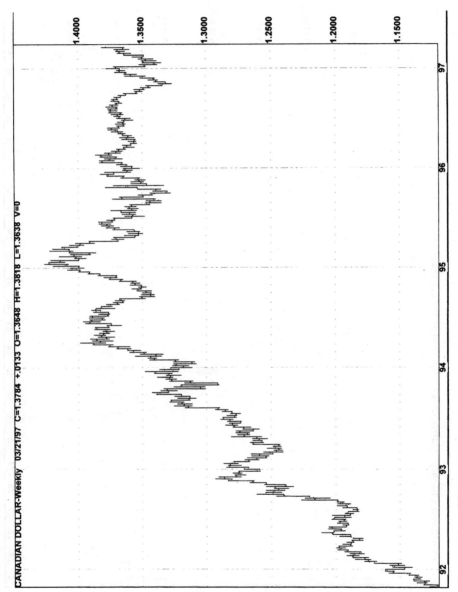

U.S. Dollar Index Monthly

U.S. DOLLAR INDEX-Monthly 03/31/97 C=95.28 +.39 O=94.98 H=96.32 L=94.73 V=0

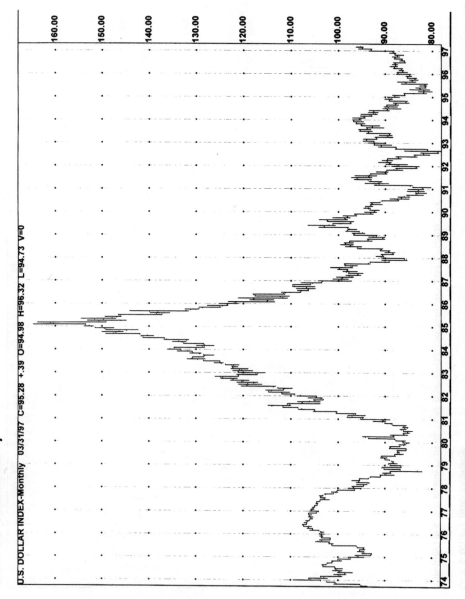

U.S. Dollar Index Weekly

U.S. DOLLAR INDEX-Weekly 03/21/97 C=95.28 -.30 O=95.67 H=95.82 L=94.73 V=0

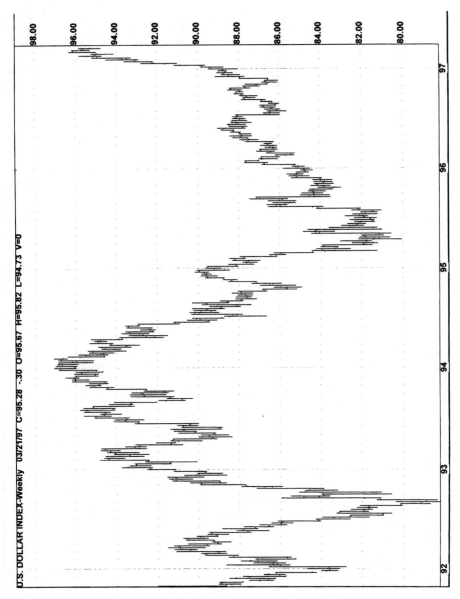

British Pound-Mark Cross Weekly

Spread (x/y) 2.7583

2.9000
2.8000
2.7000
2.6000
2.5000
2.4000
2.3000
2.2000

92 93 94 95 96 97

British Pound-Mark Cross Monthly

Spread (x/y) 2.76

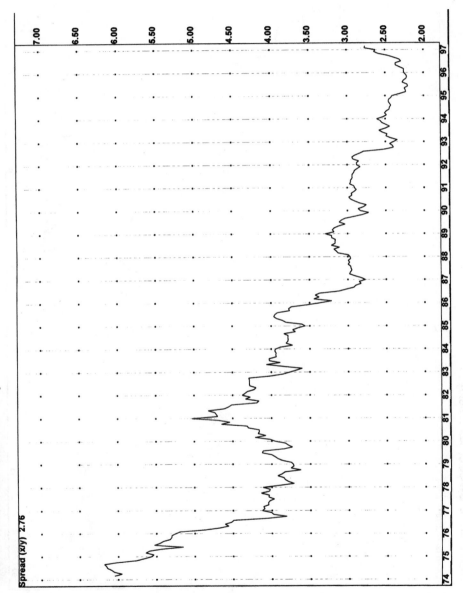

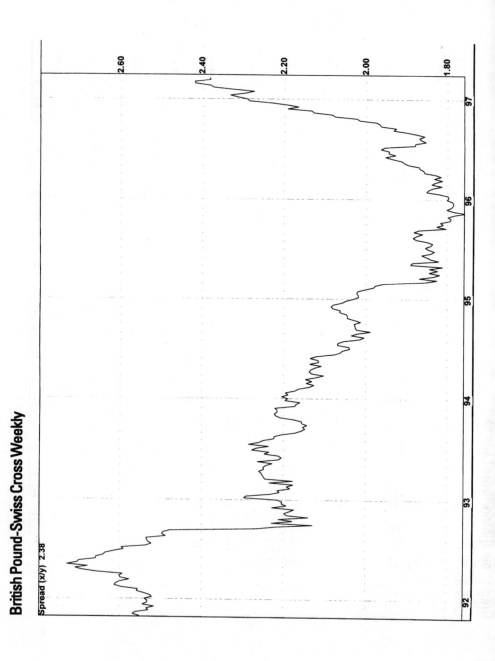

British Pound-Swiss Cross Weekly

Spread (x/y) 2.38

British Pound-Swiss Cross Monthly

Spread (x/y) 2.38

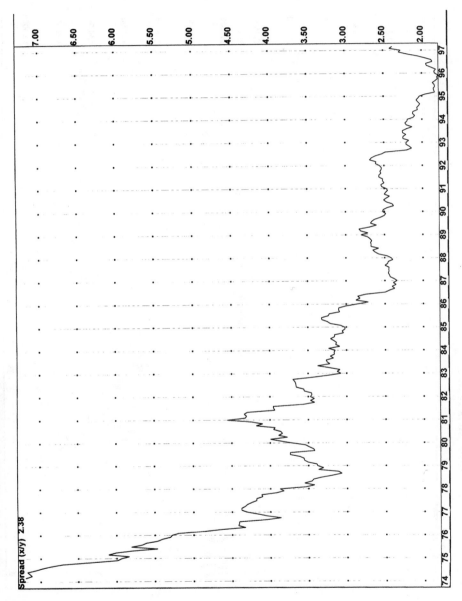

British Pound-Canadian Cross Weekly

Spread (x/y) 2.2544

2.4000
2.3500
2.3000
2.2500
2.2000
2.1500
2.1000
2.0500
2.0000
1.9500
1.9000
1.8500
1.8000

92 93 94 95 96 97

British Pound-Canadian Cross Monthly

Spread (x/y) 2.25

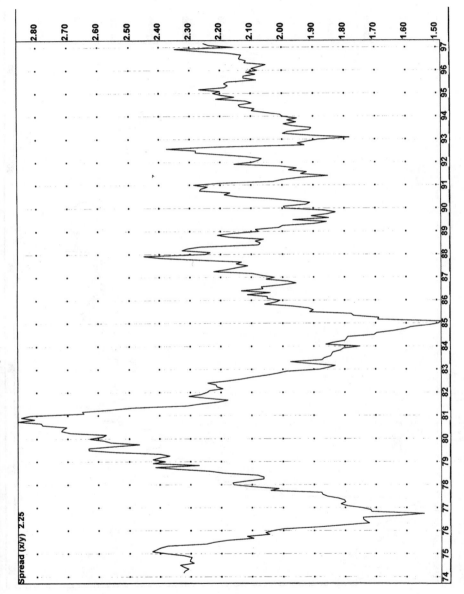

British Pound-Yen Cross Weekly

Spread (x/y) 200.59

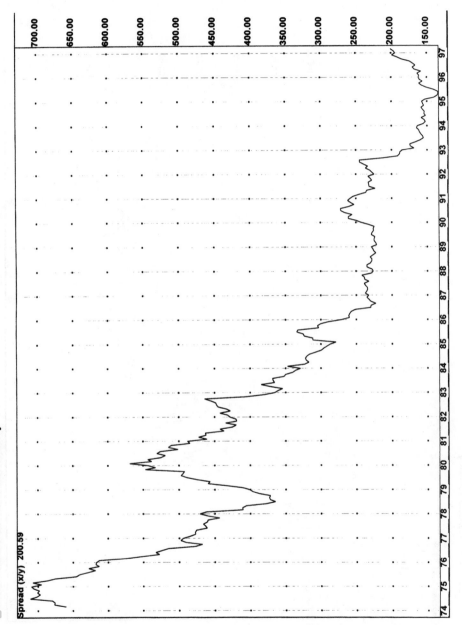

Spread (X/Y) 200.59

British Pound-Yen Cross Money

167

Canadian-Yen Cross Weekly

Spread (x/y) 88.98

Canadian Hen Cross Monthly

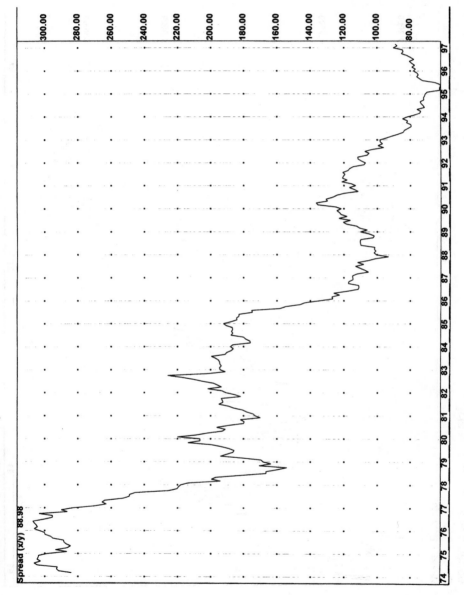

Canadian-Swiss Cross Weekly

Spread (x/y) 1.0570

Canadian-Swiss Cross Monthly

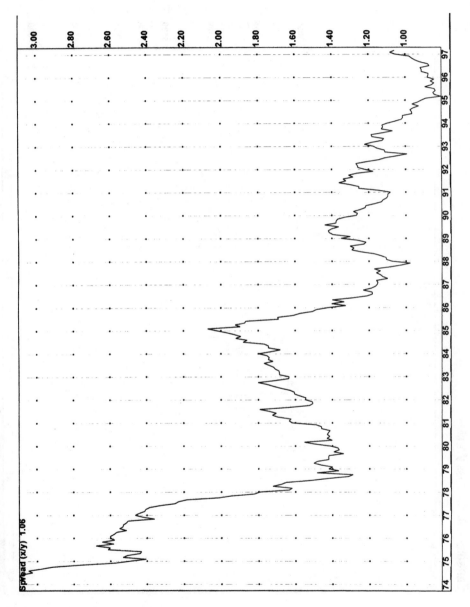

Spread (x/y) 1.06

Canadian-Mark Cross Weekly

Spread (x/y) 1.2235

172

Canadian-Mark Cross Monthly

Spread (x/y) 1.22

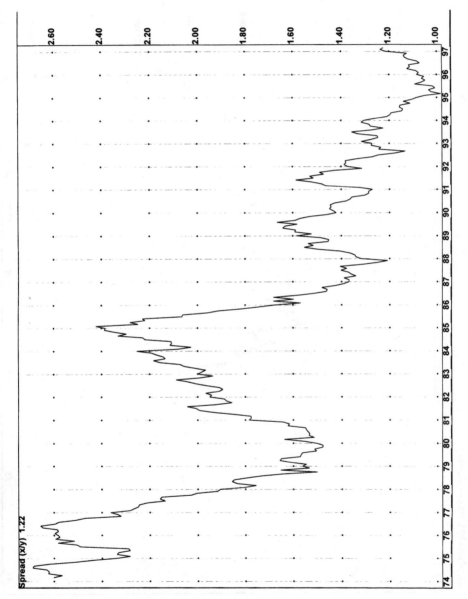

Yen-Swiss Cross Weekly

Spread (x/y) 0.011238

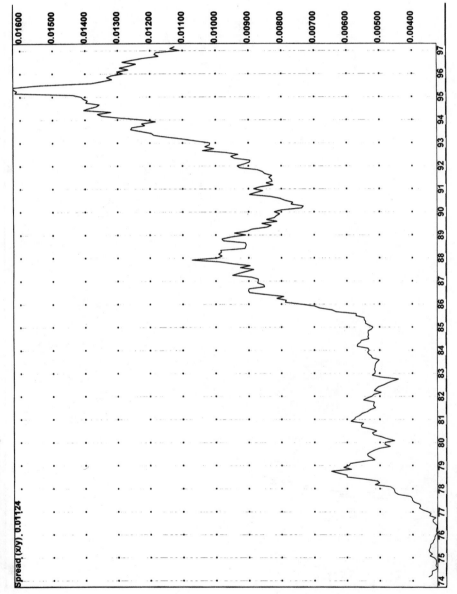

Yen-Swiss Cross Multi

Spread (x/y), 0.01124

0.01600
0.01500
0.01400
0.01300
0.01200
0.01100
0.01000
0.00900
0.00800
0.00700
0.00600
0.00500
0.00400

97 96 95 94 93 92 91 90 89 88 87 86 85 84 83 82 81 80 79 78 77 76 75 74

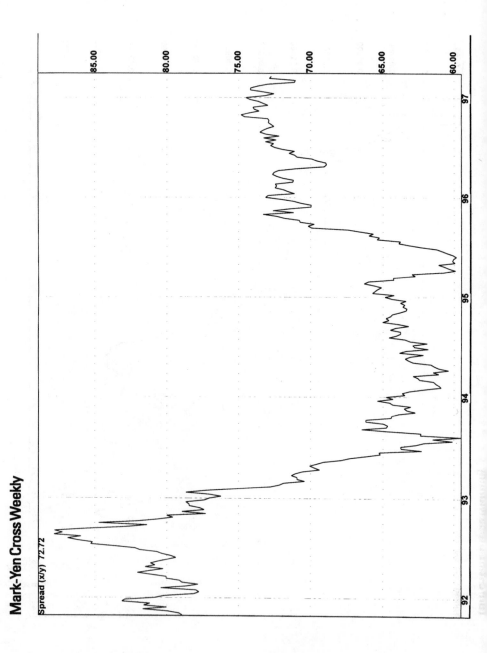

Mark-Yen Cross Weekly

Spread (x/y) 72.72

Mark-Yen Cross Monthly

Spread (x/y) 72.72

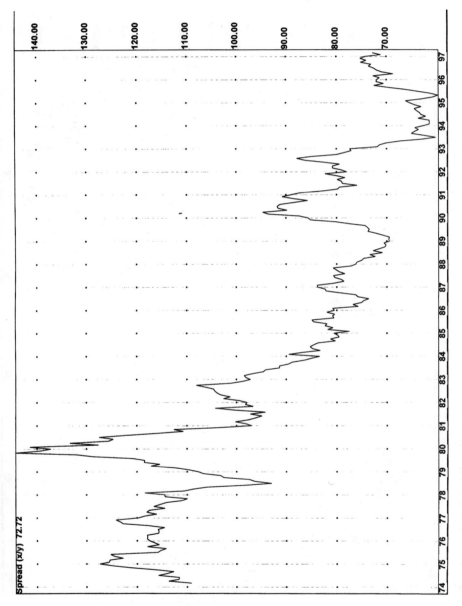

Mark-Swiss Cross Weekly

Spread (x/y) 0.8639

0.9400
0.9300
0.9200
0.9100
0.9000
0.8900
0.8800
0.8700
0.8600
0.8500
0.8400
0.8300
0.8200
0.8100

92   93   94   95   96   97

Spread (X/y) 0.8639

1.1500

1.1000

1.0500

1.0000

0.9500

0.9000

0.8500

0.8000

74 75 76 77 78 79 80 81 82 83 84 85 86 87 88 89 90 91 92 93 94 95 96 97

APPENDIX C

S.W.I.F.T. Currency Codes*

Code	Currency	Country
ADP	Andorran Peseta	Andorra
AED	UAE Dirham	United Arab Emirates
AFA	Afghani	Afghanistan
ALL	Lek	Albania
ANG	Netherlands Antillian Guilder	Netherlands Antilles
AOK	Kwanza Angola	Angola
ARA	Austral	Argentina
ATS	Schilling	Austria
AUD	Australian Dollar	Australia
		Christmas Island
		Cocos (Keeling) Islands
		Heard and Mcdonald Islands
		Kiribati
		Nauru
		Norfolk Island
		Tuvalu
AWG	Aruban Florin	Aruba
BBD	Barbados Dollar	Barbados
BDT	Taka	Bangladesh
BEF	Common Belgian Franc	Belgium
BEC	Convertible Belgian Franc	Luxembourg
BGL	Leva	Bulgaria

*Society for Worldwide Interbank Financial Telecommunication (S.W.I.F.T.).

BHD	Bahraini Dinar	Bahrain
BIF	Burundi Franc	Burundi
BMD	Bermudan Dollar	Bermuda
BND	Brunei Dollar	Brunei
BOB	Boliviano	Bolivia
BRC	Cruzeiro	Brazil
BSD	Bahamian Dollar	Bahamas
BTN	Ngultrum	Bhutan
BUK	Kyat	Burma
BWP	Pula	Botswana
BZD	Belize Dollar	Belize
CAD	Canadian Dollar	Canada
CHF	Swiss Franc	Liechtenstein
		Switzerland
CLF	Unidades de formento	Chile
CLP	Chilean Peso	Chile
CNY	Yuan Renminbi	China, People's Republic of
COP	Colombian Peso	Colombia
CRC	Costa Rican Colon	Costa Rica
CSK	Koruna	Czechoslovakia
CUP	Cuban Peso	Cuba
CVE	Cape Verde Escudo	Cape Verde
CYP	Cyprus Pound	Cyprus
DEM	Deutsche Mark	Germany, Federal Republic of
DJF	Djibouti Franc	Djibouti
DKK	Danish Kroner	Denmark
		Faeroe Islands
		Greenland
DOP	Dominican Peso	Dominican Republic
DZD	Algerian Dinar	Algeria
ECS	Sucre	Ecuador
EGP	Egyptian Pound	Egypt
ESP	Spanish Peseta	Spain
ESB	Convertible Peseta	Spain
ETB	Ethiopian Birr	Ethiopia
FIM	Markka	Finland
FJD	Fiji Dollar	Fiji
FKP	Falkland Islands Pound	Falkland Islands
FRF	French Franc	France
		French Guiana

		French Southern Territories
		Guadeloupe
		Martinique
		Monaco
		Reunion
		St. Pierre and Miquelon
GBP	Pound Sterling	United Kingdom
		Guernsey
		Channel Islands
		Isle of Man
		Jersey
GHC	Cedi	Ghana
GIP	Gibraltar Pound	Gibraltar
GMD	Dalasi	Gambia
GNF	Guinea Franc	Guinea
GRD	Drachma	Greece
GTQ	Quetzal	Guatemala
GWP	Guinea-Bissau Peso	Guinea-Bissau
GYD	Guyan Dollar	Guyana
HKD	Hong Kong Dollar	Hong Kong
HNL	Lempira	Honduras
HTG	Gourde	Haiti
HUF	Forint	Hungary
IDR	Rupiah	Indonesia
IEP	Irish Pound	Ireland
ILS	Israeli Shekel	Israel
INR	Indian Rupee	India
IQD	Iraqi Dinar	Iraq
IRR	Iranian Rial	Iran
ISK	Iceland Krona	Iceland
ITL	Lira	Italy
		San Marino
		Vatican City State
JMD	Jamaican Dollar	Jamaica
JOD	Jordanian Dinar	Jordan
JPY	Yen	Japan
KES	Kenyan Shilling	Kenya
KHR	Riel	Kampuchea, Democratic
KMF	Comoros Franc	Comoros

KPW	North Korean Won	Korea, Democratic People's Republic of
KRW	Won	Korea, Republic of
KWD	Kuwaiti Dinar	Kuwait
KYD	Cayman Islands Dollar	Cayman Islands
LAK	Kip	Lao People's Democratic Republic
LBP	Lebanese Pound	Lebanon
LKR	Sri Lanka Rupee	Sri Lanka
LRD	Liberian Dollar	Liberia
LSL	Loti	Lesotho
LUF	Luxembourg Franc	Luxembourg
LYD	Libyan Dinar	Libyan Arab Jamahiriya
MAD	Moroccan Dirham	Morocco
		Western Sahara
MGF	Malagasy Franc	Madagascar
MNT	Tugrik	Mongolia
MOP	Pataca	Macau
MRO	Ouguiya	Mauritania
		Western Sahara
MTL	Maltese Lira	Malta
MUR	Mauritius Rupee	British Indian Ocean Territory
		Mauritius
MVR	Rufiyaa	Maldives
MWK	Malawi Kwacha	Malawi
MXP	Mexican Peso	Mexico
MYR	Malaysian Ringgit	Malaysia
MZM	Metical	Mozambique
NGN	Naira	Nigeria
NIC	Cordoba	Nicaragua
NLG	Netherlands Guilder	Netherlands
NOK	Norwegian Krone	Bouvet Island
		Norway
		Svalbard and Jan Mayen Islands
NPR	Nepalese Rupee	Nepal
NZD	New Zealand Dollar	Cook Islands
		Niue Islands
		New Zealand

		Pitcairn Islands
		Tokelau
OMR	Rial Omani	Oman
PAB	Balboa	Panama
PEI	Inti	Peru
PGK	Kina	Papua New Guinea
PHP	Philippine Peso	Philippines
PKR	Pakistan Rupee	Pakistan
PLZ	Zloty	Poland
PTE	Portuguese Escudo	Portugal
PYG	Guarani	Paraguay
QAR	Quatri Rial	Qatar
ROL	Leu	Romania
RWF	Rwanda Franc	Rwanda
SAR	Saudi Ryal	Saudi Arabia
SBD	Solomon Islands Dollar	Solomon Islands
SCR	Seychelles Rupee	Seychelles
SDP	Sudanese Pound	Sudan
SEK	Swedish Krona	Sweden
SGD	Singapore Dollar	Singapore
SHP	St. Helena Pound	St. Helena
SLL	Leone	Sierra Leone
SOS	Somali Shilling	Somalia
SRG	Surinam Guilder	Surinam
STD	Dobra	São Tomé and Principe
SUR	Rouble	Byelorussian SSR
		Ukrainian SSR
		Russia
SVC	El Salvado Colon	El Salvador
SYP	Syrian Pound	Syrian Arab Republic
SZL	Lilangeni	Swaziland
THB	Baht	Thailand
TND	Tunisian Dinar	Tunisia
TOP	Pa'anga	Tonga
TPE	Timor Escudo	East Timor
TRL	Turkish Lira	Turkey
TTD	Trinidad and Tobago Dollar	Trinidad and Tobago
TWD	New Taiwan Dollar	Taiwan, Province of
TZS	Tanzanian Shilling	Tanzania, United Republic of

UGX	Uganda Shilling	Uganda
USD	U.S. Dollar Common	
USN	U.S. Dollar next day funds	United States
USD	U.S. Dollar	American Samoa
		British Virgin Islands
		British Indian Ocean Territory
		Guam
		Haiti
		Johnston Island
		Midway Islands
		Pacific Islands (Trust Territory)
		Panama
		Panama Canal Zone
		Puerto Rico
		Turks and Caicos Islands
		United States Miscellaneous
		Pacific Islands
		United States Virgin Islands
		Wake Island
UYP	Uruguayan Peso	Uruguay
VEB	Bolivar	Venezuela
YND	Dong	Vietnam
VUV	Vatu	Vanuatu
WST	Tala	Samoa
XAF	CFA Franc BEAC	Cameroon
		Central African Republic
		Chad
		Congo
		Equatorial Guinea
		Gabon
XCD	East Caribbean Dollar	Anguilla
		Antigua and Barbuda
		Dominica
		Grenada
		Montserrat
		St. Kitts-Nevis
		St. Lucia
		St. Vincent and the Grenadines
		European Union

XBA	European Composite Unit	European Union
XBB	European Monetary Unit	European Union
XBD	European Unit of Acc-17	European Union
XBC	European Unit of Acc-9	European Union
XDR	SDR IMF International Monetary Fund	
XEU	European Currency Unit (ECU)	
XOF	CFA Franc BCEAO	Benin
		Burkino Faso
		Ivory Coast
		Mali
		Niger
		Senegal
		Togo
XFU	UCI-Franc	
XPF	CFP Franc	French Polynesia
		New Caledonia
		Wallis and Futuna Islands
YER	Yemeni Rial	Yemen, Republic of
YDD	Yemeni Dinar	Yemen, Democratic
YUN	Yugoslavia Dinar	Yugoslavia
ZAL	Financial Rand	South Africa
ZAR	Rand	Lesotho
		Namibia
		South Africa
ZMK	Zambian Kwacha	Zambia
ZRZ	Zaire	Zaire
ZWD	Zimbabwe Dollar	Zimbabwe

Noncurrency S.W.I.F.T. Codes

Code	Noncurrency
XAU	Gold
XFO	Gold-Franc
XPT	Platinum
XAG	Silver
XXX	Transactions without currency

GLOSSARY

ABA: The American Bankers Association.

Abandon: Failure to exercise or offset an option before its expiration.

ABI: The Associazione Bancaria Italiana, the Italian Banking Association.

Absolute advantage, theory of: The theory that trade between nations occurs when one nation is absolutely more productive than other nations in the production of a good. Nations should export those goods for which they possess an absolute advantage and import goods for which other nations possess an absolute advantage.

Absolute rate: A quote made which is given as an absolute rate rather than in reference to a funding base such as LIBOR, U.S. treasury rates, etc. For example, rather than T-bill rate + 0.25%, the bid is expressed as 5.75% (if T-bill = 5.50%).

Acceptance bank: The financial institution with a draft drawn on it accepted by that same financial institution.

Accommodating transaction: Transaction undertaken by a central bank solely to accommodate autonomous transactions; also called compensatory transaction.

Accommodation: When the financial institution agrees to lend money or provide other special consideration to a customer, even though the customer may not be qualified to receive special treatment.

Account: The bookkeeping record of a customer's transaction and credit (or debit) balances. This record usually includes confirmation of transactions, listing of holdings and/or open positions, cash and/or cash equivalents, and beginning and ending liquidating value.

Account audit trail: A record of transactions against a specific account or list of accounts.

Account balance: The amount of money or debt in an account.

Account blocking: Occurs when a certain amount of an account is reserved for a specified period. During the blockage, the blocked amount of the account cannot be touched by the account holder. An account can be totally or partially blocked.

Account deactivation: Action of preventing any movement or action in an account.

Account executive: The broker or clerk who is assigned to work with a customer and his or her account on behalf of a financial institution.

Account fee condition: A fee condition (amount, percentage, charging date, etc.) which applies to a particular account.

Account identification: (1) A series of characters (alpha and/or numeric) used to identify a customer account or relationship. (2) The remitting financial institution's account serviced by the receiving bank. (3) The identification assigned by a financial institution, often called the account number.

Account information: Refers to all data that can be recorded in a database about an account, e.g., address, financial information.

Account number: See *Account identification.*

Account officer: A financial institution staff member who looks after one or more client account relationships.

Account position: The balance and current holdings of an account.

Account reactivation: Action of reinstating an account to its normal condition after a blocking or deactivation operation.

Account status: The status of an account often affects what and how many transactions can be performed on that account. For example, an account that is undermargined (insufficient funds) will not be allowed to add positions to the account.

Accounting: (1) An information system conveying data in financial terms, about a specific entity, that can be made reasonably precise. (2) The method of recording all transactions affecting the financial condition of a given business.

Accounts payable: Money a company owes for merchandise or services bought for delayed payment.

Accounts receivable: Money owed to a company for merchandise or services bought on credit.

Accrual (accounting):   A method of reporting income when earned and expenses when incurred, as opposed to reporting income when received and expenses when paid.

Accrued fee: A cumulative fee to be paid to or received from an account holder, but not yet due. A fee that has been earned even though the related transaction is yet incomplete.

Accrued interest: (1) The interest that has been earned, but not yet been paid. (2) Interest due but not yet paid or received as from the last interest settlement date. In the securities market, for instance, the bond buyer pays the seller the agreed price of the bond plus interest accrued since the last interest payment date up to and including the value date. The same calculations are also used in swap product transactions. (3) The interest that has accumulated since the last interest payment up to, but not including, the settlement date and that is added to the contract price of a bond transaction.

Actuals: The physical (cash) commodity or financial instrument rather than a futures or derivative contract for that commodity or financial instrument.

Adjustable peg: A provision of the Bretton Woods system by which a country had a limited right to adjust the value of its currency in terms of gold.

Administrative Law Judge (ALJ):   A CFTC official authorized to conduct a proceedings and render a decision in formal complaint procedures.

Administrative services: A department of a financial institution that carries out tasks which deal with administrative affairs of the customers, e.g., account opening, and approval, etc.

Advice of execution: A report to the executing party to give brief and early information about a transaction.

Advice: (1) The affirmation that an action has taken place. (2) A market recommendation.

Advised letter of credit: Letter of credit in which the seller's bank advises the seller about the creditworthiness of the bank issuing the letter of credit.

AFB: The French Bankers Association.

Affiliate: Two companies are affiliated when one owns less than a majority stake of the other, or when both are subsidiaries of a third company. Or, in general terms, any association between two companies that is short of a parent-subsidiary tie.

Affiliated bank: Partly owned, separately incorporated foreign banking operation of a domestic bank.

Aggregate: A total amount.

Aggregation: The policy under which all futures positions owned or controlled by one trader or a group of traders are combined to determine reporting status and speculative limit compliance (CFTC regulation).

Aggressive investment strategy: Portfolio allocation and management aimed at achieving maximum return. Aggressive investors place a high percentage of their investable assets in equity securities and a far lower percentage in safer debt securities and cash equivalents and pursue aggressive policies including trading on margin, arbitrage, and options.

Algorithm: (1) A specified mathematical process for computation. (2) A sequence of steps to be followed to perform a task. Often used when talking about computer programming.

All-in cost: The total cost of a financial transaction including interest cost, periodic charges, and all front-end compensation expressed as a per cent per annum figure.

Amendment date: The date on which an amendment or change was made.

Amendment: A request to change something. Also referred to as an amendment request or an update request.

American depository receipt (ADR): A negotiable certificate (receipt) representing a given number of shares of stock in a foreign corporation; it is bought and sold in the American securities markets, just as stock is traded. Also known as American depository share.

American Stock Exchange (AMEX): A stock exchange; a private, not-for-profit corporation, located in New York City. The third most-active market in the United States. The exchange was founded in 1842. Also called AMEX and the curb exchange.

American-style option: An option that may be exercised at any time prior to expiration.

Amortization: (1) The paying off of debt in regular installments over a period of time. (2) The ratable deduction of capitalized expenditures over a specified period of time. (3) The cost of the asset amortized when this period is over. (4)The accounting procedure that companies use to write off intangible rights or assets—such as goodwill, patents, or copyrights—over the period of their existence.

Amount of credits: The sum amount of all credit transactions, exclusive of any fees.

Amount of debits: The sum amount of all debit transactions, exclusive of any fees.

Amount: The value in units of currency.

Annual effective yield: The actual annual return on an account after interest is compounded.

Annual percentage rate (APR): The interest rate borrowers pay on a loan. A loan's up-front fees are usually factored into the APR.

Appreciate: The increase in an asset's value. A gradual increase in the value of currency, usually occurring over a period as the result of market forces of supply and demand in a system of floating exchange rates. When the value of currency is substantially changed in one moment, this is called revaluation and is due to government intervention in a fixed exchange rate currency.

Arbitrage pricing theory: A theory that if an investor earns a higher-than-normal return, it is because he or she is accepting a higher-than-normal risk.

Arbitrage: A classic trading strategy used to profit from different prices for the same security, commodity, or financial instrument in different markets. Market forces will normally ensure that these arbitrage differences are short-lived. The simultaneous purchase of one commodity against the sale of another in order to profit from distortions from usual price relationships.

Arbitration: Dispute resolution technique in which both parties agree to submit their cases to a private individual or body for resolution. A forum for the fair and impartial settlement of disputes. NFA's arbitration program provides a forum for resolving futures-related disputes.

Article 65:   The Japanese Securities and Exchange regulation, modeled on the Glass-Steagall Act in the United States. Article 65 separates merchant/investment banking from commercial banking. It does not permit a financial institution to engage in both types of banking.

Ask: An indication by a trader or a dealer of a willingness to sell a security, a futures, or other financial instrument. The price at which an investor can buy. Same as offer. See also *bid*; *quotation.*

Asked: The price that someone is willing to accept for a security, futures, or other financial instrument. The ask portion of a quote is the lowest price anyone is willing to accept at that time.

Asked Price: The price at which sellers offer securities, futures, or other financial instrument to buyers. Also called *offer price.*

Asset: Anything owned by an individual, a business, or a financial institution which has commercial or exchange value. Assets may consist of property or claims against others, in contrast to obligations or liabilities due to others. Assets may be tangible or intangible, short-term (current), or long-term (noncurrent).

Assets and liabilities: The basic classification of financial items in the financial institution's balance sheet.

Assigned arrangements: Management arrangement in which one partner in a strategic alliance assumes primary responsibility for the operations of the alliance.

Associated person (AP):   An individual who solicits orders, customers, or customer funds on behalf of a futures commission merchant, an introducing broker, a commodity trading advisor, or a commodity pool operator and who is registered with the Commodity Futures Trading Commission (CFTC) via the National Futures Association (NFA).

At or better: (1) In a buy order for securities, futures, or other financial instruments, purchasing at the specified price or under it. (2) For a sell order, selling at the specified price or above it. See also *Limit order.*

At the market: See *Market order.*

At-the-money: An option with a strike price equal to the current price of the instrument, such as a stock, upon which the option was granted.

At-the-opening order: An order that specifies it is to be executed at the opening of the market or of trading or else it is to be canceled. The order does not have to be executed at the opening price, but within the opening range of prices.

Auction market: A market in which buyers enter competitive bids and sellers enter competitive offers simultaneously.

Audit: The action of checking that the corporation, individual, partnership, or other institution is following the correct procedures as required by the regulatory authorities and by the firm's own procedures.

Authentication: Checking a request (e.g., to execute a financial transaction) to ensure that it is bona fide.

Authorization: (1) The approval of a financial transaction or a change. (2) The power of attorney.

Autonomous transaction: Transaction conducted for the economic self-interest of a market participant.

Available balance: The balance at the disposal of the account owner at the close of the statement period. The cleared balance of an account.

Available funds: Funds available for transfer or withdrawal in cash.

Average balance: The average of the daily balances over a period of time (such as a month or quarter).

Award: See *Reparations award.*

B/S: An abbreviation for *balance sheet.*

Back office: Departments in a financial institution in which the majority of the work is accounting, balancing, clearing, and bookkeeping, not directly dealing with clients.

Balance: The amount in an account. Usually includes cash, open trade equity , and securities on deposit. See also *Available balance* and *Average balance.*

Balanced investment strategy: Portfolio allocation and management aimed at balancing risk and return; a balanced portfolio may combine stocks, bonds, mutual funds, and cash equivalents.

Balance of payments (BOP): An international accounting record of all transactions made by one particular country with others during a certain time period. The difference between receipts and payments is directly reflected in the foreign exchange reserves held by the country. A negative balance of payments will result in a reduction in the country's foreign currency reserves, unless the country borrows additional foreign currency on the international markets.

Balance of trade: The difference between a country's imports and exports during a specific time period. The largest component of a country's balance of payments; it concerns the export and import of merchandise (not services).

Balance on merchandise trade: Difference between a country's merchandise exports and imports.

Balance on services trade: Difference between a country's service exports and imports.

Balance sheet: A report of a firm's financial condition at a specific time.

Balance sheet equation: A formula stating that a corporation's assets equal the sum of its liabilities plus shareholders' equity.

Balance sheet hedge: Technique for eliminating translation (exchange rate) exposure when a firm matches its assets and liabilities denominated in a given currency on a consolidated basis.

Bank: A financial institution authorized or chartered by its national regulatory authority to be designated as a bank. This term can include credit institutions, mortgage institutions, foreign central banks, and multilateral development banks.

Bank identifier code: A code used to identify financial institutions in order to facilitate automated processing of telecommunication messages in banking and related financial transaction environments. In the United States, the ABA number.

Bank rate: The minimum rate at which a bank, either alone or in conjunction with other banks in a market, lends money to other banks.

Bank-to-bank information: Any instructions or additional information for the receiving, "account with," intermediary, or beneficiary bank.

Bank to bank transfer: A transfer between banks affecting accounts held by banks, not accounts held by banks on behalf of customers.

Banker's acceptance: Draft that has been endorsed by a bank, signifying the bank's promise to guarantee payment at a designated time. A form of financing sometimes used in import/export transactions.

Banking transaction: A transaction that involves money.

Bank wire: A private telecommunication/settlement service for banks in the United States.

Barter: Form of countertrade involving exchange of goods or services between two parties without involving monetary payment.

Base currency: Currency in which general ledger and P/L accounts are maintained.

Base rate: The lowest or starting-point interest rate from which other rates are made. A standard interest rate serving as a basis for interest calculation, e.g., LIBOR.

Basis: (1) The difference between two interest rates or prices of two financial instruments. The difference between the cash price of the underlying financial instrument and the price for the related financial futures contract. (2) The difference between the cash or spot price and the price of the nearby futures contract.

Basis point: One one-hundredth of 1 percent (i.e., 0.01%), used to express interest rate and bond yield differentials. The smallest measure used in quoting yields on bonds and notes.

Basis risk: The risk of a movement between two different interest rate profiles, for example, prime lending rate and U.S. Treasury rates.

Bear market (bear/bearish): A market in which prices are declining. A period of generally failing prices and pessimistic attitudes. A trader who believes prices will move lower is called a "bear."

Beta: A measure of an investment's volatility. The lower the beta, the less risky the investment.

Beta coefficient: A means of measuring the volatility of an individual market (security, futures, financial instrument) in comparison with the market as a whole. A beta of 1 indicates that the individual market's price will move with the overall market.

Bid: An indication by a trader of a willingness to buy a security. The price at which an investor can sell.

Bid-offer spread: The difference between the bid price and the offer price.

Bills of exchange: A common term for bank bills, trade bills, note issuance facilities (NIFs), and promissory notes.

Black-Scholes model: A widely used option pricing equation developed in 1973 by Fischer Black and Myron Scholes. Used to evaluate OTC options, option portfolios, or option trading on exchanges.

Board of trade: Any exchange or association of persons who are engaged in the business of buying or selling any commodity or receiving the same for sale on consignment. It usually means an exchange where commodity futures and/or options are traded. Sometimes referred to as *Contract Market* or *Exchange.*

Bollinger bands: A method used by technical analysts. Bollinger bands are fixed lines above and below a market's average price. As volatility increases, the bands widen.

Bond: A debt instrument that pays a set amount of interest on a regular basis. The issuer promises to repay the debt on time and in full.

Bond yield: The rate of return on a bond, calculated by using the purchase price and the coupon rate.

Bonus: A premium over normal.

Book balance: The total sum of all balances and transactions of an account, regardless of other characteristics (such as the funds not yet being cleared).

Book transfer: A transfer between two accounts both serviced by the financial institution executing the transaction.

Book value: (1) The value, in terms of the currency and the amount per security, future, or other financial instrument. (2) The value of a financial instrument as shown by the accounting records. It is often not the same as how the instrument is valued by the market.

Booked: A transaction is said to have been booked when the transaction-handling program has processed the transaction; i.e., the funds may not yet be available, but the system has posted it on the book date and marked it as having, for example, a value date of two days in the future.

Booking date: The date the payment is to be booked and executed. The date the payment will be passed to the automated system to book.

Bookings: A collection of records of financial transactions processed by automated systems. Bookings are also called postings.

Bookkeeping: The process of keeping financial records. The process of analyzing and recording transactions in the accounts of an automated system.

Bottom fishing: Buying stocks whose prices appear to have bottomed out or fallen to low levels.

Bottom line: Accounting term for the net profit or loss.

Branch bank: Overseas banking operation of a home country bank that is not separately incorporated.

Break: A rapid and sharp price decline.

Break-even point: (1) The point at which gains equal losses. (2) The price a market must reach for an option buyer to avoid a loss if he or she exercises. For a call, it is the strike price plus the premium paid. For a put, it is the strike price minus the premium paid.

Broad tape: The term commonly applied to news wires carrying price and background information on securities and commodities markets. This contrasts to the exchanges' own price transmission wires, which use a narrow ticker tape.

Broker: An individual or firm that charges a fee or commission for executing buy and sell orders placed by another individual or firm; a floor broker in commodities futures trading, a person who actually executes orders on the trading floor of an exchange; an account executive (associated person) who deals with customers and their orders in commissionhouse offices.

Broker: An individual or firm who introduces the two parties in a transaction to each other. The transaction can, for example, be between two parties wanting currencies or two swap counterparties with specific interest rate or currency requirements. A firm that is a broker is referred to as a brokerage firm or house.

Brokerage fee: A fee charged by a broker for the execution of a transaction. An amount charged per transaction, or a percentage of the total value of the transaction.

Broker-dealer (BD): A person or firm in the business of buying and selling securities. A firm may act as both broker (agent) or dealer (principal), but not in the same transaction. In the United States, broker-dealers must register with the SEC and any state in which they do business.

Bucket (bucketing): Illegal practice of accepting orders to buy or sell without executing such orders on an official board of trade; the illegal use of the customer's funds without disclosing the fact of such use.

Budget: A plan of future income and expenses during a specified period.

Bull market (bull/bullish): A market in which prices are rising. A trader who believes prices will move higher is called a "bull." A news item is considered bullish if it is expected to bring on higher prices.

Bundesbank: Germany's central bank.

Bureaucratic law: Legal system based on interpretations, actions, and decisions of government employees.

Buyin: A purchase to offset, cover, or close a short position.

Buy on close: Buying securities, futures, or other financial instruments at the end of a trading session at a price within the closing range.

Buy on opening: Buying securities, futures, or other financial instruments at the beginning of a trading session at a price within the opening range.

Buy stop order: An order to buy a market that is entered at a price above the current offering price and that is triggered when the market price touches or goes through the buy stop price.

Buying hedge (or long hedge): Buying futures contracts (or other financial instruments) to protect against possible increased cost of inputs slated for futures uses. See *Hedging.*

Call: See *Call option.*

Call option: Publicly traded contract granting the owner the right, but not the obligation, to buy a specific amount of foreign currency or other financial instrument at a specified price at a stated future date. The buyer of a call option acquires the right but not the obligation to purchase a particular market at a stated price on or before a particular date.

Call option position delta's: The sum of the delta amounts of call options bought and written for each currency.

Cap: An investment product that compensates the holder when interest rates rise above a certain level.

Capital: Accumulated money, resources, or goods available for use in producing more money, resources, or goods.

Capital account: Balance of payments account that records capital transactions between residents of one country and those of other countries.

Capital and reserves: Contributed capital (capital stock and other paid-in surplus) and retained earnings (profit and loss previous years).

Capital appreciation: A rise in the market price of an asset.

Capital asset: All tangible property, including securities, real estate, and other property, held for the long term.

Capital gain: The difference between the purchase price and the sale price of an asset when the asset was sold for more than it was bought.

Capital loss: The difference between the purchase price and the sale price of an asset when the asset was sold for less than it was bought.

Capital market: The market for the purchase and sale of medium- and long-term financial instruments, such as equities, commodities, bonds, notes, swaps, and other derivatives.

Capitalization: The sum of a firm's long-term debt, stock, and surpluses. Also referred to as invested capital.

Car(s): A colloquialism for futures contract(s). It came into common use when a railroad car or hopper of corn, wheat, etc., equaled the amount of a commodity in a futures contract. See also *Contract.*

Carrying broker: A member of a commodity exchange, usually a clearinghouse member, through whom other brokers or customers clear all or some trades.

Carrying charges: Costs incurred in warehousing the physical commodity, generally including interest, insurance, and storage.

Carryover: That part of the current supply of a commodity consisting of stocks from previous production/marketing seasons.

Cash: Currency on hand and deposits immediately convertible to cash.

Cash commodity: The actual commodity or financial instrument, as opposed to a futures contract based upon the commodity or instrument. See also *Actuals.*

Cash flow: Cash receipts minus disbursements from a given asset, or group of assets, for a given period.

Cash forward sale: See *Forward contracting.*

Cash market: The underlying commodity, security, currency, or money market in which transactions for the purchase and sale of cash instruments to which futures and derivative contracts relate are carried out.

Cash price: A price quotation obtained or a price actually received in a cash market.

Cash transactions: All kinds of transactions involving the cash market.

CDs: Certificates of deposit.

Central bank: The government bank that coordinates the nation's banks and the flow of payments between different banks. May also be the central regulatory authority in a country for banks.

Central governments: The highest governing and executive bodies of the state.

Centralized cash depository: The entity controlled by a parent firm that coordinates worldwide cash flows of its subsidiaries and pools their cash reserves.

Centrally planned economy (CPE): Economy in which government planners determine price and production levels for individual firms.

Certificated stock: Stocks of a cash market that have been inspected and found to be of a quality deliverable against futures contracts, stored or deposited at the delivery points designated as regular, or acceptable for delivery by the futures exchange.

Change: The difference between the current price and the previous day's close or settlement price.

Charges: Fees associated with financial services.

Charting: The use of graphs and charts in the technical analysis of markets to plot trends of price movements, average movements of price volume, and open interest. See also *Technical analysis*.

Chicago Board of Trade (CBOT or CBT): The oldest futures exchange in the United States; established in 1848. The exchange lists agricultural commodity futures such as corn, oats, and soybeans, in addition to financial instruments, e.g., Treasury bonds and Treasury notes.

Chicago Board Options Exchange (CBOE): An exchange at the Chicago Board of Trade at which to trade stock options. The CBOE has markets in equities, options, and over-the-counter securities.

Chicago Mercantile Exchange (CME): Operates the International Monetary Market (IMM), the Index and Options Market (IOM), and the Growth and Emerging Markets (GEM)..

Churning: Excessive trading of a customer's account by a broker, who has control over the trading decisions for the account, in order to make more commissions while disregarding the best interest of the customer. This violates NASD, CFTC, and NFA rules. In the stock market, it refers to a period of heavy trading activity but few sustained price trends and little overall movement in stock market indexes.

Civil law: Law based upon detailed codification of permissible and nonpermissible activities. The world's most common form of legal system.

Claims: (1) Unsettled amounts which a financial institution is obliged to pay. (2) Legal statement of actions done or not done, e.g., claim of wrongdoing.

Clear: The formal completion of a trade.

Cleared funds: See *Available funds*.

Clearing: The procedure through which trades are checked for accuracy. Once the trades are validated, the clearinghouse or association becomes the buyer to each seller and the seller to each buyer.

Clearing member: A member of a clearinghouse or an association. All trades of a nonclearing member must be registered and eventually settled through a clearing member.

Clearing organization: An organization with which securities may be deposited for safekeeping and through which purchase and sale transactions may be realized. The two main systems in the Eurobond market are Cedel and Euroclear.

Clearing price: See *Settlement price*.

Clearinghouse: An agency connected with exchanges through which all transactions are made, offset, or fulfilled through delivery of the actual cash market and through which financial settlement is made; often, it is a fully chartered separate corporation rather than a division of the exchange proper.

Clearinghouse accounts: Accounting system used to facilitate international countertrade. A firm must balance its overall countertrade transactions but need not balance any single countertrade transaction.

Client: A client, also called party, is a person or a corporate body involved in any transaction with a financial institution.

Close: The period at the end of a trading session during which all transactions are considered to be made at the close.

Closing balance: The balance of entries posted to the account at the close of the statement period.

Closing price: The price at which transactions are made just before the close on a given day. A number of transactions are often made at this time, and they will be included over a range of prices. See also *Closing range.*

Closing range: A range of closely related prices at which transactions took place at the closing of the market; buy and sell orders at the closing might have been filled at any point within such a range.

Coffee, Sugar, and Cocoa Exchange of New York: Also known as the CSCE.

Coincident indicator: A measurable economic factor that varies directly and simultaneously with the business cycle, thus indicating the current state of the economy. See also *Lagging economic indicator* and *Leading economic indicator.*

Collateral decrease: A reduction in the financial worth of a collateral. This is usually due to changes in financial conditions (for example, changed interest rates, stock values, risk ratings).

Collateral increase: An increase in the financial worth of a collateral. This is usually due to changes in financial conditions (for example, changed interest rates, stock values, risk ratings).

Collateral items: Specific items of property that a borrower pledges as security for the repayment of a loan or as margin for an account. The pledger agrees that the pledgee will have the right to sell the collateral for the purpose of liquidating the debt or paying the margin if the pledger defaults under the terms of the pledge agreement.

Comity, principle of: The principle in international law that one country will honor and enforce within its own territory the judgments and decisions of foreign courts.

Commercial bank: A bank owned by shareholders that accepts deposits, makes commercial and industrial loans, and provides other banking services for the public. Commercial banks may not underwrite corporate securities or most municipal bonds. Also called a full-service bank.

Commission: (1) A fee charged by a broker to a customer for performance of a specific duty, such as the buying or selling of futures contracts. Banks charge commissions for issuing letters of credit, accepting drafts drawn under letters of credit, entering foreign exchange transactions for their customers, custodial services, acting as fiscal agent, etc. Fees are paid by banks to others for various services and include fees to foreign exchange brokers for arranging foreign exchange transactions. A commission must be fair and reasonable, considering all the relevant factors of the transaction. (2) Sometimes used to refer to the *Commodity Futures Trading Commission (CFTC).*

Commission broker: A member of an exchange who executes orders for the sale or purchase of financial futures contracts.

Commission merchant (also futures commission merchant, FCM): One who makes a trade, either for another member of the exchange or for a nonmember client, in his or her own name and becomes liable as principal to the other party to the transaction.

Commodity: An entity of trade or commerce, services, or rights in which contracts for future delivery may be traded. Some of the contracts currently traded are wheat, corn, cotton, livestock, copper, gold, silver, oil, propane, plywood, currencies, Treasury bills, Treasury bonds, and stock indexes.

Commodity cartel: Cartel created by producers of a good to control production and prices of that good, e.g., OPEC.

Commodity Exchange Act (CEA): The federal act that provides for federal regulation of futures trading. CEA is administered by the Commodity Futures Trading Commission.

Commodity Exchange of New York (CMX): A division of the New York Mercantile Exchange.

Commodity Futures Trading Commission (CFTC): The federal agency established by the Commodity Futures Trading Commission Act of 1974 to ensure the open and efficient operation of the futures markets. The five futures markets commissioners are appointed by the President (subject to Senate approval).

Commodity pool operator (CPO): An individual or organization which operates or solicits funds for a commodity pool. Generally required to be registered with the Commodity Futures Trading Commission.

Commodity pool: An enterprise in which funds contributed by a number of persons are combined for the purpose of trading futures contracts and/or options on futures. Not the same as a joint account.

Commodity Trading Advisor (CTA): Individual or firm that, for a fee, issues analyses or reports concerning commodities and provides advice to others trading commodity futures, options, or leverage contracts.

Common law: Law that forms the foundation of the legal system in Anglo-American countries; an accumulation of findings of judges in individual cases.

Comparative advantage, theory of: The theory that trade between countries occurs when one country is relatively more productive than others in the production of a good.

Complainant: The individual who files a complaint seeking a reparations award against another individual or firm.

Compliance department: The department within a brokerage firm that oversees the trading and market-making activities of the firm. It ensures that the employees and officers of the firm are abiding by the rules and regulations of the SEC, CFTC, NASD, and NFA exchanges and Designated Supervisory Regulatory Organizations (SROs).

Comptroller of the Currency: A Treasury Department official, appointed by the President and confirmed by the Senate, who is responsible for chartering, examining, supervising, and liquidating national banks.

Confirmation statement: A statement sent by a commission house to a customer when a transaction is made. The statement confirms the number of contracts bought or sold and the prices at which the contracts were bought or sold.

Consolidated financial statement: A financial statement combining the accounting records of a parent corporation and all its subsidiaries into a single set of statements denominated in a single currency.

Consolidation: A technical analysis term. A pause in trading activity in which price moves sideways, setting the stage for the next move. Traders are said to evaluate their positions during periods of consolidation.

Consumer Price Index (CPI):   A measure of price changes in consumer goods and services used to identify periods of inflation or deflation. The index is based on a list of specific goods and services purchased in urban areas. It is released monthly by the Department of Labor.

Consumer products: Goods and services sold for use by individual consumers.

Contingent assets: Assets recorded on a balance sheet as incoming cash flows which will materialize in the future, or whose materialization is uncertain.

Contingent liabilities: Liabilities recorded on a balance sheet as outgoing cash flows which will materialize in the future, or whose materialization is uncertain.

Contract: (1) An agreement between at least two parties to buy or sell, on certain conditions, a certain product, as a result of which a legal status concerning rights and duties of the parties exists. (2) A term of reference describing a unit of trading for a commodity.

Contract amount: The currency and the amount of an agreement.

Contract date: Date on which the contract is agreed between the parties.

Contract grades: Standards or grades of commodities listed in the rules of the exchanges which must be met when delivering cash commodities against futures contracts. Grades are often accompanied by a schedule of discounts and premiums allowable for delivery of commodities of lesser or greater quality than the contract grade.

Contract market: A board of trade designated by the Commodity Futures Trading Commission to trade futures or option contracts on a particular commodity. Commonly used to mean any exchange on which futures are traded. See also *Board of trade* and *Exchange.*

Contract month: The month in which deliveries are to be made in accordance with a futures contract.

Contract type: The details which specify the type of contract entered into by two parties.

Controlled account: See *Discretionary account.*

Controller: The managerial position in an organization given specific responsibility for financial control.

Convertible currencies: The currencies that are freely traded and accepted in international commerce; also referred to as hard currencies.

Corner: To secure control of a market so that its price can be manipulated.

Corporate banking: Banking that involves such tasks as account management, credit services, and trade finance for corporations.

Correction: A technical analysis term. A price reaction against the prevailing trend of the market. Common corrections often amount to 33 percent, 50 percent, or 66 percent of the most recent trend movement. Sometimes referred to as a *Retracement.*

Correspondent banks: Foreign banks that are engaged in an exchange of services and/or have an account or accounts with domestic banks.

Corresponding: Two banks which have opened accounts with each other and use them for financial transactions on behalf of their clients.

Cost(s):   The combination of commissions, taxes, charges, and additional costs that are involved in completing a transaction.

Cost of living: The level of prices of goods and services required for a reasonable standard of living.

Cost of recovery: Administrative costs or expenses incurred in obtaining money due the complainant. Included are costs such as administrative fees, hearing room fees, charge for clerical services, travel expenses to attend the hearing, attorney's fees, and filing costs.

Cost-push inflation: A sustained rise in prices caused by businesses passing on increases in costs to purchasers.

Council of the European Union: The decision-making body of the European Economic Union, composed of 15 members, who represent the interests of their home governments.

Counterparty: The corresponding party to a transaction. Party with whom a contract has been concluded, i.e., client, broker, other branch, other bank, or department.

Counterparty credit risk: The risk the counterparty will fail to meet its obligations under the terms agreed in all contracts, resulting in possible replacement costs. Counterparty credit risk is becoming an important factor in the derivatives markets (such as swaps).

Country code: A code which identifies the country in which a financial institution is located.

Cover: The action of offsetting a futures securities or other financial instrument transaction with an equal and opposite transaction. Short covering is a purchase to offset an earlier sale of an equal number of the same delivery month. Liquidation is a sale to offset the obligation to take delivery.

Covered: An investment strategy in which the seller owns the underlying security.

Covered-interest arbitrage: Arbitrage that exploits geographic differences in interest rates and differences in exchange rates over time.

Credit: (1) A loan to a customer. (2) An entry on the right-hand side of an account ledger. (3) A balance that shows a profit in bookkeeping.

Credit advice: A notification of a credit to the account of the receiver (account owner).

Credit institutions: In finance, this normally means financial institutions that are subject to local government regulations relating to banking (i.e., which are legally required to submit periodical financial reports to the central banking authorities). They are not mortgage institutions, multilateral development banks, and central banks.

Credit limit: (1) The maximum that a customer can borrow. (2) Maximum allowed counterparty credit risk for contracts other than foreign exchange contracts.

Cross hedging: The hedging of a cash instrument on a different, but related, futures or other derivatives market.

Cross rate: An exchange rate between two foreign currencies. Two different currencies compared to the same third currency.

CTR: Currency Transaction Report.

Currency: A medium of exchange that circulates in an economy. Also refers to a country's official unit of exchange. The currency may be represented by a currency code.

Currency code: The ISO code identifying the currency.

Currency future: Publicly traded contract involving the sale or purchase of a standardized amount of foreign currency at a stated price with delivery at a stated future date.

Currency option: Publicly traded contract giving the owner the right, but not the obligation, to sell or buy a standardized amount of foreign currency at a price at a stated future date. See also *Call option; Put option.*

Currency revaluation: The changing of the value of one currency in terms of another by the legal authority (usually a central bank) responsible for that currency.

Currency unit of monetary exchange: The local currency of a country that is the authorized media of circulation and the basis for recordkeeping.

Current account: Balance of payments account that records exports and imports of goods and services, investment income, and gifts.

Current assets: Cash and other assets that are expected to be converted into cash within the next twelve months, such as cash and equivalents, accounts receivable, inventory, and prepaid expenses.

Current delivery (month): The futures contracts which will come to maturity and become deliverable during the current month; also called spot month.

Current rate method: The technique used to consolidate the financial statements of a foreign subsidiary when the subsidiary's functional currency is the subsidiary's home currency.

Current value: The costs of replacement of an asset on the date of valuation, or the proceeds from continued use or sale of the asset on the date of valuation, whichever is the lower.

CUSIP: Committee on Uniform Securities Identification Procedures.

Customer collateral: The collateral guaranteed or pledged by the customer as security for financial transactions.

Customer daily position: A statement produced daily showing the position of a customer's account or group of accounts.

Customer segregated funds: See *Segregated account.*

Customer: A client registered in the files of a financial institution under a unique customer number.

Day order: An order that if not executed expires automatically at the end of the trading session of the day it was entered.

Day traders: Traders who take positions in the market and then liquidate them prior to the close of the trading day.

Deal: This is a bargain made to buy or sell a currency.

Deal amount: The currency and the quantity of the currency purchased/sold multiplied by the deal price.

Deal date: The date on which the deal was made.

Deal price: An ISO term; the currency code and the price or percentage price of the deal.

Dealer: An individual or company that buys and sells financial instruments for its own account and customer accounts.

Dealer option: A put or call on a physical commodity, not originating at or subject to the rules of an exchange, written by a firm which deals in the underlying cash commodity.

Dealing 2000: A foreign exchange system sold by Reuters.

Debit: A sum owed.

Debit balance: Accounting condition in which the trading losses in a customer's account exceed the amount of equity in the customer's account.

Debt: Financial instrument representing money owed, such as bonds, notes, mortgages, and other forms of paper that indicate the intent to repay an amount owed.

Debt financing: Raising money for working capital or for capital expenditures by selling commercial paper, bonds, bills, or notes to individual or institutional investors. In return for the money lent, the individuals or institutions become creditors and receive a promise to repay principal and interest on the debt.

Debt service: The schedule for repayment of interest and principal on an outstanding debt.

Deck: All of the unexecuted orders in a floor broker's possession.

Default: (1) Failure to pay principal or interest on a financial obligation. It can also refer to a breach or nonperformance of the terms of a debt instrument. (2) The failure to perform on a futures contract as required by an exchange.

Deferred delivery: The distant delivery month in which futures or options trading is taking place, as distinguished from the nearby futures delivery month.

Deflation: A decline in the overall price level of goods and services, which results in increased purchasing power of money. The opposite of inflation.

Deliverable grades: See *Contract grades.*

Delivery: The tender and receipt of an actual cash commodity or warehouse receipt or other negotiable instrument covering such market, in settlement of a futures contract or other forward financial transaction.

Delivery date: The date on which a financial instrument is to be/have been delivered/ received.

Delivery month: A calendar month during which a futures or options contract matures and becomes deliverable.

Delivery notice: Notice from the clearinghouse of a seller's intention to deliver the physical commodity against a short futures position; it precedes and is distinct from the warehouse receipt or shipping certificate, which is the instrument of transfer of ownership.

Delivery points: Those locations designated by commodity exchanges at which stocks of a commodity represented by a futures contract may be delivered in fulfillment of the contract.

Delivery price: The official settlement price of the trading session during which the buyer of futures contracts receives, through the clearinghouse, a notice of the seller's intention to deliver and the price at which the buyer must pay for the commodities represented by the futures contract.

Delivery risk: Risk between currency settlement hours outside the country involved and the actual settlement hours in the country of the currency.

Delta: A measure of the relationship between an option price and its underlying futures contract or stock price. Delta measures how rapidly the value of an option moves in relation to the underlying value. It is the change in an option's price divided by the change in the price of the underlying instrument. An option whose price changes by $1 for every $2 change in the price of the underlying instrument has a delta of 0.5.

Delta hedge: The partial offset of the exchange risk of a currency option by an opposite open currency spot position in the same foreign currency.

Demand: A consumer's desire and willingness to pay for a good or service. See also *Supply*.

Demand-pull inflation: An increase in prices that occurs when demand exceeds supply.

Depreciation: A decline in value.

Depression: A severe downturn in an economy that is marked by falling prices, reduced purchasing power, and high unemployment.

Depth of the market: The transaction size that can be dealt with in a market without causing a price change. Shallow (thin) markets usually have wide spreads and substantial price fluctuations during a short period of time. Deep markets tend to have relatively narrow spreads and stable prices.

Derivative: A complex investment whose value is derived from or linked to some underlying financial asset, such as a stock, bond, currency, or mortgage. Derivatives may be listed on exchanges or traded privately over the counter. For example, derivatives may be futures, options, or mortgage-backed securities.

Devaluation: The government's reduction of the value of its currency in relation to the currency of other countries. A devaluation produces a substantial decrease in an exchange rate.

Differential: The difference between two values (such as a bid/offer price) for a currency.

Dip: A slight decline in a market's price followed by a rise.

Direct exchange rate: Price of a foreign currency in terms of the home currency; also called a direct quote.

Direct exporting: Product sales to customers located outside the firm's home country.

Direct quote: See *Direct exchange rate*.

Direct sales: Selling products to final consumers.

Discount: (1) A downward adjustment in price allowed for delivery of stocks of a commodity of lesser than deliverable grade against a futures contract. (2) Sometimes used to refer to the price difference between futures of different delivery months, as in the phrase "July at a discount to May," indicating that the price of the July future is lower than that of the May. (3) In general, the amount by which one market price is less than another.

Discount brokers: Brokers who charge lower commissions than full-service brokers.

Discount rate: The interest rate charged by the Federal Reserve on loans to member banks. This rate influences the rates these financial institutions then charge to their customers.

Discovery: The process which allows one party to obtain information and documents relating to the dispute from the other party(ies) in the dispute.

Discretionary account: An arrangement by which the holder of the account gives written power of attorney to another, often a broker, to make buying and selling decisions without notification to the holder; often referred to as a managed account or controlled account.

Disinflation: A slowdown in the rate of price increases. Disinflation occurs during a recession, when sales drop and retailers are unable to pass higher prices along to consumers.

Distribution: Process of getting a firm's products and services to its customers.

Dividend/interest rate: An ISO term; the amount of income per share/unit expressed in terms of the currency, the amount, and, when necessary, the period for which the income was paid/received.

Dow Jones: A U.S. publishing and information services group; owns and operates the Telerate service.

Dow Jones averages: The most widely quoted and oldest measures of change in stock prices.

Dow Jones Industrial Average: The most commonly watched U.S. securities index.

Economic and Monetary Union (EMU): Organization created by the Maastricht Treaty whose goal is to create a single currency for the EU, thereby eliminating exchange-rate risks and the costs of converting currencies for intra-EU trade.

Economic exposure: Impact on the value of a firm's operations of unanticipated exchange-rate changes.

Economic indicators: Statistics used to analyze business conditions and make forecasts.

Economic union: A form of regional economic integration that combines features of a common market with coordination of economic policies among its members, such as the European Union (EU).

Edge Act corporation: Bank that is located outside its parent bank's home state and provides international banking services.

Elasticity: A characteristic of commodities which describes the interaction of the supply, demand, and price of a commodity. A commodity is said to be elastic in demand when a price change creates an increase or decrease in consumption. The supply of a commodity is said to be elastic when a change in price creates changes in the production of the commodity. Inelasticity of supply or demand exists when either supply or demand is relatively unresponsive to changes in price.

Electronic funds transfer (EFT): Any method of electronically moving money between accounts (between banks).

Electronic trading: The computerized matching of buyers and sellers of financial instruments. GLOBEX, Project A, and Access are examples.

Embargo: A ban on the exporting and/or importing of goods.

Equity: The dollar value of a futures account if all open positions were offset at the current market price. In securities markets, it is the part of a company's net worth that belongs to shareholders.

Euro bonds: Bonds issued by a borrower outside its own country. The bonds are denominated in a currency foreign to the borrower or the purchaser or both.

Euro currency: A deposit in a bank outside the depositor's country of origin. Most deposits are U.S. dollar deposits, although nearly all major Western currencies are represented.

Euro dollars: U.S. dollars deposited in banks outside the borders of the United States.

Euro loans: Loans of dollar-denominated deposits in banks outside the United States, or of other deposits in banks outside the depositor's country of origin.

Euro markets: Euro bond and Euro loan markets.

European Commission: Twenty-person group that acts as the European Union's administrative branch of government and proposes all EU legislation.

European Currency Unit (ECU):   A monetary unit created in 1979 by nine European nations to promote currency stability in the European Union. The European Currency Unit consists of weighted amounts of the national currencies of members of the European Monetary System. The value of the European Currency Unit in relation to other currencies is published daily in newspapers.

European Monetary Institute (EMI):   An organization created by the Maastricht Treaty as a preliminary step in establishing a European Central Bank. It plays an important role in promoting economic and monetary union among EU members.

European Monetary System (EMS):   An exchange rate system established by a 1979 agreement among members of the European Union to manage currency relationships among themselves.

European Union (EU):   An intergovernmental organization of 12 Western European nations created under the Maastricht Treaty of December 1991, having its own institutional structures and decision-making framework. Prior to the Maastricht Treaty, the organization was known as the European Community or the Common Market. Its members are Belgium, Denmark, France, Germany, Greece, Italy, Luxembourg, the Netherlands, Portugal, Spain, and the United Kingdom. Its council of ministers and the European Commission are based in Brussels, Belgium, and its parliament is based in Strasbourg, France.

European-style option: An option that may be exercised only on its expiration date.

Exchange: An association of persons or entities engaged in the business of buying and selling futures and/or options, usually involving an auction process. Also called a *Board of trade* or *Contract market.*

Exchange rate: The price at which one currency can be traded for another currency. The price of one country's currency in terms of another country's currency. (1) Direct quotation: One unit of foreign currency expressed as a number of units of the local currency. (2) Indirect quotation: One unit of the local currency expressed as a number of units of the foreign currency

Exchange rate mechanism (ERM):   An agreement among European Union members to maintain fixed exchange rates among themselves within a narrow band.

Exchange risk: The risk of market fluctuation of an asset or liability denominated in a foreign currency, such as the ownership of a currency (spot or forward) or trade account payable in foreign currency.

Execution: (1) The completion of an order for a transaction. (2) The carrying out of an instruction.

Execution date: The date on which a trader wishes to exercise an option.

Exercise: By exercising an option, the buyer elects to accept the underlying market at the option's strike price.

Exercise date: The date on which the buyer of an option chooses to exercise the buyer's right under the option contract with the seller of the option.

Exercise date and striking price: The last day on which the option can be exercised, as well as the currency and price at which the market can be purchased or sold, on or before that date.

Exercise price: The price at which the buyer of a call (put) option may choose to exercise his or her right to purchase (sell) the underlying futures contract. Also called strike price or strike.

Exotic option: Any of a class of options with unusual underlying assets or terms. For example, rainbow options depend on the amount by which one asset outperforms another.

Expense: Cost incurred.

Expiration date: Generally the last date on which an option may be exercised or a transaction made.

Expiry: Occurs when a condition is no longer valid or applicable.

Exporting: Selling products of one country for use or resale in other countries.

Exposure: A possible loss of value caused by changes in market value, interest rates, or exchange rates.

Face value: The monetary value of a bond printed on its face. Face value and market value usually differ.

FDIC: The Federal Deposit Insurance Corporation. A U.S. body that regulates and insures the U.S. banking system.

Fed: The short name for the U.S. Federal Reserve Banks.

Fed funds: See *Federal funds.*

Federal debt: The total amount the federal government owes because of past deficits.

Federal deficit: The amount of money the federal government owes because it spent more than it received in revenue for the past year.

Federal funds: (1) U.S. dollars on deposit at a Federal Reserve Bank in the United States. (2) Reserves traded between commercial banks in the United States for overnight use. The minimum amount is U.S. $1,000,000.

Federal Open Market Committee (FOMC):   A committee of the Federal Reserve Banks that makes decisions concerning the Fed's operations to control the money supply. The FOMC's chief mechanism is the purchase and sale of government securities, which increases or decreases the money supply. It also sets key interest rates, such as the discount rate and Fed fund rate.

Federal Reserve: The central bank of the United States that sets monetary policy. The Federal Reserve and FOMC oversee money supply, interest rates, and credit with the goal of keeping the U.S. economy and currency stable. Governed by a seven-member board, led by the Federal Reserve Chairman, the Fed includes 12 regional Federal Reserve Banks, 25 branches, and all national and state banks that are part of the system. Also called the *Fed.*

Federal Reserve Banks: The U.S. Federal Reserve Banks.

Federal Reserve Board (FRB):   A seven-member board that directs the operations of the Federal Reserve system. FRB members are appointed by the President, subject to approval by Congress.

Fedwire: An electronic payment service operated by the U.S. Federal Reserve system as a private wire network for transfers between financial institutions having accounts at the Federal Reserve Bank. Also known as Federal Reserve Wire Network.

Fee: Fees are all interests, charges, taxes, or commissions which have to be paid or received for certain transactions or services to or from a customer.

Fee accrual: A way of recognizing that an expense (or revenue) and the related liability (or asset) can increase over time and not as signaled by an specific cash transaction.

Fee base rate: A rate expressed as a percentage.

Feed ratios: The variable relationships of the cost of feeding animals to market weight sales prices, expressed in ratios, such as the hog/corn ratio. These serve as indicators of the profit return or lack of it in feeding animals to market weight.

Fibonacci number (or sequence): The sequence of numbers (0, 1, 2, 3, 5, 8, 13, 21, 34, 55, 89, 144, 233 . . .), used in technical analysis, discovered by the Italian mathematician Leonardo de Pise in the thirteenth century. It is the mathematical basis of the Elliott wave theory: The first two terms of the sequence are 0 and 1, and each successive number is the sum of the previous two numbers.

Fiduciary: A person legally appointed and authorized to hold assets in trust for another person and manage those assets for the benefit of that person.

Fiduciary duty: Responsibility imposed by operation of law which requires a broker to act with special care in the handling of a customer's account.

FIFO: First in, first out.

Financial alliance: A strategic alliance in which two or more firms work together to optimize resources and/or reduce the financial risks associated with a project.

Financial derivative: A financial instrument whose return derives from an underlying bond, stock, commodity, currency, or other asset.

Financial engineer: An individual who designs or develops innovative financial instruments and processes. Someone who formulates creative solutions to financing problems.

Financial engineering: The activities of a financial engineer.

Financial institution: An organization primarily related to providing financial (monetary) services established to offer and perform services specifically. These services can include loans, leases, banking, cashiering, foreign exchange, issuance of guarantees or pledges, brokerage, portfolio management, custody or trust services, and/or credit card services.

Financial instruments: Also known as financial products or simply as instruments; includes bonds, stocks, derivatives, and other financial representations of assets.

Financial risk: The risk of a loss in relation to expectations.

Financial transaction: A transaction which affects or is expected to affect an account balance.

First notice day: First day on which notices of intention to deliver cash commodities against futures contracts can be presented by sellers and received by buyers through the exchange clearinghouse.

Fiscal policy: The federal tax, budget, and spending policies set by Congress or the President. These policies can affect tax rates, interest rates, and government spending.

Fiscal year: The 12-month period that a corporation or government uses for bookkeeping purposes.

Fixed assets: Accounts that contain all nonmonetary assets, the services of which are to be received over a period longer than one accounting period. Can include accumulated depreciation accounts and capital leasing accounts.

Fixed exchange-rate system: The international monetary system in which each government tries to maintain the price of its currency in terms of other currencies.

Fixed rate: A rate agreed beforehand for future interest payments.

Flat yield curve: A chart showing the yields of debt instruments with short maturities as equal to the yields of long-term debt instruments.

Flexible (or floating) exchange-rate system: The system in which currency exchange rates are determined by supply and demand.

Floating rate: An interest rate for a debt instrument that will change as interest rates change.

Floor: (1) The lowest rate to which a financial market is allowed to fall. (2) The trading floor of an exchange.

Floor broker: An individual who executes orders on the trading floor of an exchange for any other person or entity.

Floor traders: Members of an exchange who are personally present, on the trading floors of the exchanges, to make trades for themselves.

Foreign bonds: Bonds issued by entities of one country to an entity of a second country and denominated in the second country's currency.

Foreign central banks: Central banks outside the country of domicile of an entity.

Foreign currency: (1) Any currency other than the local currency. (2) Within the spectrum of flow of payments, foreign currencies are all currencies, with the exception of the currency of the home country.

Foreign currency (exchange):   All currencies other than the base currency.

Foreign exchange: Trading one country's currency for another country's currency. Money instruments used to make payments between countries. Trading derivatives of foreign currencies such as forwards, options, and swaps. Also known as FX or forex.

Foreign exchange book: See *Forex book.*

Foreign exchange closing rates: The foreign currency exchange rates at the close of trading.

Foreign exchange market: Market in which foreign currencies are bought and sold and exchange rates between currencies are determined. Also called the Forex market.

Foreign exchange position statement: A report showing the foreign currency contracts and positions held by a customer.

Foreign exchange risk (exchange rate risk):   Risk that the market value of a firm, measured in the base currency, is exposed to fluctuations in foreign exchange rates.

Foreign incoming transfer: A transfer of funds between two banks in different countries.

Foreign transfer: Transfers of money in foreign currency from one account to another. One of the accounts will be in the local currency; the amount which has to be debited/ credited will be calculated using the exchange rate.

Forex: See *Foreign exchange.*

Forex book: The department of a financial institution in which foreign exchange transactions are recorded per currency.

Forward: Usually means a rate or price of a financial instrument or an event which is in the future.

Forward contracting: A cash transaction common in many industries, including commodities, in which the buyer and seller agree upon delivery of a specified quality and quantity of goods at a specified future date. Specific price may be agreed upon in advance, or there may be agreements that the price will be determined at the time of delivery on the basis of either the prevailing local cash price or a futures price.

Forward discount: The difference between the lower forward and the higher spot price of a currency, expressed as an annualized percentage.

Forward exchange rate: A currency exchange contract that traders have agreed upon for a future forward date. The forward rate is usually for one, two, three, or six months and is often referred to as 30-day forward, 60-day forward, etc.

Forward FX purchases (sales): Accounts which contain all FX purchases (sales) with a future value date.

Forward limit: The maximum allowed counterparty credit risk for foreign exchange contracts.

Forward market: A market for foreign exchange involving delivery of currency at some date in the future.

Forward points: The difference between the spot rate and the forward rate for a specific foreign currency, measured in pips.

Forward premium: The difference between the higher forward and the lower spot price of a currency, expressed as an annualized percentage.

Forward rate: An exchange rate for delivery on a date later than the spot date.

Forward spread: The premium or discount of forward (i.e., future) foreign exchange swap contracts and the forward spot rates.

Forward trading: Trading in which actual delivery and settlement is made at a future date. Forward trade occurs in the commodity, foreign exchange, stock, bond, and futures markets.

Forward valuation: A valuation based upon a date in the future.

Free trade: Trade between nations that is unrestricted by governmental actions.

Front office: The department of a financial institution involving direct contact with customers.

Full-service brokers: Brokers who execute buy and sell orders, research investments, help investors develop and meet investment goals, and give advice to investors. They charge a commission for their work.

Fully disclosed account: An account carried by a futures commission merchant or other financial institution in the actual name of the individual customer; it is the opposite of an omnibus account.

Functional currency: The currency of the principal economic environment in which a firm operates.

Fund: Money for investment.

Fundamental analysis: An approach to the analysis of markets which examines the underlying factors which will affect the supply and demand of the market, overall economy, industry conditions, etc. See also *Technical analysis*.

Funding risk: See *Liquidity risk*.

Funds transfer transaction: Movement of funds directly between two parties involving no intermediaries other than a payment or communications service.

Future value (FV): The value of a cash flow, expressed as a cash flow, for a certain future date, by compounding at the appropriate interest rate.

Futures commission merchant (FCM): An individual or organization which solicits or accepts orders to buy or sell futures contracts or commodity options and accepts money or other assets from customers in connection with such orders. The individual or organization must be registered with the Commodity Futures Trading Commission.

Futures contract: A standardized, binding agreement to buy or sell a specified quantity or grade of a commodity at a later date, i.e., during a specified month. Futures contracts are freely transferable and can be traded only by public auction on designated exchanges.

Futures Industry Association (FIA): The national trade association for the futures industry.

Futures option: An option on a futures contract.

FX: See *Foreign exchange.*

FX book: See *Forex book.*

Gap: In technical analysis, a trading day during which the daily price range is completely above or below the previous day's range.

General Agreement on Tariffs and Trade (GATT): A trade pact ratified in 1994 to cut tariffs worldwide, reduce agricultural subsidies, standardize copyright and patent protection, and set up arbitration panels. The institution changed its name to the World Trade Organization after the trade pact was ratified.

General ledger: An accounting book in which trade transactions, debits, and credits are recorded.

Generally accepted accounting principles (GAAP): Guidelines that explain what should be done in specific accounting situations as determined by the Financial Accounting Standards Board.

Geographic arbitrage: See *Two-point arbitrage.*

Global bonds: Large, liquid bond issues designed to be traded in numerous capital markets worldwide.

Global corporation: An organization that treats the world as a single marketplace and strives to create standardized goods and services to meet the needs of customers worldwide.

GLOBEX: A global, after-hours electronic system for trading in futures and options. A Reuters system for the Chicago Mercantile Exchange.

Gold standard: The international monetary system based on the willingness of countries to trade their paper currencies for gold at a fixed rate.

Goods: Physical, tangible products.

Government security: A debt obligation of the U.S. Treasury, backed by the full faith, credit, and taxing power of the U.S. government and regarded as having no risk of default. The government issues short-term Treasury bills, medium-term Treasury notes, and long-term Treasury bonds.

Grantor: A person who sells an option and assumes the obligation but not the right to sell (in the case of a call) or buy (in the case of a put) the underlying futures contract or commodity at the exercise price.

Great Depression: The worldwide economic depression generally regarded as having begun with the stock market collapse of October 29, 1929. It continued through most of the 1930s.

Greenwich Mean Time (GMT): The time at the meridian at Greenwich, England, used as the basis for standard time throughout most of the world.

Gross domestic product (GDP): The measure of the market value of goods and services produced in a country. It includes consumption, government purchases, investments, and exports minus imports. In the United States it is calculated by the Commerce Department.

Gross national product (GNP): The dollar value of all goods and services produced in a nation's economy. Unlike GDP, it includes goods and services produced abroad.

Gross processing margin (GPM): Refers to the difference between the cost of a raw material and the combined sales income of the product(s) which results from processing.

Group of Seven (G-7): An organization of the seven major industrialized nations, whose leaders meet annually to discuss monetary and fiscal issues. The countries are the United States, Canada, Britain, France, Italy, Germany, and Japan.

Hard assets: Also known as tangible assets. These investments tend to perform well during inflationary times. Gold and other precious metals are the best-known hard assets.

Hard currencies: The currencies that are freely tradeable. Also called convertible currencies.

Hard loan policy: The World Bank lending policy requiring that loans be made only if they are likely to be repaid.

Head and shoulders: A technical analysis chart pattern that has three peaks resembling a head and two shoulders. The market's price moves up to its first peak (the left shoulder), drops back, then moves to a higher peak (the top of the head), drops again, but recovers to another, lower peak (the right shoulder). A head and shoulders top typically forms after a substantial rise and indicates a market reversal. A head and shoulders bottom (an inverted head and shoulders) indicates a market advance.

Head office: The office of a financial institution that is legally registered as the main office of the firm.

Hedge: An investment made in order to reduce the risk of an adverse price movement. See also *Hedging.*

Hedge-ratio: The proportion of underlying currencies, securities, or options needed to hedge a written option.

Hedging: A transaction strategy used by dealers and traders in foreign exchange, commodities, and securities, as well as farmers, manufacturers, and other producers, to protect against severe fluctuations in exchange rates and market prices. A current sale or purchase is offset by contracting to purchase or sell at a specified future date.

Home country: The country in which a firm's headquarters is located.

Hurdle rate: The minimum rate of return a firm or investor finds acceptable for capital investments.

IMF conditionality: The restrictions placed on economic policies of countries receiving International Monetary Fund loans.

Import of the services of capital: The payments a country's residents make on capital supplied by foreigners.

Import tariff: A tax levied on goods entering a country.

Importing: Buying products or raw materials from other countries for use or resale in one's own country.

Imports: Goods and services one country purchases from another country.

In-the-money: An option having intrinsic value. A call is in-the-money if its strike price is below the current price of the underlying futures contract. A put is in-the-money if its strike price is above the current price of the underlying futures contract.

Inconvertible currencies: Currencies that are not freely traded. Also called soft currencies.

Indirect exchange rate: The price of the home currency in terms of the foreign currency. Also called indirect quote.

Indirect exporting: The sale of a firm's products to a domestic customer, who exports the product either in its original form or a modified form.

Indirect quote: See *Indirect exchange rate.*

Industrial products: Goods and services sold primarily for use by industry.

Inelasticity: A characteristic that describes the interdependence of the supply, demand, and price of a commodity. A commodity is inelastic when a price change does not create an increase or decrease in consumption; inelasticity exists when supply and demand are relatively unresponsive to changes in price. See also *Elasticity.*

Inflation: Inflation is a time of generally rising prices.

Initial margin: Customers' funds required at the time a futures or forex position is established, or an option is sold, to ensure performance of the customer's obligations. Margin in futures or forex markets is not a down payment, as it is in securities. See also *Margin.*

Inside information: Material information that has not been made available to the general public.

Insider: An individual having access to material nonpublic information about a corporation. Insiders include directors, officers, and stockholders who own more than 10% of any class of equity security of a corporation.

Insider trading: (1) The legal trading of securities by corporate officers based on information available to the public. (2) The illegal trading of securities by any investor based on information not available to the public.

Institutional investor: A person or organization that trades securities or other financial instruments in large enough quantities or dollar amounts that it qualifies for special treatment and/or lower commissions. Institutional investors are protected by regulations because it is assumed that they are more knowledgeable and better able to protect themselves.

Interest: The charge or cost for using money; expressed as a percentage rate per period.

Interest amount: The amount of interest payable (receivable) over the full life of a fixed deposit (or loan).

Interest arbitrage: Using foreign exchange swap contracts to earn a higher rate of return in the market of another currency.

Interest charges: A type of fee charged to an account.

Interest maturity date: The date on which interest calculation ends for a specific interest rate. Also called interest date.

Interest period: The time period between interest start date and interest maturity date.

Interest-rate swap: A derivative in which one entity agrees to pay a fixed interest rate in return for receiving a floating interest rate from another entity.

Interest risk: The risk that the market value of a firm is exposed to fluctuations in interest rates.

Interest settlement date: Date on which interest has to be settled as per the terms of a contract.

Interest start date: The date on which interest calculation starts.

Interindustry trade: An international trade involving the exchange of goods produced in one industry in one country for goods produced in another industry in a different country.

Intermediaries (import or export): Third parties that specialize in facilitating imports and exports.

Internalization advantages: The factors affecting the desirability of a firm producing a good or service itself, rather than relying on local firms to control production.

Internalization theory: The theory stating that foreign direct investment occurs because of the high costs of entering into production or procurement contracts with foreign firms.

International Accounting Standards Committee (IASC): The international organization having the mission to harmonize the national accounting standards used by various nations.

International bank credit analyst: A company which rates the creditworthiness of banks.

International Bank for Reconstruction and Development (IBRD): The official name of the World Bank. See also *World Bank.*

International Banking Facility (IBF): An entity of a U.S. bank that is exempted from domestic banking regulations as long as it provides only international banking services.

International business: Cross-border commercial transactions with individuals, private firms, and/or public-sector organizations.

International Development Association (IDA): World Bank affiliate that specializes in loans to less developed countries.

International Finance Corporation (IFC): World Bank affiliate specializing in the development of the private sector in developing countries.

International Fisher effect (IFE): The observation that differences in nominal interest rates among countries are due to differences in their expected inflation rates.

International investments: The capital invested by residents of one country in businesses or other opportunities in another country.

International Monetary Fund (IMF): The agency created by the Bretton Woods Agreement to promote international monetary cooperation after World War II. It makes loans and provides other services intended to stabilize world currencies and promote orderly and balanced trade. Member nations may obtain foreign currency when needed, making it possible to make adjustments in their balance of payments without currency depreciation.

International Monetary Market (IMM): A division of the Chicago Mercantile Exchange.

International monetary system: The system by which countries value and exchange their currencies.

International Options Market (IOM): A division of the Chicago Mercantile Exchange.

International strategic management: A comprehensive and ongoing management planning process aimed at developing and implementing strategies that enable a firm to compete effectively internationally.

International Swap Dealers Association (ISDA): The main body representing swap dealers. It develops guidelines for the swaps markets and products. ISDA controls the master agreement for swaps.

International trade: The trading of goods, services, or assets between a person or organization located in one country and a person or organization located in another country.

International trading company: A firm directly engaged in international trade (importing and exporting) of goods for its own account.

Intracorporate transfer: The selling of goods by a firm in one country to an affiliated firm in another country.

Intraindustry trade: The trade between two firms in different countries involving the exchange of goods produced by the same industry.

Intrinsic value: The absolute value of the in-the-money amount, that is, the amount that would be realized if an in-the-money option were exercised. See also *In-the-money.*

Introducing Broker (IB): A firm or individual that solicits and accepts commodity futures orders from customers but does not accept money, securities, or property from the customer. An IB must be registered with the Commodity Futures Trading Commission and must carry all of its accounts through an FCM on a fully disclosed basis.

Inverted market: Futures or forward market in which the nearer months are selling at premiums over the more distant months; it is, characteristically, a market in which supplies are currently in shortage.

Inverted yield curve: Long-term debt instruments having lower yields than short-term debt instruments.

Investment: Expenditure on real or financial assets with the expectation of an increase in value.

Investment banker: A bank in the business of raising capital for corporations and municipalities. It may not accept deposits or make commercial loans.

Invisible supply: Uncounted stocks of a commodity in the hands of wholesalers, manufacturers, and producers which cannot be identified accurately; the stocks are outside commercial channels but theoretically available to the market.

Invoicing currency: The currency in which an international transaction is invoiced.

Irrevocable letter of credit: Letter of credit that cannot be changed without the consent of all parties—buyer, seller, and the issuing bank.

Issuer: (1) An entity, such as a corporation or municipality, that offers its securities for sale. (2) The creator of an option: The issuer of an over-the-counter option is the option writer, and the issuer of a listed option is the options clearing corporation.

Jamaica Agreement: The agreement among central bankers, made in 1976, allowing each country to adopt whatever exchange-rate system it wished.

Joint venture: A special form of strategic alliance created when two or more firms agree to work together and jointly in a specific business enterprise.

Keynesian economics: The economics theory that active government intervention in the marketplace is the best method of ensuring economic growth and stability.

Knock-in option: An option activated only when the price of the option's underlying instrument or market reaches a certain level above or below an agreed-upon range.

Knock-out option: An option that becomes worthless when the price of the option's underlying instrument or market reaches a previously agreed-upon point.

Lagging economic indicators: A composite of seven economic measurements that tend to trail developments in the economy as a whole. Lagging indicators are believed to confirm long-term trends. These indicators are duration of unemployment, ratio of inventories to sales, index of labor costs per unit of output, average prime rate, outstanding commercial and industrial loans, ratio of outstanding consumer installment credit to personal income, and consumer price index for services.

Last trading day: Day on which trading ceases for the maturing (current) delivery month.

Leading economic indicators: A composite of 11 economic measurements that tend to change in the economy as a whole. Leading indicators are believed to predict changes in the economy. The components are average work week, unemployment claims, orders for consumer goods, slower deliveries, plant and equipment orders, building permits, durable order backlog, materials prices, stock prices, M2 money supply, and consumer expectations.

Leads and lags strategy: Money management technique in which a multinational corporation attempts to increase its holding of currencies and assets denominated in currencies that are expected to rise in value, and to decrease its holdings of currencies and assets denominated in currencies that are expected to fall in value.

Letter of credit: A document issued by a bank promising to pay the seller a specific amount if all conditions specified in the letter of credit are met. It's used mostly in foreign trade but also domestically to guarantee payment of securities for other financial transactions.

Leverage: Essentially, leverage allows an investor to establish a position in the marketplace by depositing funds that are less than the value of the contract. The use of borrowed assets by a business to enhance the return to the owner's equity.

Leverage contract: A standardized agreement calling for the delivery of a commodity, with payments against the total cost spread out over a period of time. Its principal characteristics include standard units and quality of a commodity and terms and conditions of the contract, payment and maintenance of margin close out, by offset or delivery (after payment in full), and no right to or interest in a specific lot of the commodity. Leverage contracts are not traded on exchanges.

Leverage transaction merchant (LTM): The firm or individual through whom leverage contracts are entered. LTMs must be registered with the Commodity Futures Trading Commission.

Liabilities: The claims against a corporation or other entity. They include accounts payable, wages and salaries, dividends, taxes, and obligations such as bonds, debentures, and bank loans. A legal obligation to pay a debt owed.

Life of contract: Period between the beginning of trading in a particular futures contract or other derivative and the expiration of trading in the delivery month.

Limit move: A price that has advanced or declined the limit permitted during one trading session as fixed by the rules of a contract market.

Limit order: An order in which the customer sets a limit on either price or time of execution, or both, as contrasted with a market order, which implies that the order should be filled at the most favorable price as soon as possible.

Lingua franca: Common language.

Liquid assets: Assets consisting of cash and other assets readily convertible into cash without a substantial loss in value.

Liquid market: A market where selling and buying can be accomplished easily due to the presence of many interested buyers and sellers. See also *Liquidity*.

Liquidation: (1) The sale (or purchase) of futures contracts or other derivatives to offset the obligation to take (or make) delivery. (2) The process of converting stock or other assets into cash.

Liquidity: The ease of converting an asset to cash.

Liquidity market: A broadly traded market where buying and selling can be accomplished with small price changes and bid and offer price spreads are narrow.

Liquidity risk: The risk of insufficient liquidity to meet cash flow requirements on a certain date in the future. Also known as funding risk.

Loan program: It is the primary means of government agricultural price support operations. The government lends money to farmers at announced rates, using the crops as collateral. Default on these loans is the primary method by which the government acquires stocks of agricultural commodities.

Local central banks: The central bank(s) in the country of domicile of a financial institution's foreign office.

Local currency: Legal tender of the country where a firm is located.

London Interbank Offer Rate (LIBOR): The interest rate that London banks charge each other for short-term Euro currency loans. A floating interest rate that serves as a base for many lending agreements.

London Metal Exchange (LME): An exchange that has markets in aluminum, tin, copper, lead, nickel, and zinc.

London Stock Exchange: Formally known as the International Stock Exchange of the United Kingdom and the Republic of Ireland Limited, or ISE. Has markets in equities, options, unlisted (USM), and U.K. ADR (American Depository Receipts) securities.

Long: To own (buy) a security, currency, futures contract, commodity, or derivative.

Long hedge: Buying futures contracts to protect against possible increased prices of commodities. See also *Hedging*.

Long position: An excess of assets (and/or forward purchase contracts) over liabilities (and/or forward sale contracts) in the same currency. A dealer's position when net purchases and sales leave him or her in a net-purchased position. See also *Net position*.

Long-term product: (1) A product having a maturity or history of five years or longer. (2) A product having a long-term lifetime stipulated by a regulating authority, usually a central bank.

Long-term portfolio investments: Portfolio investments with maturities of more than one year.

Louvre Accord: The agreement made in 1987 among central bankers to stabilize the value of the U.S. dollar.

M1: A category of the money supply that includes all coins, currency, and demand deposits (that is, checking accounts and NOW accounts).

M2: A category of the money supply that includes M1 in addition to all time deposits, savings deposits, and noninstitutional money-market funds.

M3: A category of the money supply that includes M2 in addition to all large time deposits, institutional money-market funds, short-term repurchase agreements, and certain other large, liquid assets.

Maastricht Treaty: See *Treaty on European Union.*

Macropolitical risk: The political risk affecting all firms operating within a country.

Maintenance margin: The amount of money that must be maintained on deposit while futures and other derivative positions are open. If the equity in a customer's account drops under the maintenance margin level, the broker must issue a call for money that will restore the customer's equity in the account to required initial levels. See also *Margin.*

Managed float: A flexible currency exchange system in which government intervention plays a major role in determining exchange rates. Also called a dirty float.

Margin: (1) In the futures industry, it is an amount of money deposited by both buyers and sellers of futures contracts to ensure performance against the contract. It is not a down payment. (2) In the stock market, the amount of cash that must be put up in a purchase of securities. If the margin requirement is 50%, the buyer must put up 50% of the purchase price and borrow the rest.

Margin account: A brokerage account allowing customers to buy securities and/or other financial instruments with money borrowed from the brokerage.

Margin call: A call from a brokerage firm to a customer to bring margin deposits back up to minimum levels required by exchange regulations; similarly, a request by the clearing-house to a clearing member firm to make additional deposits to bring clearing margins back to minimum levels required by clearinghouse rules. A demand upon an investor to put up more collateral for securities bought on credit.

Markdown: The difference between the highest current bid price among dealers and the lower price that a dealer pays to a customer.

Market: (1) Any area or condition where buyers and sellers are in contact for doing business together. (2) The generic term for a financial instrument.

Market arbitrage: The simultaneous purchase and sale of the same security, futures, or other financial instrument in different markets to take advantage of a price disparity be-tween the two markets.

Market order: An order to buy or sell futures contracts, stocks, or other financial instru-ments which is to be filled at the best possible price and as soon as possible. A limit order, in contrast, may specify requirements for price or time of execution.

Market risk: The potential for an investor to experience losses owing to daily fluctuations in the prices at which a financial instrument can be bought or sold.

Market timing: Shifting money in and out of investment markets in an effort to take advantage of rising prices and avoid being stung by downturns.

Market value: The price at which investors buy or sell a financial instrument at a given time. Market value is determined by actual bids and offers made by buyers and sellers.

Market value (fair market price): Price (value) determined at arm's length between a willing buyer and a willing seller, each acting rationally in his or her own self-interest. May be estimated in the absence of a monetary transaction.

Markup: The difference between the lowest current offering price among dealers and the higher price a dealer charges a customer.

Match trading: Financial transactions made outside of an auction or negotiation process. Buy and sell orders for the same financial instrument, at the same price, are paired and executed, often by computer.

Matching orders: Simultaneously entering identical (or nearly identical) buy and sell orders for a financial instrument to create the appearance of active trading in that market.

Maturity: Period within which a futures contract can be settled by delivery of the actual commodity; the period between the first notice day and the last trading day of a commodity futures contract.

Maturity date: (1) Date on which the principal amount of a note, draft, acceptance, bond, or other debt instrument becomes due and payable. Also, termination or due date on which an installment loan must be paid in full. (2) The agreed-upon date on which a fixed loan/ deposit matures. (3) When a bond expires and the loan must be paid back in full.

Maximum price fluctuation: See *Limit move.*

MCE: Mid-America Commodity Exchange.

Medium term: (1) A financial product having a lifetime between one to five years. (2) A product having a medium-term lifetime as stipulated by a regulating authority, such as a central bank.

Member firm: (1) A broker-dealer in which at least one of the principal officers is a member of the New York Stock Exchange, another exchange, a self-regulatory organization, or a clearing corporation. (2) A member of the National Futures Association.

Mercantilism: The economic belief that a nation's wealth is measured by its holdings of gold and silver.

Merchandise export: The sale of a good to a resident of a foreign country.

Merchandise import: The purchase of a good from a resident of a foreign country.

Micropolitical risk: The political risk that affects only specific firms or a specific industry operating within a country.

Minimum price fluctuation: See *Point.*

Misrepresentation: An untrue or misleading statement concerning a material fact relied upon by a customer when making a decision about an investment.

Momentum indicator: A line that is plotted to represent the difference between today's price and the price of a fixed number of days ago. Momentum can be measured as the difference between today's price and the current value of a moving average. Often referred to as a momentum oscillator.

Monetary aggregates: Measures of a country's money supply. See *M1, M2,* and *M3.*

Monetary authority: The government entity in charge of executing regulations, which have to be fulfilled by financial institutions.

Monetary base: The sum of reserve accounts of financial institutions at Federal Reserve banks and currency in circulation. It is the ultimate source of the nation's money supply and is controllable, to some degree, by Federal Reserve monetary policy.

Monetary policy: A government's efforts to control its money supply; in the United States, the actions of the Federal Reserve Bank.

Money: A medium of exchange; currency.

Money supply: The total stock of bills, coins, loans, credit, and other liquid instruments in the economy. See also *M1*, *M2*, and *M3*.

Moving average: A mathematical procedure to smooth or eliminate the fluctuations in data. Moving averages emphasize the direction of a trend, confirm trend reversals, and smooth out price and volume fluctuations or "noise" that can confuse interpretation of the market.

Multicurrency: A system that can process transactions and post balances in more than one currency.

Multilateral Investment Guarantee Agency (MIGA): World Bank affiliate that offers political-risk insurance to investors in developing countries.

Multilateral netting: The netting of transactions between three or more business or trading units.

Multinational corporation (MNC): An incorporated firm that has extensive involvement in international business, engages in foreign direct investment, and/or owns or controls value-adding activities in more than one country.

Multinational enterprise (MNE): A business that may or may not be incorporated and has extensive involvement in international business.

Multinational organization (MNO): Any organization—profit-making or nonprofit—with extensive international involvement.

Multiplier effect: The expansion of the money supply that results from a Federal Reserve System member bank being able to lend more money than it takes in. A small increase in bank deposits generates a far larger increase in available credit.

Mutual fund: An investment company that continuously offers new equity shares in an actively managed portfolio of securities. All mutual fund shareholders participate in the gains or losses of the fund. The shares are redeemable on any business day at the net asset value. Each mutual fund's portfolio is invested to match the objective stated in the offering prospectus.

National Association of Securities Dealers, Inc. (NASD): A self-regulatory body that regulates and registers security deals. NASD oversees the NASDAQ and NASDAQ International markets.

National Association of Securities Dealers Automated Quotation System (NASDAQ): The nationwide electronic quotation system for up-to-the-minute bid and asked quotations on over-the-counter stocks.

National competitive advantage, theory of: The theory that states success in international trade is based upon the interaction of four elements: factor conditions, demand conditions, related and supporting industries, and firm strategy, structure, and rivalry.

National Futures Association (NFA): The industrywide, self-regulatory organization of the futures industry.

Nationalization: The transfer of property from a privately owned firm to the government.

NAV per share: Net asset value. The value of a mutual fund share, calculated by dividing the total net asset value of the fund by the number of shares outstanding. The value of a mutual fund share is calculated once a day, based on the closing market price for each security in the fund's portfolio. It is computed by deducting the fund's liabilities from the total assets of the portfolio.

Nearby: The nearest delivery months of a futures or forward market.

Nearby delivery (month): The futures contract delivery month closest to maturity.

Negotiable certificate of deposit (CD): An unsecured promissory note issued with a minimum face value of $100,000. It documents a time deposit of funds with the issuing bank and is guaranteed by the bank.

Negotiable order of withdrawal (NOW) account: An interest-bearing checking account through which the customer is permitted to write drafts against money held on deposit.

Neomercantilists: The modern supporters of mercantilism, sometimes called protectionists, who think that a country should erect barriers of trade to protect its industries from foreign competition.

Net change: The difference between the closing price of a financial instrument on the trading day reported and the previous day's closing price. In over-the-counter transactions, the term refers to the difference between the closing bids.

Net domestic product (NDP): The calculation of the annual economic output of a nation adjusted to account for depreciation. It is calculated by subtracting the amount of depreciation from the gross domestic product.

Net income: The amount left after a company's taxes and all other expenses have been paid.

Net performance: An increase or decrease in net asset value exclusive of additions, withdrawals, and redemptions.

Net position: (1) A financial institution has a position in foreign currency when its assets—including futures contracts to purchase, and liabilities, including futures contracts, to sell—in that currency are not equal. An excess of assets over liabilities is called a net "long" position, and liabilities in excess of assets result in a net "short" position. A long net position in a currency which is depreciating results in a loss, because with each day, that position (asset) is convertible into fewer units of local currency. A short position in a currency which is appreciating represents a loss, because with each day, satisfaction of that position (liability) costs more units of local currency. (2) The difference between the open long (buy) contracts and the open short (sell) contracts held by any one entity in any one futures contract month or in all months combined.

Net worth: The amount by which assets exceed liabilities.

Net-off: To apply one cash flow against another.

Netting: The process of combining many transactions for a financial institution or clearinghouse into a single amount. It reduces credit and liquidity risks associated with market activities.

New asset value: The value of each unit of a commodity pool or mutual fund. It is a calculation of assets minus liabilities plus or minus the value of open positions (marked-to-the-market) divided by the number of units.

New York Stock Exchange (NYSE): The largest stock exchange in the United States. It is a corporation, operated by a board of directors, responsible for administering the Exchange and member activities, listing securities, overseeing the transfer of members' seats on the Exchange, and determining whether an applicant is qualified to be a specialist.

No-load fund: A mutual fund sold without a commission or sales charge. The shares are distributed directly by the investment company.

Nominal price: Declared price for a futures or forward market used in place of a closing price when no recent trading has taken place in that particular delivery month. Typically it is an average of the bid and asked prices.

Nominal yield: The interest rate stated on the face of a financial obligation (such as a bond or promissory note).

Nondisclosure: Failure to disclose a material fact to a customer regarding an investment.

Nontariff barrier (NTB): A governmental regulation, policy, or procedure other than a tariff that has the effect of restricting international trade.

Normal yield curve: When long-term debt instruments have higher yields than short-term debt instruments.

Normalizing: Adjusting data, such as a price series, to put it within normal or more standard range. A technique sometimes used to develop a trading system.

Note: A short-term debt security, usually maturing in five years or less. See also *Treasury note*.

Notice day: See *First notice day*.

Notice of delivery: See *Delivery notice*.

NPV: 1. Net present value. 2. No par value.

NYFE: New York Futures Exchange.

NYMEX: New York Mercantile Exchange.

OCP: Open currency position.

Offer: An indication of willingness to sell at a given price, also referred to as an ask, or asking price. The opposite of bid.

Official reserves account: Balance of payments account that records changes in official reserves owned by a central bank.

Official settlements balance: Balance of payments balance that measures changes in a country's official reserves.

Office of the Comptroller of the Currency (OCC): A U.S. regulatory body that has a role in the regulation of foreign banks operating in the United States.

Offset: The liquidation of a purchase of a futures contract, forward, or other financial instrument through the sale of an equal number of the same delivery months; or the covering of a short sale of futures forward or other financial instrument through the purchase of an equal number of the same delivery months. Either action transfers the obligation to make or take delivery of the actual financial instrument to someone else.

Offset obligations: Agreement between a multinational corporation and a host government in which the multinational corporation agrees to provide economic benefit to the host government in return for the purchase of a good or service by the host government.

Offset purchases: A form of countertrade in which a portion of the exported good is produced in the importing country.

Omnibus account: An account carried by one futures commission merchant or financial institution with another where the transactions of two or more persons are combined, rather than designated separately, and the identity of the individual accounts is not disclosed.

Open: The period at the beginning of a trading session during which all transactions are considered made "at the open."

Open currency position (OCP): (1) The net sum of the open currency spot position and the open currency forward position, being the measure of the foreign exchange risk. (2) The open currency position is the difference between assets and liabilities priced in foreign currency, plus the forward (conditional and unconditional) forex purchase and sales. The open currency position is the measure of the foreign exchange risk.

Open interest: The total number of futures contracts or market position of a given commodity which have not yet been offset or fulfilled by delivery of the actual commodity; the total number of open transactions where each transaction has a buyer and a seller.

Open outcry: Method of public auction for making bids and offers in the trading pits or rings of commodity exchanges.

Open trade equity: The unrealized gain or loss on open positions.

Opening range: The range of closely related prices at which transactions took place at the opening of the market; buying and selling orders at the opening might be filled at any point within such a range.

Operating expenses: The day-to-day costs of running a business.

Operating income: The profit realized from the operation of a business.

Option: An agreement that represents the right to buy or sell a specified amount of an underlying security, such as a stock, bond, futures contract, at a specified price within a specified time. The purchaser acquires a right, and the seller assumes an obligation. Stock options are traded on several exchanges, including the Chicago Board of Options Exchange, the American Stock Exchange, the Philadelphia Stock Exchange, the Pacific Stock Exchange, and the New York Stock Exchange; futures options are traded on all U.S. futures exchanges; over-the-counter options are traded with a wide variety of financial institutions.

Option buyer: The party who pays a premium to obtain the rights under an option.

Option contract: The right, but not the obligation, to buy or sell a specific quantity of an underlying instrument on or before a specific date in the future. The seller of the option has the obligation to sell the underlying instrument (in the case of a put option) or buy it from the option buyer (in the case of a call option) at the exercise price if the option is exercised.

Option delta amount: The product of an option's principal amount and its respective delta calculated according to Black and Scholes.

Option forward purchase: The purchase of a foreign currency for delivery between two future specified dates at a specified price.

Option forward sale: The sale of a foreign currency for delivery between two future specified dates at a specified price.

Option period: The period between the start date and the expiry date of an option contract.

Option premium: The money, securities, or property the buyer pays to the writer (grantor) for granting an option contract, thus conveying the rights of the option to the buyer.

Option seller/writer: The party who is obligated to perform if an option is exercised by the option buyer.

Order execution: The handling of a customer order by a broker, including receiving the order verbally or in writing from the customer, transmitting it to the trading floor of the exchange where the transaction takes place, and returning confirmation (fill price) of the completed order to the customer.

Order to buy: An instruction sent by a client, or his or her authorized representative, to buy a given quantity of an identified financial instrument under specified conditions.

Order to sell: An instruction sent by a client, or his or her authorized representative, to sell a given quantity of an identified financial instrument under specified conditions.

Orders: See *Limit order, Market order,* and *Stop order.*

Original margin (initial margin): The term applied to the initial deposit of margin money required of clearing member firms by clearinghouse rules.

Out-of-the-money: A call option with a strike price higher, or a put option with a strike price lower, than the current market value of the underlying asset. A put option is out-of-the-money when the price of the underlying asset is above the option's exercise price. An option contract is out-of-the-money when there is no benefit to be derived from exercising the option immediately.

Over-the-counter derivative: A financial instrument whose value is designed to track the return on commodities, stocks, bonds, currencies, or some other benchmark that is traded over-the-counter or off organized exchanges. Also called an OTC derivative.

Over-the-counter (OTC) market: Trading in financial instruments transacted off organized exchanges. OTC trading includes transactions among market-makers and between market-makers and their customers. OTC trading takes place often over computer and telephone networks that link brokers and dealers around the world.

Overall foreign currency limit: Maximum allowed total open currency position on a particular point in time, expressed in an agreed-upon currency.

Overbought: A technical analysis term that the market price has risen too steeply and too fast in relation to underlying fundamental or other factors.

Overseas Private Investment Corporation (OPIC): U.S. government agency that promotes U.S. international business activities by providing political risk insurance.

Oversold: A technical analysis term for a market price that has experienced much more and stronger selling than the fundamentals justify.

Oversold: Negative open currency position.

Ownership advantages: When resources owned by a firm provide the firm a competitive advantage over its industry rivals.

P&L: Profit and loss account.

P/E: See *Price/earnings ratio.*

Paper gold: See *Special drawing rights.*

Par: (1) 100% of principal value. (2) The dollar amount assigned to a security by the issuer.

Par value: Official price of a currency in terms of gold.

Parity: Equal standing.

Participating forward: A financial instrument which combines a forward foreign exchange deal with a put or call option.

Participation: A direct or indirect interest in the equity of a company. Active involvement in a market.

Partnership: A form of business organization in which two or more individuals or entities manage a business and are equally and personally responsible for its debts and liabilities.

Passive income: Earnings received from a rental property, limited partnership, or other enterprise in which the individual is not actively involved.

Passive loss: A loss incurred through a passive investment.

Pegging: Stabilizing a country's currency through its purchase or sale by the country's central bank. The gold standard pegged the value of a country's currency to gold.

Per capita income: The average income per person in a country.

Personal income (PI): An individual's total earnings from wages, passive business enterprises, and investments.

Pip: Unit that expresses differences between exchange rates. The minimum incremental price change in the interbank markets.

Pit: A specially constructed arena on the trading floor of some exchanges where trading is conducted by open outcry. On some exchanges, the term "ring" designates the trading area.

Plaza Accord: The agreement in 1985 among central banks to allow the U.S. dollar to fall in value.

Pledged amount: The whole or a part of the principal amount of a collateral that will be used as a security for a financial transaction.

Pledged percentage: The percentage of the principal amount of a collateral that will be used as security for a financial transaction.

Pledging: Pledging is the action of putting up anything as security for a loan or other financial transaction.

Point: The minimum fluctuation in prices or options premiums. Also called *Tick*.

Point balance: A statement prepared by futures commission merchants or financial institutions to show profit or loss on all open positions by computing them to an official closing or settlement price.

Political risk: Change in the political environment that may adversely affect the value of a firm.

Political risk assessment: The systematic analysis of the political risks when operating a foreign country or making an investment in a foreign financial instrument.

Pool: See *Commodity pool*.

Portfolio: A selection of financial instruments held by a person or institution. Portfolios are often designed to spread investment risk.

Portfolio manager: The entity responsible for investment strategy and managing day-to-day portfolio trading.

Position: A market commitment. For example, a buyer of futures contracts is said to have a long position, and, conversely, a seller of futures contracts is said to have a short position.

Position limit: The maximum number of futures contracts that one can hold in certain regulated commodities, according to the provisions of the CFTC.

Position management: Managing various financial positions of a firm so that they do not exceed the established guidelines for the firm.

Position trader: A trader who either buys or sells financial instruments and holds them for an extended period of time, as distinguished from the day trader, who will normally initiate and liquidate positions within a single trading session.

Premium: (1) The amount that an option buyer pays to an option seller. (2) The difference between the higher price paid for a financial instrument and the financial instrument's face amount at issue. (3) The additional payment allowed by exchange regulations for delivery of higher-than-required standards or grades of a commodity against a futures contract. In speaking of price relationships between different delivery months of a given commodity, one commodity is said to be trading at a premium over another when its price is greater than that of the other.

Present value (PV): The value of a future cash flow expressed as today's cash flow by discounting at the appropriate interest rate.

Price limit: Maximum price advance or decline from the previous day's settlement price, permitted for futures in one trading session by the rules of the exchange.

Price-earnings (PE) ratio: Comparing the prices of different common stocks by determining how much the market is willing to pay for a share of each corporation's earnings. Calculated by dividing the market price stock by the earnings per share.

Primary market: The principal market for the purchase and sale of a cash commodity.

Prime rate: The minimum interest rate that commercial banks charge their prime or most creditworthy customers.

Principal: A person who is a principal of an entity. (1) A principal may be a sole proprietary, general partner, officer, director, or person occupying a similar status or performing similar functions, having the power to exercise a control over the activities of the entity. (2) Any holder or any beneficial owner of 10% or more of an entity.

Private wires: Wires leased by various firms and news agencies for the transmission of information to branch offices and subscriber clients.

Privatization: The sale of publicly owned property to private investors.

Proceeding clerk: The member of the CFTC's staff in the Office of Proceedings who maintains the Commission's reparation docket, assigns reparation cases to an appropriate CFTC official, and acts as custodian of the records of proceedings.

Producer: A person or entity that produces (grows, mines, etc.) a commodity.

Product: (1) A finished consumer good. (2) A "packaged" financial instrument, e.g., an investment product..

Production alliance: A strategic alliance in which two or more firms manufacture products or provide services in a shared facility.

Productivity: The economic measure of efficiency summarizing the value of outputs relative to the value of inputs.

Promissory note: An agreement to pay a borrowed amount on a future date.

Public elevators: Grain storage facilities, licensed and regulated by state and federal agencies, in which space is rented out to whoever is willing to pay for it; some are also approved by the commodity exchanges for delivery of commodities against futures contracts.

Purchase and sale (P&S) statement: A statement sent by a financial institution to a customer when a futures or options position or other financial instrument has been liquidated or offset. The statement shows the number of positions bought or sold, the gross profit or loss, the commission, other fee charges, and the net profit or loss on the transaction. Sometimes combined with a confirmation statement.

Purchase price: The total actual cost paid by a person for entering into a financial transaction.

Purchasing power parity (PPP):   The theory stating that prices of tradeable goods, when expressed in a common currency, will tend to equalize across countries as a result of exchange-rate changes.

Put option: An option that gives the option buyer the right, but not the obligation, to sell the underlying financial instrument at a particular price on or before a particular date, e.g., the right but not obligation to sell foreign currency at a certain rate.

Put spread: The selling of a put or puts at a lower strike price to pay for a put or puts at a higher strike.

Pyramiding: The use of profits on existing futures or forward positions as a margin to increase the size of the position, normally in successively smaller increments.

Quad: An economic grouping of countries consisting of Canada, the European Union, Japan, and the United States.

Qualitative analysis: A research technique that deals with factors that cannot be precisely measured, such as employee morale and management expertise.

Quantitative analysis: A research technique that deals with measurable assets, such as the value of assets and the cost of capital.

Quotation: The actual price, or the bid or ask price, of a security, commodity, futures, option, currency, or other financial instrument at a particular time. Often called quote.

Quote: See *Quotation.*

Rally: An upward movement of prices.

Rally top: The point where a rally stalls. A bull move will usually make several intermediate rally tops over its life.

Random walk theory: The theory that the past movement or direction of the price of a stock or other market cannot be used to predict its future movement or direction.

Range: The difference between the high and low price during a given period—a single trading session, a week, a month, etc.

Rate: A percentage or measure of value. See also *Cross rate.*

Reaction: A short-term countertrend movement of prices.

Real estate investment trust (REIT):   A trust which invests in a variety of real estate. REITs are managed by one or more trustees.

Receivership: A situation, such as bankruptcy, in which a receiver has been appointed. A receiver is a person appointed by a court to take custody of, control, or manage property or funds, pending judicial action.

Recession: A downturn in economic activity, lasting from 6 to 18 months. Generally two consecutive quarters of decline in a nation's gross domestic product.

Record date: The date on which a shareholder must own a company's stock to be entitled to receive a dividend.

Recovery: An upward movement of prices following a decline. In a business cycle, the period after a recession when the gross domestic product increases.

Re-exporting: The process of importation of a good into a country for immediate exportation.

Registered commodity representative (RCR): See *Associated person (AP)*; *Broker.*

Reparations award: The amount of damages (usually monetary) a respondent may be ordered to pay to a complainant.

Reporting currency: The currency in which the financial accounts and statements of the reporting entity are maintained or expressed.

Reporting limit: Sizes of futures positions set by the exchange and/or by the CFTC at or above which commodity traders must make daily reports to the exchange and/or the CFTC as to the size of the position by commodity, by delivery month, and according to the purpose of trading, i.e., speculative or hedging.

Reset date: The date a financial contract or agreement with a floating rate ends.

Resistance: In technical analysis, the price level where a trend stalls. Prices must build momentum to move through resistance. It is the opposite of a support level.

Respondents: The individuals or firms against which a complaint has been filed and a reparations award is sought.

Retender: The right of holders of futures contracts who have been tendered a delivery notice through the clearinghouse to offer the notice for sale on the open market, liquidating their obligation to take delivery under the contract; it is applicable only to certain commodities and only within a specified period of time.

Retracement: In technical analysis, price movement in the opposite direction of the prevailing trend. Also described as a *Correction.*

Return on equity (ROE): A calculation of a corporation's profitability, specifically its return on assets, calculated by dividing after-tax income by tangible assets.

Return on investment (ROI): The profit or loss resulting from a financial transaction, often expressed as an annual percentage rate.

Revaluation/marking to market: Determining the value or replacement costs of positions at the market prices on a particular moment in time. Revaluation may be required due to changes in currencies, interest rates, or the market value of a collateral.

Revenue: The money a firm takes in, including interest earned and receipts from sales, services provided, rents, and royalties.

Revocable letter of credit: A letter of credit that can be changed by a financial institution without the consent of the buyer and the seller.

Ring: A circular area on the trading floor of an exchange where traders and brokers stand while executing trades. Some exchanges use pits rather than rings.

Risk: The potential of losing money.

Risk management: Management to control and monitor the risks of a bank, financial institution, business entity, or individual.

Rolling settlement: A system of settling exchange transactions where each trade has to be paid for in full at the end of the settlement period. The alternative settlement method is called trading account settlement.

Round lot: A quantity of a commodity equal in size to the corresponding futures contract for the commodity, as distinguished from a job lot, which may be larger or smaller than the contract.

Round turn: The combination of an initiating purchase or sale of a futures contract or other financial instrument and offsetting sale or purchase of an equal number of futures contracts or other financial instruments of the same specifications. Commissions and fees for transactions are charged on the round turn.

Royalty: Compensation paid by a licensee to a licenser.

Safe keeping account: An account in which securities are deposited or withdrawn.

Sample grade: In commodities, usually the lowest quality acceptable for delivery in satisfaction of futures contracts.

Sanctions: Government-imposed restraints or restrictions against commerce with a foreign country.

Scalper: A speculator on the trading floor of an exchange who buys and sells rapidly, with small profit or losses, holding positions for only a short time during a trading session. Typically, a scalper will stand ready to buy at a fraction below the last transaction price and sell at a fraction above, thus creating market liquidity.

Secondary market: A market for financial instruments which have been previously issued.

Secured amount: The amount of a facility which is secured by one or more items of collateral.

Securities and Exchange Commission (SEC): The federal agency created by Congress to regulate the securities markets and protect investors. It has five commissioners appointed by the President of the United States and approved by the Senate. The SEC enforces the Securities Act of 1933, the Securities Exchange Act of 1934, the Trust Indenture Act of 1939, the Investment Company Act of 1940, and the Investment Advisers Act of 1940.

Securities Investor Protection Corporation (SIPC): A nonprofit membership corporation created by an act of Congress to protect clients of brokerage firms that are forced into bankruptcy. Membership is composed of all brokers and dealers registered under the Securities Exchange Act of 1934, all members of national securities exchanges, and most NASD members. SIPC provides customers of these firms up to $500,000 coverage for cash and securities held by the firms (although coverage of cash is limited to $100,000).

Security: Under the Securities Exchange Act of 1934, a security is any note, stock, bond, investment contract, debenture, certificate of interest in profit-sharing or partnership agreement, certificate of deposit, collateral trust certificate, preorganization certificate, option on a security, or other instrument of investment. Also categorized as securities are interests in oil and gas drilling programs, real estate condominiums and cooperatives, farmland or animals, commodity option contracts, whiskey warehouse receipts, multilevel distributorship arrangements, and merchandising marketing programs.

Security deposit: See *Margin*.

Segregated account: A special account used to hold and separate customers' assets from those of the broker or firm.

Sell: To convey ownership of a security or other asset for money or value.

Selling hedge: Selling futures contracts to protect against possible decreased prices of the underlying cash market which will be sold in the future.

Sell-off : A period of intensified selling in a market that pushes prices sharply lower.

Service exports and imports: The trade involving intangible products between residents of different countries.

Services: Functions or tasks that have value.

Settlement price: (1) The closing price, or a price within the range of closing prices, which is used as the official price in determining net gains or losses at the close of each trading session. (2) Payment of any amount of money under a contract.

Short: To have sold a cash commodity, a commodity futures contract, or other financial instrument; a long, in contrast, is to have bought a cash commodity or futures contract.

Short covering: Trades that reverse, or close out, short-sale positions.

Short hedge: Selling futures to protect against possible decreasing prices of an underlying cash market. See also *Hedging.*

Short interest: Total number of shares of a given stock that have been sold short and not yet repurchased.

Short selling: In the stock market, a trading strategy that anticipates a drop in a share's price. Stock or another financial instrument is borrowed from a broker and then sold, creating a short position.

Short squeeze: Occurs when the price of a financial instrument rises sharply, causing many short sellers to buy the security to cover their positions and limit losses.

Short term: A product having a lifetime as stipulated by a regulating authority, usually a central bank.

Short-term portfolio investments: Portfolio investments with maturities of one year or less.

SIMEX: Singapore International Monetary Exchange.

Society for Worldwide Interbank Financial Telecommunication (S.W.I.F.T.): A private, international telecommunication service for member banks and qualified participants.

Soft currencies: See *Inconvertible currencies.*

Soft loans: Loans made by the World Bank group that are not expected to be repaid.

Special drawing rights (SDRS): Credits granted by the IMF that can be used to settle transactions among central banks; also called paper gold.

Specific tariff: A tax assessed as a specific amount per unit of weight or other standard measure.

Speculator: One who attempts to anticipate price changes and make profits through the sale and/or purchase of financial instruments. A speculator with a forecast of advancing prices hopes to profit by buying futures contracts and then liquidating at a higher price. A speculator with a forecast of declining prices hopes to profit by selling and then buying at a lower price in the future.

Spot: Market for the immediate delivery of the product and immediate payment. May also refer to the nearest delivery month of a futures contract.

Spot commodity: See *Cash commodity.*

Spot contract: Contract with a present delivery date.

Spot date: The maturity date.

Spot market: A market for buying or selling commodities or foreign exchange for immediate delivery and for cash payment.

Spot price: The actual price at which a particular cash commodity or financial instrument can be bought or sold immediately.

Spot rate: Exchange rate for delivery on the spot date.

Spread (or straddle): (1) The purchase of one futures or forward delivery month against the sale of another futures or forward delivery month of the same commodity. The purchase of one delivery month of one futures or forward against the sale of the same delivery month of a different futures or forward. The purchase of one future or forward in one market against the sale of that future or forward in another market, to take advantage of and profit from the distortions from the normal price relationships that sometimes occur. (2) In a quotation, the difference between the bid and the ask prices of a market. (3) The difference between two or more prices.

Standard price policy: The pricing policy of a firm that charges the same price for its products and services regardless of where they are sold.

Statement of open orders: A statement, sent by a firm which has accepted one or several orders to buy and/or sell financial instruments, that identifies those orders that have not been executed.

Stop loss: A risk-management technique used to close out a losing position at a given point. A stop loss order is placed at the given point.

Stop order: An order that becomes a market order when a particular price level is reached. A sell stop is placed below the market; a buy stop is placed above the market. Sometimes referred to as a stop loss order.

Strategic alliance: A business arrangement in which two or more firms choose to cooperate for mutual benefit.

Strategic goals: The major objectives of a firm pursuing a particular course of action.

Strategic planning: The process of developing an international strategy.

Strategy: Making and carrying out plans to achieve a goal. More of an art than a science.

Strike price: A specified price at which an investor can buy or sell an option's underlying financial instrument. The exchange rate, interest rate, or market price that is guaranteed by an option transaction.

Subordinate loan: A loan to a customer that is subordinated to (comes after or is junior to) other claims.

Subsidiary bank: A separately incorporated overseas banking operation.

Super 301: A trade law provision under which the United States identifies trade practices it considers unfair and against which it can apply sanctions.

Supply: The total amount of a good or service available for purchase by consumers.

Support: A price level at which a declining market has stopped falling. Once this level is reached, the market trades sideways for a period of time or rebounds. It is the opposite of a resistance price range.

Sustainable competitive advantage: The advantage over competitors that can be sustained over time.

Swap: An agreement or contract that exchanges one financial instrument's return for another's.

Swap market: The international capital market in which two firms can exchange financial obligations.

Swap rate/swap points: Price for a swap contract expressed as the difference between the two rates involved, respectively spot/forward and forward, measured in pips.

Swap transactions: Transactions involving the simultaneous purchase and sale of a foreign currency with delivery at two different points in time.

S.W.I.F.T.: Society for Worldwide Interbank Financial Telecommunication.

Switch: Liquidation of a position in one delivery month of a futures or forward and simultaneous initiation of a similar position in another delivery month of the same market. When used by hedgers, this tactic is referred to as "rolling forward" the hedge.

Tariff: A tax placed on an imported good.

Tax havens: Countries that charge low, often zero, taxes on incomes and offer an attractive business climate.

Technical analysis: An approach to analysis of markets and anticipated trends of market prices. It examines the technical factors of market activity. Technicians normally examine patterns of price range, rates of change, changes in volume of trading, and open interest. These data are often charted to show trends and formations which serve as indicators of likely future price movements.

TED spread: The difference, or spread, between yields on Treasury bills and those on Euro dollars.

Tender: The act on the part of the seller of futures contracts of giving notice to the clearinghouse that he or she intends to deliver the physical commodity in satisfaction of the futures contract.

Term: In finance this normally means a distinction is made according to the general criteria original and remaining. A further distinction is made according to the special criteria longest and average.

Theta: Measures the change in the theoretical value of an option when the outstanding time before it expires is changed.

Thin market: See *Depth of the market.*

Three-point arbitrage: An arbitrage based upon exploiting the difference between the direct rate of exchange between two currencies and their cross-rate of exchange using a third currency.

Tick: A minimum upward or downward movement in the price of securities, futures, or other financial instruments.

Time value: Any amount by which an option premium exceeds the option's intrinsic value.

Tort laws: The laws covering wrongful acts, damages, and injuries.

Total open currency position: The sum of the absolute values of the open currency positions, expressed in an agreed-upon currency.

Total return: An investment's total return reflects not only the income that it pays out from interest or dividends, but also any change in its share price or principal value.

Trade: The exchange of goods, services, or assets between one person or organization and another.

Trade execution date and place: The day and the place (e.g., stock exchange or other market) where the deal was agreed/executed.

Trade in invisibles: British term for trade in services.

Trade in visibles: British term for merchandise trade.

Traders: People who negotiate prices and execute buy and sell orders, either on behalf of an investor or for their own account.

Trading halt: A pause in the trading of a particular security on one or more exchanges, usually in anticipation of a news announcement or to correct an order imbalance.

Trading range: An established set of price boundaries with a high and a low price within which a market will spend a marked period of time.

Transaction costs: (1) The costs of negotiating, monitoring, and enforcing a contract. (2) All the costs of executing a financial transaction.

Transaction currency: The currency in which an international transaction is denominated.

Transaction exposure: The financial risks of an international transaction affecting exchange rate movements after the firm is legally obligated to the transaction.

Transaction fee: A fee charged for transaction activity.

Transit tariff: A tax levied on goods as they pass through one country on route to another.

Translation: The process of transforming the accounting statements of a foreign subsidiary into the home country's currency.

Treasury bill: A marketable U.S. Treasury debt security with a maturity of less than one year.

Treasury bond: A marketable, fixed-interest U.S. Treasury debt security with a maturity of more than ten years.

Treasury management: The management of financial flows and their currency and interest rate risks.

Treasury note: A marketable, fixed-interest U.S. Treasury debt security with a maturity of between one and ten years.

Treaty of Rome: The treaty signed in 1957 that established the European Economic Community.

Treaty on European Union: The treaty signed in 1992 to further economic and political integration of the EC's members. Commonly known as the Maastricht Treaty.

Trendline: A line that connects a series of highs or lows in a trend. The trendline can represent either support (as in an up trendline) or resistance (as in a down trendline). Consolidations are marked by horizontal trendlines.

Triad: The grouping of countries that dominate the world economy—the European Union, Japan, and the United States.

Triffin paradox: The paradox that resulted from reliance on the U.S. dollar as the primary source of liquidity in the Bretton Woods system. For trade to grow, foreigners needed to hold more dollars; the more dollars they held, the less faith they had in the U.S. dollar, thereby undermining the Bretton Woods system.

Triple-witching hour: Slang for the quarterly expiration of stock-index futures, stock-index options, and options on individual stocks. Trading associated with the expirations inflates stock market volume and can cause volatility in prices. Occurs on the third Friday of March, June, September, and December.

Trough: The end or bottom of a period of declining business activity throughout the economy.

Two-point arbitrage: The purchase of an investment product in one geographic market for immediate resale in a second geographic market in order to profit from a price difference between the markets. Also called geographic arbitrage.

Two-tiered pricing policy: The pricing policy of a firm setting one price for domestic sales and a second price for international sales.

Unauthorized trading: Purchase or sale of commodity futures, options, or other financial instruments for a customer's account without the customer's permission.

Underlying futures contract: The specific futures contract that the option conveys the right to buy (in the case of a call) or sell (in the case of a put).

Value date: (1) The date on which the funds are at the disposal of the receiver. (2) The date when funds due from a financial transaction are required to be delivered. (3) The date when the amount relating to a financial transaction is actually to affect the balance of the account.

Variable limit: A price system that allows price movements for larger than normally allowed price movements under certain conditions. In periods of extreme volatility, some exchanges permit trading and price levels to exceed regular daily limits. At such times, margins may be automatically increased.

Variation margin call: A mid-session call by a clearinghouse on a clearing member, requiring the deposit of additional funds to bring clearing margin monies up to minimum levels in relation to changing prices and the clearing member's net position.

Volatility: (1) A measure by which an exchange rate is expected to fluctuate over a given period. (2) A measure of a commodity's tendency to move up and down in price based on its daily price history over a period of time.

Volume of trade: The number of contracts, shares, or other financial instruments traded during a specified period of time.

Voluntary Export Restraint (VER): The promise by a country to limit its exports of a good to another country.

Warehouse receipt: Document guaranteeing the existence and availability of a given quantity and quality of a commodity in storage; it is commonly used as the instrument of transfer of ownership in both cash and futures transactions.

Windfall: An unexpected profit because of favorable changes in the market price, exchange rate, or interest rates.

World Bank: A financial institution that fosters economic development, especially in the Second and Third Worlds. Also known as the International Bank for Reconstruction and Development.

World Bank Group: The organization consisting of the World Bank and its affiliated organizations.

World Trade Organization (WTO):   The successor organization to the GATT. Founded in 1995, it oversees international trade issues, resolves trade disputes, and enforces the GATT trade pact.

Writer: See *Grantor.*

Yield: The annual rate of return on an investment, as paid in dividends or interest. It is expressed as a percentage.

Yield curve: Comprised of the market yields to maturity of a specific category of debt markets.

Yield spread: The difference in the yield between various debt markets.

Yield to maturity: The internal rate of return yielded by a financial instrument held to maturity.

INDEX